# MACINTOSH METHODOLOGIES IN THEORY AND PRACTICE

A technical guide for experienced users

formerly *Macs For Dummies*

## BY D. WELCH POGUE

Includes advanced treatment of these topics:
- ◆ Invoking the commencement of A/C 120V electric power to the CPU unit
- ◆ Propelling the cursor-control module on a horizontal plane
- ◆ Insertion and removal of magnetic-oxide data storage media

Look, we use the word *Dummies* on the cover with affection and a twinkle in the eye. Still, we understand if you're not thrilled about leaving a book on your desk called *Macs For Dummies*.

We hear you. And we've got the perfect solution: just rip off the real cover of the book! This phony cover will be all that's left. Leave it on your desk in plain sight, so everybody will know what a computer whiz you are.

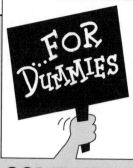

™

# References for the Rest of Us

## COMPUTER BOOK SERIES FROM IDG

Are you intimidated and confused by computers? Do you find that traditional manuals are overloaded with technical details you'll never use? Do your friends and family always call you to fix simple problems on their PCs? Then the *". . . For Dummies"*™ computer book series from IDG is for you.

*". . . For Dummies"* books are written for those frustrated computer users who know they aren't really dumb but find that PC hardware, software, and indeed the unique vocabulary of computing make them feel helpless. *". . . For Dummies"* books use a lighthearted approach, a down-to-earth style, and even cartoons and humorous icons to diffuse computer novices' fears and build their confidence. Lighthearted but not lightweight, these books are a perfect survival guide to anyone forced to use a computer.

> *"I like my copy so much I told friends; now they bought copies."*
>
> **Irene C., Orwell, Ohio**

> *"Quick, concise, nontechnical, and humorous."*
>
> **Jay A., Elburn, IL**

> *"Thanks, I needed this book. Now I can sleep at night."*
>
> **Robin F., British Columbia, Canada**

Already, hundreds of thousands of satisfied readers agree. They have made *". . . For Dummies"* books the #1 introductory level computer book series and have written asking for more. So if you're looking for the most fun and easy way to learn about computers look to *". . . For Dummies"* books to give you a helping hand.

## IDG BOOKS

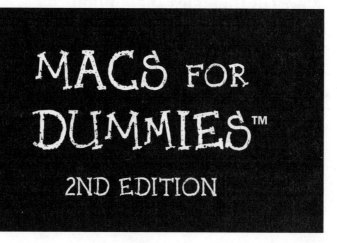

# MACS FOR DUMMIES™
## 2ND EDITION

**by David Pogue**

Foreword by John Kander

## IDG
## BOOKS

IDG Books Worldwide, Inc.
An International Data Group Company
San Mateo, California ◆ Indianapolis, Indiana ◆ Boston, Massachusetts

# Macs For Dummies 2nd Edition

Published by
**IDG Books Worldwide, Inc.**
An International Data Group Company
155 Bovet Road, Suite 310
San Mateo, CA 94402

Library of Congress Catalog Card No.: 93-80357

ISBN: 1-56884-051-9

Printed in the United States of America

10 9 8 7 6 5 4 3 2

Distributed in the United States by IDG Books Worldwide, Inc.

Distributed in Canada by Macmillan of Canada, a Division of Canada Publishing Corporation; by Computer and Technical Books in Miami, Florida, for South America and the Caribbean; by Longman Singapore in Singapore, Malaysia, Thailand, and Korea; by Toppan Co. Ltd. in Japan; by Asia Computerworld in Hong Kong; by Woodslane Pty. Ltd. in Australia and New Zealand; and by Transword Publishers Ltd. in the U.K. and Europe.

For information on where to purchase IDG Books outside the U.S., contact Christina Turner at 415-312-0633.

For information on translations, contact Marc Jeffrey Mikulich, Foreign Rights Manager, at IDG Books Worldwide; FAX NUMBER 415-358-1260.

For sales inquiries and special prices for bulk quantities, write to the address above or call IDG Books Worldwide at 415-312-0650.

 is a trademark of IDG Books Worldwide, Inc.

COMPUTER
BOOK SERIES
FROM IDG

# Acknowledgments

I can't tell you how much I've appreciated the patience of everyone whose projects got back-burnered for the sake of this book: Carol Person and Adrian Mello of *Macworld;* Freddie Gershon and the gang at Music Theatre International; the lovely Dr. O'Sullivan; Joe, Allison, Max, and *Downtown Local;* and Poppa, for whose creative chromosomes I'll thank him personally at his 104th birthday.

Thanks to the unbelievably supportive, enthusiastic people at IDG Books: publisher John Kilcullen; my editors Marta Partington and Jeremy Judson; and everyone in the sprawling universe of IDG Books voicemail. Thanks, too, to Londa Holsinger for her borrowed wit.

Above all, thanks to my students: the ranks of born-again Mac nuts whose first steps, questions, and impressive strides constitute my research.

The publisher would like to give special thanks to Patrick J. McGovern, without whom this book would not have been possible.

# Credits

**Publisher**
David Solomon

**Managing Editor**
Mary Bednarek

**Acquisitions Editor**
Janna Custer

**Production Manager**
Beth Jenkins

**Senior Editors**
Sandy Blackthorn
Diane Graves Steele

**Production Coordinator**
Cindy L. Phipps

**Acquisitions Assistant**
Megg Bonar

**Editorial Assistant**
Patricia R. Reynolds

**Project Editors**
Marta Justak Partington
Jeremy Judson

**Technical Reviewer**
Dennis Cohen

**Production Staff**
Tony Augsburger
Valery Bourke
Mary Breidenbach
Sherry Gomoll
Drew Moore
Gina Scott

**Proofreader**
Charles A. Hutchinson

**Indexer**
Sherry Massey

**Book Design**
University Graphics

# About the Author

Ohio-bred David Pogue never touched a computer — nor wanted to — until Apple Computer suckered him into it by selling Macs half-price at Yale, from which he graduated *summa cum laude* in 1985. Since then, Pogue has merged his two loves — the musical theatre and Macs — in every way he could dream up: by writing manuals for music programs like Finale; by being the computer-consultant guy for Broadway musicals like *Carrie* and Lincoln Center's *Anything Goes*; by teaching Mac music seminars around the country; and by becoming the Mac guru to every Broadway and Hollywood creative-type he could get his hands on — Mia Farrow, Carly Simon, Mike Nichols, Stephen Sondheim, and others.

In his other life, Pogue is a straight-ahead theatre musician, having conducted 1½ Broadway shows (the second one flopped out of town), played piano for some Off-Broadway productions, and composed a number of small-time musicals. In his other life, he's a magician, and teaches courses in magic in New York City.

And in his *other* other life, Pogue is a Contributing Editor for *Macworld* magazine. His column, *The Desktop Critic,* appears in the magazine each month.

With his former Yale roommate and current *Macworld* writer, Joseph Schorr, Pogue wrote the 1000-page, 3-disk, fact-filled best-seller, *Macworld Macintosh SECRETS*.

In between crises, Pogue wrote a novel called *Hard Drive* — a Macintosh techno-thriller, which was published last year by the Berkley Publishing Group.

Pogue's résumè also boasts some real accomplishments, like winning the Ohio spelling bee in seventh grade, being the only nonlawyer in three generations, and getting a Viewer Mail letter read on David Letterman.

# About IDG Books Worldwide

Welcome to the world of IDG Books Worldwide.

IDG Books Worldwide, Inc., is a division of International Data Group, the world's largest publisher of computer-related information and the leading global provider of information services on information technology. IDG publishes over 194 computer publications in 62 countries. Forty million people read one or more IDG publications each month.

If you use personal computers, IDG Books is committed to publishing quality books that meet your needs. We rely on our extensive network of publications, including such leading periodicals as *Macworld*, *InfoWorld*, *PC World*, *Computerworld*, *Publish*, *Network World*, and *SunWorld*, to help us make informed and timely decisions in creating useful computer books that meet your needs.

Every IDG book strives to bring extra value and skill-building instruction to the reader. Our books are written by experts, with the backing of IDG periodicals, and with careful thought devoted to issues such as audience, interior design, use of icons, and illustrations. Our editorial staff is a careful mix of high-tech journalists and experienced book people. Our close contact with the makers of computer products helps ensure accuracy and thorough coverage. Our heavy use of personal computers at every step in production means we can deliver books in the most timely manner.

We are delivering books of high quality at competitive prices on topics customers want. At IDG, we believe in quality, and we have been delivering quality for over 25 years. You'll find no better book on a subject than an IDG book.

John Kilcullen
President and C.E.O.
IDG Books Worldwide, Inc.

IDG Books Worldwide, Inc. is a division of International Data Group. The officers are Patrick J. McGovern, Founder and Board Chairman; Walter Boyd, President. International Data Group's publications include: **ARGENTINA's** Computerworld Argentina, InfoWorld Argentina; **ASIA's** Computerworld Hong Kong, PC World Hong Kong, Computerworld Southeast Asia, PC World Singapore, Computerworld Malaysia, PC World Malaysia; **AUSTRALIA's** Computerworld Australia, Australian PC World, Australian Macworld, Network World, Reseller, IDG Sources; **AUSTRIA's** Computerwelt Oesterreich, PC Test; **BRAZIL's** Computerworld, Mundo IBM, Mundo Unix, PC World, Publish; **BULGARIA's** Computerworld Bulgaria, Ediworld, PC & Mac World Bulgaria; **CANADA's** Direct Access, Graduate Computerworld, InfoCanada, Network World Canada; **CHILE's** Computerworld, Informatica; **COLOMBIA's** Computerworld Colombia; **CZECH REPUBLIC's** Computerworld, Elektronika, PC World; **DENMARK's** CAD/CAM WORLD, Communications World, Computerworld Danmark, LOTUS World, Macintosh Produktkatalog, Macworld Danmark, PC World Danmark, PC World Produktguide, Windows World; **EQUADOR's** PC World; **EGYPT's** Computerworld (CW) Middle East, PC World Middle East; **FINLAND's** MikroPC, Tietoviikko, Tietoverkko; **FRANCE's** Distributique, GOLDEN MAC, InfoPC, Languages & Systems, Le Guide du Monde Informatique, Le Monde Informatique, Telecoms & Reseaux; **GERMANY's** Computerwoche, Computerwoche Focus, Computerwoche Extra, Computerwoche Karriere, Information Management, Macwelt, Netzwelt, PC Welt, PC Woche, Publish, Unit; **HUNGARY's** Alaplap, Computerworld SZT, PC World, ; **INDIA's** Computers & Communications; **ISRAEL's** Computerworld Israel, PC World Israel; **ITALY's** Computerworld Italia, Lotus Magazine, Macworld Italia, Networking Italia, PC World Italia; **JAPAN's** Computerworld Japan, Macworld Japan, SunWorld Japan, Windows World; **KENYA's** East African Computer News; **KOREA's** Computerworld Korea, Macworld Korea, PC World Korea; **MEXICO's** Compu Edicion, Compu Manufactura, Computacion/Punto de Venta, Computerworld Mexico, MacWorld, Mundo Unix, PC World, Windows; **THE NETHERLAND'S** Computer! Totaal, LAN Magazine, MacWorld; **NEW ZEALAND's** Computer Listings, Computerworld New Zealand, New Zealand PC World; **NIGERIA's** PC World Africa; **NORWAY's** Computerworld Norge, C/World, Lotusworld Norge, Macworld Norge, Networld, PC World Ekspress, PC World Norge, PC World's Product Guide, Publish World, Student Data, Unix World, Windowsworld, IDG Direct Response; **PANAMA's** PC World; **PERU's** Computerworld Peru, PC World; **PEOPLES REPUBLIC OF CHINA's** China Computerworld, PC World China, Electronics International, China Network World; **IDG HIGH TECH BEIJING's** New Product World; **IDG SHENZHEN's** Computer News Digest; **PHILLIPPINES'** Computerworld, PC World; **POLAND's** Computerworld Poland, PC World/Komputer; **PORTUGAL's** Cerebro/PC World, Correio Informatico/Computerworld, Macin; **ROMANIA's** PC World; **RUSSIA's** Computerworld-Moscow, Mir-PC, Sety; **SLOVENIA's** Monitor Magazine; **SOUTH AFRICA's** Computing S.A.; **SPAIN's** Amiga World, Computerworld Espana, Communicaciones World, Macworld Espana, NeXTWORLD, PC World Espana, Publish, Sunworld; **SWEDEN's** Attack, ComputerSweden, Corporate Computing, Lokala Natverk/LAN, Lotus World, MAC&PC, Macworld, Mikrodatorn, PC World, Publishing & Design (CAP), Datalngenjoren, Maxi Data, Windows World; **SWITZERLAND's** Computerworld Schweiz, Macworld Schweiz, PC & Workstation; **TAIWAN's** Computerworld Taiwan, Global Computer Express, PC World Taiwan; **THAILAND's** Thai Computerworld; **TURKEY's** Computerworld Monitor, Macworld Turkiye, PC World Turkiye; **UNITED KINGDOM's** Lotus Magazine, Macworld, Sunworld; **UNITED STATES'** AmigaWorld, Cable in the Classroom, CD Review, CIO, Computerworld, Desktop Video World, DOS Resource Guide, Electronic News, Federal Computer Week, Federal Integrator, GamePro, IDG Books, InfoWorld, InfoWorld Direct, Laser Event, Macworld, Multimedia World, Network World, NeXTWORLD, PC Games, PC Letter, PC World Publish, Sumeria, SunWorld, SWATPro, Video Event; **VENEZUELA's** Computerworld Venezuela, MicroComputerworld Venezuela; **VIETNAM's** PC World Vietnam

 The text in this book is printed on recycled paper.

# Say What You Think!

Listen up, all you readers of IDG's international bestsellers: the one — the only — absolutely world-famous ...*For Dummies* books! It's time for you to take advantage of a new, direct pipeline to the authors and editors of IDG Books Worldwide.

In between putting the finishing touches on the next round of ...*For Dummies* books, the authors and editors of IDG Books Worldwide like to sit around and mull over what their readers have to say. And we know that you readers always say what you think.

So here's your chance. We'd really like your input for future printings and editions of this book — and ideas for future ...*For Dummies* titles as well. Tell us what you liked (and didn't like) about this book. How about the chapters you found most useful — or most funny? And since we know you're not a bit shy, what about the chapters you think can be improved?

Just to show you how much we appreciate your input, we'll add you to our Dummies Database/Fan Club and keep you up to date on the latest ...*For Dummies* books, news, cartoons, calendars, and more!

Please send your name, address, and phone number, as well as your comments, questions, and suggestions, to our very own ...*For Dummies* coordinator at the following address:

### ...For Dummies Coordinator
IDG Books Worldwide
3250 North Post Road, Suite 140
Indianapolis, IN 46226

(Yes, Virginia, there really is a ...*For Dummies* coordinator. We are not making this up.)

Please mention the name of this book in your comments.

Thanks for your input!

# Contents at a Glance

# Table of Contents

# Foreword

It is certainly no surprise to me that I was asked to write the Foreword for this book. After all, I was David Pogue's first dummy. When we met five years ago, I was an aging composer, wearily putting quill pen to parchment, surrounded by mountains of erasers. The world of computers was as foreign to me as the craters of the moon.

Then along came Mr. Pogue, fresh from Yale, who guided me patiently and painlessly into the joyful world of Macintosh. He made it all seem so simple. And the Mac, my new friend, was helpful as well, with little admonitions like, "Are you sure you want to do this?" or apologies like, "I'm sorry I can't find this. If you find it for me, I promise I'll remember where it is next time." I was soon convinced that this machine really cared about me. In a short time, I became a mouse maniac.

Since then, I have written the scores for two musicals, two films, and countless letters of complaint to my Congressmen on this wonderful contraption, thanks to my two wise, kind friends, David and the Mac.

In this book, you'll find many reminders, explanations, and shortcuts. *Macs for Dummies, 2nd Edition* will stay by me at my desk. After all, once a dummy . . .

John Kander

*John Kander, with lyricist Fred Ebb, has written the scores for* Cabaret; Chicago; Zorba; New York, New York; *and the Tony-award winning musical* Kiss of the Spider Woman.

# Introduction

· · · · · · · · · · · · · · · · · · · · · · · · · · · · · · · · · · · · · · · · · · · · · · · · · · · · · · · ·

## *A Formal Welcome to the 20th Century*

Something has driven you to learning the computer — your friends, your job, or fate. In any case, you couldn't have chosen a better time; technology and price wars have made computers comprehensible, affordable, and almost fun. The Macintosh, of course, is the primary example.

In 1984, the ad people called the Macintosh "the computer for the rest of us." The implication was that *other* computers were hard to learn. Previous computers required you to learn jargon, have technical skill, and memorize dumb keyboard codes. The Macintosh was as simple as a toaster — nothing to assemble, nothing to install, no manual to puzzle through.

And sure enough, the first Mac pretty much fit that description. Its factory-sealed case meant that you didn't have to install any parts (like you do on IBM-style computers). Unless you were a real soldering gunslinger, the first Macintosh wasn't expandable. It was a complete, self-contained unit. You unpacked it and plugged it in. Like a toaster.

But Apple Computer learned about a funny catch-22 in the computer business. The people who influence computer sales (like computer magazines, consultants, industry spokespeople) all were people who *liked* the jargon, the keyboard codes, the messy circuit board stuff! These were people who prided themselves on having *mastered* the convoluted, dim-witted design of pre-Mac computers . . . people who not only didn't appreciate the simplicity of the Macintosh but actually *resented* it. In reviews, editorials, and interviews, the Powers That Were said over and over again that the Macintosh would never survive unless Apple opened it up. Let people expand it, customize it, juice it up, just like IBM owners had been required to do for years.

Alas, that movement pushed the Mac out of its "computer for the rest of us" mold. Suddenly there were more models. They became available in separate modular pieces, so you had more to shop for. The computer weenies who ruled the press started imposing all their terminology and tech-talk on this poor little machine. Macintosh user groups sprang up — they're everywhere now — where you'd hear talk like, "How can I accelerate my 25MHz SE/30 fast enough to get a decent frame rate out of QuickTime 1.6?" or "How much RAM do I need for virtual memory on my 80MB Quantum?"

The Mac wasn't a toaster anymore.

# Why a Book for Dummies?

Today, you'd be justified in saying that the Mac sometimes seems almost as intimidating as the computers it was supposed to replace. The way the techno-nerds throw jargon around (and the way the pages of Mac magazines have slowly been filling up with stories about Ethernet Hubs and 9600 bps modems with MNP and v42.BIS error-correction protocol), you'd think the Mac was the private property of the dweeby intelligentsia all over again.

It's not. You hold in your hands a primal scream: "It's *not* as complicated as they try to make it sound!" Really, truly, almost everything said by the computer salespeople and magazines and books and computer consultants of the world is more complicated than it has to be. (Ever study psychology? A person who uses jargon where simple English would do is trying to underscore the listener's ignorance.)

This book is designed to help you

- Translate the tech-talk into useful information
- Weed out the stuff you'll never need to know
- Navigate the hype when it comes to buying things
- Learn the Macintosh and get useful things done

By the way, of *course* you're not a dummy. Two pieces of evidence tell me so: for one thing, you're learning the Mac, and for another, you're reading this book! But I've taught hundreds of people how to use their Macs, and an awful lot of them start out saying they *feel* like dummies when it comes to computers. Society surrounds us with fast-talking teenagers who grew up learning English from their Nintendo sets; no wonder the rest of us sometimes feel left out.

But you're no more a dummy for not knowing the Mac than you were before you knew how to drive. Learning the Mac is like learning to drive: after a lesson or two, you can go anywhere your heart desires.

So when we say *Dummies,* we're saying it with an affectionate wink. Still, if the cover bothers you even a little — I'll admit it, you wouldn't be the first — please rip it right off. The inner cover, we hope, will make you proud to have the book lying in plain sight on your desk.

# *How to Use This Book (Other Than as a Mousepad)*

If you're starting from the very, *very* beginning, you might want to start this book from the end — with **Appendix A,** where you can find out how to buy a Mac (and which one to get) without getting scammed. It also contains an idiot-proof guide to setting up your computer.

**Chapter 1** assumes that you do, in fact, have a Mac, and that it's been plugged in. You'll find out how to turn it on and off, for starters. In 10 minutes (or 20 if you're trying to watch TV simultaneously), you'll have mastered the raw basics of driving your Mac.

Then there's something, if you'll forgive me, called **Chapter 1½.** It's my attempt to play down the technical nature of the topic— the difference between memory and disks — by not devoting a full scary chapter to it.

**Chapter 2**'s a Mac lesson for the absolute beginner: how to use the mouse (and what a mouse *is*), how to use menus — that kind of thing. In **Chapter 3,** you'll do some actual work; it includes a word processing lesson that won't destroy your self-esteem.

Once you've got your ideas typed into the computer, you'll want to print your work; that's one of the Mac's strong suits. **Chapter 4** lays bare the mysteries of printing and using typefaces.

**Chapter 5** has the all-important "Faking Your Way Through the Top Ten Programs," an indispensable guide for anybody who wants to look cool without actually expending any effort. And speaking of software, **Chapter 6** explains those icons inside the all-important System Folder and attempts to answer man's primal question: "What *is* all that junk?"

In **Chapter 7,** you get to read about all the expensive equipment you can plug *into* the Mac: modems, scanners, and all that good stuff. By the time you get to **Chapter 8,** you'll be ready to start sailing with a priceless potpourri of sizzling shortcuts. You'll find out about the creative vandalism the Mac lets you do: colorizing the screen, recording your own sounds, and using utility programs that help you get extra mileage out of your computer.

If you were clever enough to buy a Performa — a special breed of Macintosh that comes with preinstalled software and has some special features for beginners — then **Chapter 9** has your name on it. Likewise, for the peripatetic among us, PowerBook (and Newton!) owners will thrill to the insights of **Chapter 10.** It shows you, among other things, how to coax every last milliwatt of juice from your laptop's batteries.

When anything goes wrong, turn to **Chapter 11,** "When Bad Things Happen to Good Machines," the mother of all troubleshooting sections. It identifies the snafus you're most likely to encounter, how to prevent them, and what to do about them. Read **Chapter 12** when the stuff in this book is starting to seem old hat, and you're ready to push off into the wider world of computing.

The book winds down with **Appendix B**, the Resource Resource (which lists contact info for a number of important Mac companies and organizations), and **Appendix C**, the Techno-Babble Translation Guide. (You'd probably call it a glossary.)

## Macintosh conventions

Macintosh conventions? Sure. They're called Macworld Expos, and there's one in Boston and one in San Francisco each year.

## Conventions in this book

Oh, *that* kind of convention. First, I'm going to take the liberty of defining terms in the margin whenever I think it'd be helpful to a wide-eyed, terrorized novice. If you already know the term, great — just breeze on by; that's why it's in the margins.

Second, I'm going to satisfy those beginners who have a recessive geek gene in their DNA, those who actually *want* to learn more about what's going on under the hood, with occasional sidebars on technoid topics. They'll be clearly marked with titles like "Stuff you'll never need to know." Unless you're actually interested, rest assured that you can live a rich and rewarding life without ever reading a word.

Finally, so that we'll be eligible for some of the more prestigious book-design awards, I've marked some topics in the main text with these icons:

Nerdy stuff that's OK to skip but will fascinate the kind of people who read Tom Clancy novels.

You can never, *ever* damage your Mac by "doing something wrong" (other than by pouring Diet Coke into the air vents or something). Occasionally, though, I'll alert you that there's a potential risk to your work.

The former Speaker of the House. Also a shortcut so you can show off.

Denotes an actual You-Try-It Experience. Hold the book open with a nearby cinder block, put your hands on the computer, and do as I say.

Indicates a deep glimpse into the psychology of Mac users: why people who already *know* how to use the damn things, for example, love to intimidate people who *don't.*

# Why a Mac?

If there's one single *atom* of computer phobia in your bloodstream, but you need a computer, get a Macintosh. Trust me. And trust the ten million former computer phobes who are now happily computing away.

## A free psychological confirmation of your taste and intelligence

You've heard it a thousand times: the Macintosh is the most user-friendly computer. What does that *mean?* In concrete terms?

For one thing, there's a lot less to install and set up. When you buy an IBM computer, for example, you're likely to spend your first weekend hunched over an open computer case filled with wiring. You squint at the manual that's filled with techno-babble and get depressed that you, a well-educated, perfectly good English speaker, can't understand the first thing it's saying. With a Macintosh, of course, you basically just plug it in and press the On switch.

And another thing: there's a lot less to memorize when you use a Macintosh. Because the commands are all listed on the screen (in *menus*), you don't have to remember that Control-Alt-Escape-semicolon is the Print command. In the IBM world, of course, every single program has different commands in different places with different *keyboard shortcuts.* Out of 10,000 Macintosh programs, there are probably five that don't have exactly the same major commands in exactly the same menus with exactly the same keyboard shortcuts.

There are a bunch of other reasons you've done the right thing to go for the Mac — the screen looks better, it's easy to expand, it's the easiest to learn, and it has all kinds of high-tech goodies like a microphone for recording your own sounds. Of course, the last reason that a Mac is superior *is* that it's superior; it entitles you to gloat about owning the world's most hip, technologically evolved, shrewd computer.

## *Apple and obsolescence*

Apple is the gigantic Silicon Valley computer company that started out as a couple of grungy teenagers in a garage. It's the target of incredible love and hate from the Macintosh community. Each time Apple introduces a new Macintosh model, you can bet that it's faster, more powerful, and less expensive than the model *you* already bought. Thus, the mixed passions — people love Apple for coming up with such great products but feel cheated at having paid so much for a suddenly outdated machine.

Feel whatever you want, of course. But if you're going to buy a computer, accept the fact that your investment is going to devalue faster than real estate in Three Mile Island.

Here's a promise: No matter how carefully you shop or how good a deal you get on a Macintosh today, it's going to be discontinued by Apple in two years. (It'll still *work* just fine, and be more or less up-to-date, for about five years.) Yeah, I know — it's a cruel, irritating fact, but it's a fact nonetheless.

With that quick and inevitable computer death looming, how can people psych themselves into laying out $3,000 for a computer? Simple: They believe that in those few short years, the computer will speed them up enough, and enhance their productivity enough, to cover the costs easily.

That's the theory, anyway.

# Part I
## For the Absolute
## Mac Virgin

### The 5th Wave

THE COMMITTEE FOR THE PROLIFERATION OF MACINTOSH COMPUTERS FINALLY PAY A VISIT TO LARRY.

# In this part...

There are three general ways to learn how to work your Mac. You can prevail upon the good graces of your local computer dealer, who, having pocketed your money already, would just as soon have you blow away. You can read the manuals, which have about as much personality as a walnut. Or you can read a book like this one. (Then again, no book is quite like this one.)

Tough choice, huh?

In this part, you'll learn, as kindly and gently as possible, what you need to know to get up and running on your Mac system — and nothing else. So take off your thinking cap and enjoy your journey through this utopia we call the Mac world.

# Chapter 1

# How to Turn On Your Mac
# (and What to Do Next)

- - - - - - - - - - - - - - - - - - - - - - - - - - - - - - - - - - - - - - - -

### In This Chapter

▶ How to turn your Mac on (and off)

▶ Confronting weird new words like mouse and menu

▶ Doing windows

▶ Mindlessly opening and closing folders

- - - - - - - - - - - - - - - - - - - - - - - - - - - - - - - - - - - - - - - -

*1*f you haven't bought a Mac yet, go *immediately* to Appendix A. Don't speak to any salesperson until you've read it.

If you have bought a Mac, but it's sitting in cardboard boxes on your living-room floor, read the second half of Appendix A, where you'll be gently guided through the not-harrowing-at-all experience of plugging everything in.

At this moment, then, there should be a ready-to-roll Mac on your desk and a look of fevered anticipation on your face.

# I Took Off the Shrink-Wrap! Now What?

## Switching the Mac on

In this very first lesson, you'll be asked to locate the On button. To keep life interesting, Apple has decreed that this switch shall be In a Different Place on Every Different Mac Model. Fortunately, after you know where yours is, it'll pretty much stay in that spot for as long as you own your Mac.

First, figure out which Mac model you have. Apple came up with a clever and sophisticated method for letting you know which model you have: they painted its name right on the plastic front.

Now find your model listed here. Then find the power button!

| | |
|---|---|
| Macintosh Classic<br>Macintosh Classic II<br>Performa 200<br>Macintosh Plus<br>Macintosh SE or SE/30 | These are the so-called *compact* Macs. As you look at the Mac from the front, the On/Off switch is in the middle of the rear left edge. It's a rocker switch; when the top half is pushed in, the computer is on. |
| Macintosh LC-almost-anything<br>Performa 400 through 476<br>Quadra 605 | As you look at the Mac from the front, the switch is at the rear right corner. It's another rocker switch; the On position is marked by a straight line, and the Off position is marked by a circle. Nobody can ever remember which is which. You may want to think of it this way: the *O* stands for *Off*. (Of course, it also stands for *On* . . . and they wonder why people are intimidated by computers?) |
| Color Classic<br>LC 520<br>Performa 550 | And the 1040-Form Award for Consternation and Confusion goes to . . . these Macs. They actually have *two* power switches. First, there's a rocker switch on the back edge of the machine; it allows the current to reach the Mac. Turn it on today and forget it forever.<br><br>But turning on that back-panel switch doesn't actually start up your Mac. To do that, you have to press the power key on the keyboard. It's a key all by itself with a left-pointing triangle on it.<br><br>So, to recap: turning on the back panel switch does nothing until you press the keyboard power button. On the other hand, pressing the keyboard button does nothing *unless* you've also turned on the back-panel switch. This is great stuff.<br><br>Oh, and by the way, your Mac's monitor goes off by itself if you don't use the computer for awhile. To wake it up when you come back from lunch, click the mouse button. (Read on for details on mice and buttons.) |
| Mac II-anything<br>Quadra-almost-anything<br>Centris 650 | The On switch is on the keyboard. It's a key all by itself with a left-pointing triangle on it:<br><br> |

| | |
|---|---|
| Quadra (Centris) 610<br>Quadra (Centris) 660AV | These odd birds have a round nub of an On/Off button on the front panel, on the right side. |
| PowerBook | You have to flip open the back panel, which can be a pain. You'll then see the round, concave power button. |
| PowerBook Duo | Press the rubber capsule-shaped button on the keyboard. (There's an identical button on the back.)<br><br>When you insert the Duo into a Duo Dock, you turn on the whole schmear by pressing the big left-triangle key on your keyboard. |

Was your hunt for the elusive On Switch successful? Then turn the Mac on!

You should hear a ding or a chord, and after a few seconds, an image appears on the screen.

## *What you'll probably see*

After a moment, you should see the smiling Macintosh on the screen. It looks like this:

A few seconds after that, the words "Welcome to Macintosh" appear. Then the gray or tinted pattern, called the *desktop,* appears. Congratulations! You've arrived.

Skip ahead to "Your First Moments Alone Together."

---

## The big triangle button on the keyboard

If you've just read all about turning on the Mac, you may have noticed that, for many models, the big obvious-looking left-pointing-triangle key on the keyboard is the On switch.

If you have a Mac that uses some other mechanism for On, you may have wondered why *your* keyboard nonetheless has the big obvious-looking triangle key. And you probably wondered: if it doesn't turn my Mac on, then what *does* that cryptic, Picasso-esque key do?

And the answer, if you have a compact Mac or certain Centris models, is: absolutely nothing.

## Techie terms not worth learning

You may occasionally hear cocky teenagers tell you to "boot up." No, they're not taking you fly-fishing. That's computerese for turning on the Mac. You also hear people say *power up, start up,* and just *boot.*

Furthermore, after the computer is on, you're sometimes asked to turn it off and on again. This is called *rebooting,* or *restarting,* or sometimes *turning it off and on again.*

## *What you might see*

The very first time you turn on your Mac, there's a chance that you'll see a disk with a blinking question mark like this:

The Mac, in its charming, universal, picture-based language of love, is trying to tell you that it can't find a disk to start up from. More specifically, it can't find an electronic *System Folder,* which is where the Mac's instructions to itself live. (You'll find more about this all-important folder in Chapter 6.)

If you see the blinking question mark icon, you've just met your first computer problem. Now is as good a time as any to dog-ear the pages of Chapter 11, "When Bad Things Happen to Good Machines." This problem, and many others, is explained — and solved — for you there.

In this case, you have to give the Mac a disk containing a System Folder, or it will sit there like an idiot and blink at you until the warranty expires. The easiest way to provide it with a System Folder is to locate those white-labeled System floppy disks that came with the Mac. (They don't, alas, come with Performa models or the PowerBook 145b; and you get a silvery compact disc, instead of white floppies, if you bought a Mac with a built-in CD-ROM player. You know who you are.)

The one that contains a System Folder is called Disk Tools. Insert the disk into the slot on the front of the computer — metal side first, label side up. And then read Chapter 11 for the full troubleshooting scoop.

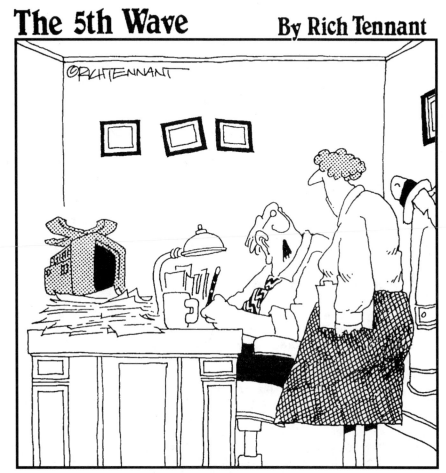

"IT'S NOT THAT IT DOESN'T WORK AS A COMPUTER, IT JUST WORKS BETTER AS A PAPERWEIGHT."

# *Your First Moments Alone Together*

As any gadget lover can tell you, the most exciting period of appliance owner-ship comes at the very beginning. You're gonna love this stuff. Read on, MacDuff!

## *The big turn-off*

Before we get into 3-D color graphs, space-vehicle trajectories, and DNA analysis, maybe you'd better learn how to turn the Mac off.

You already know where the On/Off switch on a compact, LC, or Performa Mac is. On the fancier Macs, the power-on button on the keyboard won't work to turn it off. You have to find the tiny, round, pea-sized On/Off button at the rear of the machine — it's on the left as you look at the back of the machine.

But turning off the Mac by chopping off its power is a no-no, according to Apple (although I've never heard of it hurting anything). The preferred method is to use the Shut Down command; we'll get to that in a moment.

## *Moving the mouse*

The mouse is the gray, soap-sized plastic box on the desk beside your key-board. Having trouble visualizing it as a rodent? Think of the cord as its tail, and (if it helps you) draw little eyeballs on the sloping side facing you.

Now then, roll the mouse across the desk (or mouse pad), keeping the cord pointed away from you. See how the arrow pointer moves across the screen? For the rest of your life, you'll hear that pointer called the *cursor*. And for the rest of your life, you'll hear moving the mouse called *moving the mouse*.

Try lifting the mouse off the desk and waving it around in midair like a remote control. Nothing happens, right? The mouse only controls the cursor when it's on a flat surface. (A ball on the bottom of it detects movement and moves the cursor accordingly.) That's a useful feature — it lets you pick up the mouse when you run out of desk space, but the cursor will stay in place on the screen. Only when you set the mouse down and begin to roll it again will the cursor continue moving.

If you have a PowerBook, by the way, you don't have a mouse. Studies have shown that rolling a gray, soap-sized plastic box across the thigh of the guy next to you on the airplane can have, ergonomically and socially speaking, unpleasant results. Therefore, you've been given a *trackball* instead. It's essentially an upside-down mouse. The principle is the same: roll the ball away from you, and the cursor moves up the screen. And instead of a square mouse button, you have two crescent-shaped buttons around the trackball. Both buttons act like the mouse button; they're identical in function.

I won't mention this mouse/trackball distinction again, OK? If you're smart enough to have bought a PowerBook, you're smart enough to translate "mouse" into "trackball" in your head.

## What's on the menu?

Let's try some real computing here. Move the cursor up to the white strip at the top of the screen. It's called the *menu bar,* named after a delightful little pub near Cupertino. Touch the arrow on the word Special.

**The 5th Wave**         **By Rich Tennant**

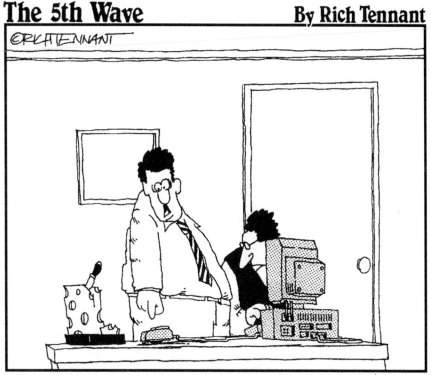

"THERE! THERE! I TELL YOU IT JUST MOVED AGAIN!"

Pointing to something on the screen in this way has a technical term: *pointing*. (Think you're going to be able to handle this?)

Now put your index finger on the button on the mouse, and press the button down. Hold it down. Don't let go.

If all went well, you should see a list of commands drop down from the word Special, as shown in the following figure. Keep holding down the button.

```
Special
 Clean Up Window
 Empty Trash

 Eject Disk      ⌘E
 Erase Disk...

 Restart
 Shut Down
```

Congratulations — you've learned how to *click the mouse* (by pressing the button), and you've also learned to *pull down a menu* (the list of commands). Try letting go of the mouse button; the menu disappears.

## Shutting down

Click the word Special (in the menu bar) again. This time, when the list of commands appears, *keep the button pressed* and roll the mouse downward so that each successive command turns black. In Mac jargon, you're *dragging* the mouse (moving with the button pressed). And when each menu command turns black, it's said to be *highlighted*.

The only commands that don't get highlighted are the ones that are dimmed, or "grayed out." They're dimmed because they don't make any sense at the moment. For example, if there's no disk in the floppy-disk drive, choosing Eject Disk wouldn't make any sense (and it wouldn't work, either). So the Mac makes it gray, which means it's unavailable to you.

---

### For budget-Mac owners only

When you use the Shut Down command on a compact Mac (or an LC or Performa 400), the computer doesn't go all the way off. Instead, it just tells you (with a message on the screen) that it's *ready* to be turned off. Now you have to reach around to the back and physically push the switch off, to the — position. Or was it the ○ position?

Roll the mouse all the way down to the words Shut Down so that they're highlighted.

If you've had enough for one session, release the mouse button — the Mac turns itself off.

Hey, you've only read the first few pages of this book, and already you can turn your Mac on and off! *Told* you it was no harder than a toaster.

If your thirst for knowledge is unquenched, and you want to slog ahead with this lesson, then don't let go of the button yet. Instead, slide the cursor off the menu in any direction, and *then* let go of the mouse button. The menu snaps back up like a window shade and nothing else happens. (You only activate a menu command when you release the mouse while the cursor is *on* a command.)

When you're ready to forge forth, read on.

## *Moving things around on the desktop*

Take a look around the Mac screen. You've already encountered menus (those words File, Edit, View, and so on at the top of the screen). Near the upper-right corner of the screen, you should see an icon (a small symbolic picture). If your Mac is brand new, that icon is called Macintosh HD.

Icons represent everything in the Mac world. They all look different: one represents a letter you wrote, another represents the Trash can, another represents a floppy disk you've inserted. Here are some examples of icons you'll probably be seeing before long:

You can move an icon by dragging it. Try this:

1. Point to the Trash icon.

2. Drag it to a new position (move the mouse while the button's down).

Hey, this thing isn't so technical after all, right?

Other than the fact that there's a Trash can, nobody's really sure why they call this "home-base" screen the desktop. It has another name, too: the *Finder.* It's where you file all your work into little electronic on-screen file folders, so you'll be able to *find* them again later.

Used in a sentence, you might hear it like this: "Well, no wonder you don't see the Trash can. You're not in the Finder!"

## *Icons, windows, and Macintosh syntax*

Point to the hard-disk icon (a rectangular box, probably called Macintosh HD — for Hard Disk) in the upper-right corner of the screen. A hard disk is like a massive floppy disk. It's the filing cabinet that contains all your work, all your files, and all your software.

So how do you see what's in it? Where do you get to see its table of contents?

It turns out that any disk icon can be *opened* into a window, where you'll see every item inside listed individually. The window has the same name as the icon you opened. (It may already be open. If there's a window open on your screen, choose Close Window from the File menu. Choose Close Window again and again, until there are no windows open on your screen.)

Before we proceed, though, it's time for a lesson in Macintosh syntax. Fear not; it's nothing like English syntax. In fact, everything you do on the Macintosh has this format: noun-verb. Shakespeare it ain't, but it's sure easy to remember.

Let's try a noun-verb command, shall we?

1. Click the hard-disk icon in the upper-right corner of the screen.

   It should turn black, indicating that it's *selected.* Good job — you've just identified the *noun.*

2. Move to the File menu and choose Open.

| File | |
|---|---|
| **New Folder** | ⌘N |
| **Open** | ⌘O |
| Print | ⌘P |
| **Close Window** | ⌘W |
| | |
| **Get Info** | ⌘I |
| **Sharing...** | |
| Duplicate | ⌘D |
| **Make Alias** | |
| **Put Away** | ⌘Y |
| | |
| **Find...** | ⌘F |
| **Find Again** | ⌘G |
| | |
| **Page Setup...** | |
| **Print Desktop...** | |

You guessed it — Open is the *verb*. And, sure enough, your hard disk *opens* into a window, where you can see its contents.

Did any of that make sense? In the world of Macintosh, you always specify *what* you want to change (using the mouse), and then you use a menu command to specify *how* you want it changed. You'll see this pattern over and over again: *select* something on the screen and then *apply* a menu command to it.

Look over the contents of your hard-drive window. See the following figure. (Everybody's got different stuff, so what you see on your screen won't exactly match these illustrations.) There are all kinds of neat things you can do to a window. They're worth learning — you're going to run into windows *every-where* after you start working.

CLOSE BOX—Click here to close the window. It's the same as choosing Close Window from the File menu.

TITLE BAR—Drag anywhere in this striped area to move the entire window.

ZOOM BOX—Click here to make the window large enough to show all its contents.

VERTICAL SCROLL BAR— It's white, indicating that you're seeing every-thing in the window (top to bottom).

SIZE BOX—Drag in any direction to make the window bigger or smaller.

HORIZONTAL SCROLL BAR—It's gray, indicating that you're not seeing everything in the window (there's something off to the side). You can drag the little square from side to side to adjust your view of the window.

Go ahead and try out some of the little boxes and scroll bars. Click them. Tug on them. Open the window and close it again. No matter what you do, *you can never hurt the machine by doing "the wrong thing."* That's the wonderful thing about the Macintosh: it's the Nerf appliance.

Now try this. Make sure your hard drive window is open. See the System Folder? Even if you don't, here's a quick way to find it: quickly type *SY* on your keyboard.

Presto, the Mac finds the System Folder (which happens to be the first thing that begins with those letters) and highlights it, in effect dropping it in front of you, wagging its tail.

## All systems are go

If nothing happened when you typed SY, your Mac may not be using the trendy new software known as System 7. Absorb the wisdom of Chapter 6 if you care what this means.

For the moment, glance at the upper-right corner of your screen. Do you see this icon ⍰ ?

If so, you have System 7. Congratulations. If not, you have System 6. Whether or not you're "System 7 savvy" will make a big difference, both to your under-standing of this book and to your ability to get dates at computer club meetings.

Because all Macs made since 1991 come with System 7, for the rest of this book I'm going to assume that you're using System 7 (or 7.1 or 7-point-anything). If your Mac is really old, and you've determined that you've got System 6, watch the margins for special notes that refer to the differences between the two systems.

## Double-clicking in theory and practice

Anyway, moving on: try pressing the arrow keys on your keyboard — right, left, up, down. The Mac highlights neighboring icons as you do so.

Suppose that you want to see what's in the System Folder. Of course, using your newfound noun-verb method, you could (1) click the System Folder to select it, and then (2) choose Open from the File menu.

But that's the sissy way. Try this power shortcut: point to the System Folder icon so that the tip of the arrow cursor is squarely inside the picture of the folder. Keeping the mouse still, click twice in rapid succession. With stunning originality, the Committee for the Invention of Computer Terminology calls this advanced computing technique *double-clicking*.

If all went well, your double-click opened a new window, showing you the contents of the System Folder. (If it didn't work, you probably need to keep the mouse still or double-click faster.)

Remember this juicy golden rule: *Double-click means "open."*

In your Mac life, you'll be asked (or tempted) to click many an item on-screen: buttons that say "OK"; tools that look like paintbrushes; all manner of multiple-choice buttons. In every one of these cases, you're supposed to click *once*.

*Only* when you want to *open* something do you double-click. Got it?

## Multiple windows

Now you should have two windows open on the screen: the hard-disk window and the System Folder window. (The System Folder window may be covering the first one up; they're like overlapping pieces of paper on a desk.)

Try this: Click the title bar of the System Folder window (just one click; remember that double-clicking is used exclusively for opening something). Drag the title bar downward until you can see the hard drive window behind it. See the following figure.

You can tell that this window is in back because its title bar is white. Just click anywhere in the window to bring it to the front.

You know that this window is the top window because its title bar is striped.

Take a stress-free moment to experiment with these two windows: click the back one to bring it forward; then click the one that was in front to bring it to the front again.

If you need any more help fooling around with these windows, the Macintosh manual has a complete tutorial.

## Using a list view

There's one more aspect of windows that will probably make Type A personalities squirm with delight. Up 'til now, you've been viewing the contents of your disk as a bunch of icons. Nice, but wouldn't it be neat to see things alphabetically?

1. Make sure the System Folder is the active window (the one in front).

   We're going to use the System Folder because it's got a lot of stuff in it.

   Next, you're going to use a menu. Remember how to choose a menu command? Point to the menu's name and hold down the mouse button.

2. Locate the View menu at the top of the screen. From it, choose By Name.

   Suddenly, the big icons are replaced by a neat alphabetical list of the window's contents.

---

## For would-be weenies only (nonessential info)

When you view a window's contents in a list, each folder *within* the window is marked by a tiny triangle. The triangle points to the right.

You can open one of these folders-within-the-folder in the usual way, if you wish — by double-clicking. But it's much more satisfying for neat freaks to click the *triangle* instead. In the following figure, the before-and-after view of the Control Panels folder (inside the System Folder) shows how much more organized you can be.

When you click the triangle, in other words, your window becomes like an outline. The contents of that subfolder are indented. To "collapse," or close, the folder, click the downward-pointing triangle.

One more trick: See the words Size, Kind, and so on (at the top of the window)? Click any of these words. Instantly the Mac re-sorts everything in the window, based on the word you clicked. Example: Click Size, and you'll see the largest files listed first.

| ☐ System Folder ▤ | | |
|---|---|---|
| 17 items     22.5 MB in disk     54.3 MB available | | |
| Name | Size | Kind |
| ▷ ☐ Apple Menu Items | 105K | folder |
| ☐ Clipboard | 56K | file |
| ▷ ☐ Control Panels | 291K | folder |
| ▷ ☐ Extensions | 1,235K | folder |
| ☐ Finder | 356K | file |
| ☐ Note Pad File | 3K | file |
| ▷ ☐ Preferences | 20K | folder |
| ▷ ☐ PrintMonitor Documents | zero K | folder |

| ☐ System Folder ▤ | | |
|---|---|---|
| 22 items     22.5 MB in disk     54.3 MB available | | |
| Name | Size | Kind |
| ▷ ☐ Apple Menu Items | 105K | folder |
| ☐ Clipboard | 56K | file |
| ▽ ☐ Control Panels | 78K | folder |
| ☐ Color | 12K | contr |
| ☐ General Controls | 17K | contr |
| ☐ Monitors | 41K | contr |
| ☐ Mouse | 9K | contr |
| ▷ ☐ Extensions | 1,235K | folder |

## *The easiest homework you've ever had*

To reinforce your budding mouse skills, here's a pathetically easy assignment. Find the icon in your hard drive window called either Macintosh Basics or Mouse Practice. (Macintosh Basics/Mouse Practice comes with every Mac sold in the last few years. If you can't find it anywhere, call up whatever store sold you the Mac and ask about it. And if you still can't get ahold of it, don't sweat. I'll try to hit most of the same points as we go along.)

It's a clever, animated introduction to the Mac, and it shows you America's favorite computer skills (the ones you just learned): pointing, clicking, and dragging. Ponder the sidebar below if you need a refresher.

Here's how you use the Macintosh Basics program:

1. Open the Macintosh Basics (or Mouse Practice) folder, if necessary, by pointing to it and double-clicking.
2. Point to the little Macintosh Basics man (or Mouse Practice Woman) and double-click *that*.

From there, just follow the instructions on the screen. Turn down the corner of this page, and pick up here when you're ready to go on. By the time you finish, you'll have earned your MMA — Master of Mouse Activity.

## Remedial mousing for the repetition lover

In the event you couldn't find your Macintosh Basics/Mouse Practice program, here's a rehash of the essential mouse skills you're supposed to have learned.

First, there's *pointing*. That's where you touch the tip of the arrow cursor on something.

You've already *clicked*, too — that's where you point to something and then click the mouse button. If you're pointing to an icon, like the Trash can, it turns black to show that it's selected.

If you point to an icon and hold the mouse button down, you can move the cursor and the icon will move along with it. The act of moving the mouse while the button's down is called *dragging*.

Finally, you're sometimes asked to *double-click* something. That is, hold the mouse still and press the mouse button twice fast. Feels great.

## Pit stop

If you're panting from the mental exertion of learning so many new things at one sitting, go get something from the fridge. Believe it or not, you've already learned more than half of the skills required for operating a Mac.

Shut the Mac down now, if you want (by choosing the Shut Down command from the Special menu — but you knew that). Chapter 1½ is something of a chalk-talk to help you explain what's really happening inside the computer's puny brain.

# Top Ten Similarities Between You and Your Mac

Before you move boldly forward to the next chapter, ponder the significance of the following interesting — nay, frightening — similarities between you and your computer.

1. Both weigh between 5 and 15 pounds when first displayed in public.

2. Both have feet on the bottom.

3. Both have slots to provide adequate ventilation of the innards.

4. Both react to the movement of a nearby mouse.

5. Both sometimes crash when asked to do too much at once.

6. Both have a central button.

7. Both light up when turned on.

8. With considerable effort, both may be made to work with IBM computers.

9. Both may be connected to a phone line for days at a time.

10. Both have a built-in 1.4MB SuperDrive. (Well, OK, *you* probably don't, but you don't want to be *exactly* like your computer, do you?)

# Chapter 1½
# High-Tech Made Easy

## Understanding How a Mac Works

I'm a little worried about sticking this chapter so close to the front of the book. Plenty of people firmly believe that the Mac has a personality — that when something goes wrong, the Mac is being cranky; and when a funny message appears on the screen, the Mac is being friendly. Don't let the following discussion of cold, metal, impersonal circuitry ruin that image for you; the Mac *does* have a personality, no matter what the wireheads say.

For the first time, you're going to have to roll up your brain's sleeves and chew on some real, live computer jargon. Don't worry — you'll feel coolly professional and in control by the time it's over. And it's a short chapter. Only *half* a chapter, really. That should make it easier to contemplate reading pages of chalk talk.

### Storing things with floppy disks

Human beings, for the most part, store information in one of two places. Either we retain something in our memory — or, if it's too much to remember, we write it down on the back of an envelope.

Computers work pretty much the same way (except they're not quite as handy with envelopes). They can either store what they know in their relatively pea-brained *memory,* which we'll cover in a moment, or they can write it down. A computer writes stuff down on computer disks.

**Floppy disk:** *A hard 3½ - inch square thing that data is stored on.*

The most common kind of disk is the floppy disk. Unfortunately for your efforts to understand the Mac, its floppy disks aren't floppy, and they're not disks. They're actually hard plastic squares, 3 ½ inches on a side.

Inside the protective hard shell, though, there's a circle of the same shiny brown stuff that tapes are made of. (I suppose that means there really is a floppy disk in there.) Anyway, instead of recording a James Taylor song or a Bruce Willis movie, as audio or videotapes would do, the computer records your documents: a letter to Aunt Millie, your latest financial figures, or notes for your novel.

# INSIDE A DISK

Sliding shield

Plastic case

Protective liner

Sector
Track

Floppy disk

Write-protect hole

Plastic case

Here's what a floppy disk would look like if you blew it apart with plastic explosives. In the middle, sandwiched between the two protective Stridex pads, there lies a shiny plastic disk to which you entrust your sacred data.

Floppy disks come in several capacities, but even the largest one only holds about 1,000 pages' worth of data. That may seem like a lot, but that's just text. Pictures, for instance, take up much more space; that same floppy disk can probably only hold one or two color pictures. You can see, then, that floppies aren't very handy for storing lots of information.

## Conceptualizing the hard disk

Every Mac made since 1987 has an even better storage device built inside it — a *hard disk*. The concept of a hard disk confuses people because it's hidden inside the Mac's case. Since you can't see it or touch it, it's sort of conceptual — like beta-carotene or God, I guess. But it's there, and a hefty chunk of your Mac's purchase price pays for it.

Hard disks differ from floppy disks in a few critical ways. A hard disk delivers information to the computer's brain about ten times faster than a floppy; holds about 100 times more; and costs about 500 times as much. (Floppies are dirt cheap.)

Why all this talk of disks? Because this is where your life's work is going to live when the computer is shut off.

And by the way, don't be confused if you hear (or see) the terms *hard disk* and *hard drive* used interchangeably — they're the same thing.

# *Understanding memory*

OK. Now we get to the good stuff: how a computer really works. I know you'd just as soon not know what's going on in there, but this is mental broccoli: it's good for you, and later in life, you'll be glad you were forced to digest it. If, at this point, your brain is beginning to hemorrhage, skip this section entirely and find serenity in Chapter 2.

There's actually a significant difference between a Mac's memory and *your* memory (besides the fact that yours is probably much more interesting). When the Mac is turned off at night, it forgets *everything.* It becomes a dumb, metal-and-plastic doorstop. That's because a computer's memory, just like yours, is kept alive by electrical impulses. When you turn off a Mac, the electricity stops.

Therefore, each time you turn on a Mac, it has to re-learn everything it ever knew, including the fact that it's a computer, what kind of computer it is, how to display text, how many days until your warranty expires, and so on. Now we arrive at the purpose of those disks we've been droning on about; that's where the computer's knowledge lives when the juice is off. Without a disk, the Mac is like someone with a completely hollow skull (and we've all met *that* type). If you're ever unlucky enough to experience a broken hard drive, you'll see how exciting a Mac can be without any disks: it shows a completely gray screen with a small blinking question mark in the middle (I've met a few people like *that,* too).

When you turn on the Mac, there's whirring and blinking; the hard disk inside begins spinning. When it hits about 3,600 rpm, the Mac starts reading the hard disk (or, if the analogy helps you, it "plays" the disk like a record player). It finds out: "Hey, I'm a Mac! And this is how I display text!" and so on. The Mac is reading the disk and copying everything it reads into *memory.*

Memory is really neat. After something's in memory, it's instantaneously available to the computer. The Mac no longer has to read the disk to learn something. Memory is also expensive; it's really a bunch of complicated circuits etched onto a piece of silicon the size of a stick of gum.

Because it's expensive, most people's Macs have far less memory than disk space. For example, even if your hard disk holds every issue of *National Geographic* ever published, you're probably only going to *read* one article at a time. So the Mac reads "African Tribal Women: Pierced Noses in the Desert" from your hard disk, loads it into memory, and displays it on the screen. So it doesn't matter that your Mac's memory doesn't hold as much as your entire hard disk; the hard disk is used for *long-term, permanent* storage of *lots* of things, and memory is used for *temporary* storage while you work on *one thing at a time.*

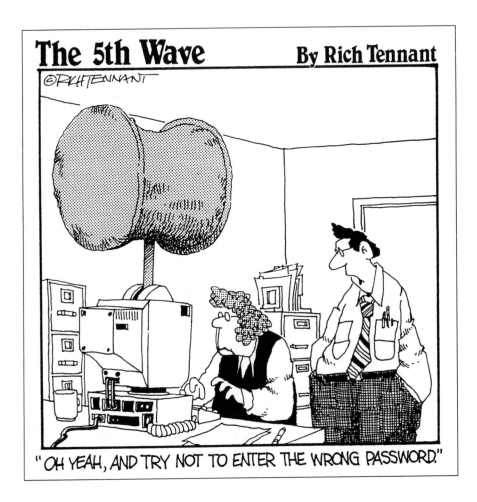

# Who's Meg?

You often hear computer jocks talk about megs. Only rarely are they referring to Meg Ryan and Meg Tilly. Meg is short for *megabyte*. So is MB. (*Mega*=1,000,000 and *byte*=$\frac{1}{1,000,000}$ of a megabyte. That was fun, wasn't it?)

**Megabyte:** *A unit of memory or storage capacity, nicknamed meg or abbreviated MB. One meg equals 1,024 kilobytes, or K; a K is about one page of a romance novel.*

What's highly confusing to most beginners is that memory (fast, expensive, temporary) and hard-disk space (permanent, slower) are measured in the same units: megabytes. A typical Mac has four or eight megs of memory (silicon chips), but 80 or 120 megs of hard-disk space (spinning platters).

With this vital fact in mind, see if you can answer the following paradoxical dinner party question:

"*How many megs* does your Macintosh have?"

The novice's answer: "Um . . . say, have you tried those little cocktail weenies?"

The partly-initiated's reply: "I . . . I think 80?"

The truly enlightened response: "What do you mean, how many megs? Are you referring to *memory* or to *hard-disk storage space?* . . . Here, have a cocktail weenie. . . ."

## Understanding RAM

**RAM:** *When the Committee for Arbitrary Acronyms ratified this abbreviation, it probably stood for Random Abbreviation for Memory. Supposedly, it really stands for Random Access Memory, whatever that means.*

Let's add another term to your quickly-growing nerd vocabulary list. It pains me to teach you this word because it's one of those really meaningless terms that was invented purely to intimidate people. Trouble is, you're going to hear it a lot, so you may as well be prepared.

It's RAM. You pronounce it like the goat. RAM is memory. A typical Mac has four or eight megs of RAM (in other words, of memory).

## Putting it all together

OK. Now that you know where a computer's information lives, let me take you on a tour of the computer's guts. Let's get into our little imaginary Disney World tram. Keep your hands and feet inside the car at all times.

When you turn on the Mac, as noted earlier, the hard disk spins, and the Mac copies certain critical information into its memory.

So far, the Mac only knows that it's a computer. It doesn't know anything else that's stored on your hard disk; it doesn't know about African Tribal Women or your new screenplay, or how much you owe on your credit card — yet.

To get any practical work done, you now have to transfer the article (or screenplay or spreadsheet) into memory; in Macintosh terminology, you have to *open a file*. In Chapter 2, you'll find out how easy and idiot-proof this is. Anyway, after you open a file, it appears on the screen. (It's in memory now.)

While your document is on the screen, you can make changes to it. This, of course, is why you bought a computer in the first place. You can delete a sentence from your novel or move a steamy scene to a different chapter (the term for this process is *word processing*). If you're working on your finances, you can add a couple of zeros to your checking-account balance (the term for this process is *wishful thinking*). All without any eraser crumb or whiteout.

Perceptive readers (who haven't already gotten bored and gone off to watch TV) will recognize that you're making all of these changes to what's in *memory*. The more you change the screenplay that's up on the screen, the more it's different from that *permanent* copy that's still on your disk, safe and sound.

At this point, you're actually in a pretty precarious position. Remember that memory is sustained by electricity. In other words, if your four-year-old mistakes the Mac's power cord for a handy suckable plaything and jerks it out of the wall, then the electricity will stop, the screen will go blank, and all the changes you've made disappear forever. You're left with the original copy on the disk, of course, but any work you've done on it vanishes, along with anything else in the Mac's memory.

However, every Mac program has a simple command, called Save, that saves your work back onto the hard disk. That is, the computer updates the original copy that's still on the hard disk, and you're safe. Even if a sun storm wipes out all power plants in the Northern Hemisphere, your novel or letter or spreadsheet is safe on the disk, even though the Mac's memory gets wiped out. Most people use the Save command every five or ten minutes so that their work is always up-to-date and preserved on the disk. (You'll learn how to use the Save command in Chapter 3.)

## *"I lost all my work!"*

So that you'll quit worrying about it, the precariousness of memory accounts for the horror stories you sometimes hear from people who claim that they lost their work to a computer. "I was on volume Y of the encyclopedia I've been writing," they'll say, "and I lost all of it because of a computer glitch!"

Now you can cry crocodile tears and then skip back to your office with a smirk. Now *you* know what happened. They probably worked for hours with some document on the screen but forgot to use the Save command. Then, when the unthinkable happened — someone tripped on the power cord — sure enough, all the changes they'd made got wiped out. A simple Save command would have stored everything neatly on the hard disk.

# Top Ten Differences Between Memory and a Hard Disk

May you never confuse memory with a hard disk again.

1. You usually buy memory two or four megs at a time. Hard disks usually come in 40-, 80-, and 160-meg sizes (and on up).

2. Memory comes as chips on a little minicircuit board. A hard disk is a big box made of metal (and sometimes encased in plastic).

3. You can only install memory inside the computer (something you usually hire a local guru to do). A hard disk may be either inside the Mac (an *internal* drive) or a separate box you just plug into the back (an *external* drive).

4. Memory delivers information to the Mac's brain almost instantly. The hard disk sometimes seems to take forever.

5. Memory is sometimes called RAM. A hard disk has no abbreviation.

6. Not every Mac has a hard disk (about 11 people still use very old models with nothing but floppy disks). But every Mac has memory.

7. When the Mac is reading some information off a hard disk, a little light flickers on and off (usually on the front of your Mac or on the case of an external hard disk). You can't tell when the Mac is getting information from RAM.

8. As a very general rule, RAM costs about $45 per meg, and hard drive space averages about $10 per meg.

9. Memory's contents disappear when you turn off the computer. A disk's contents stay there until you deliberately throw them away.

10. You can trick the Mac into thinking that some of your *hard-disk* space is RAM (called *virtual memory*). You can also trick the Mac into thinking that some of your RAM is a disk (called a *RAM disk*). (Actually, I guess this is really a similarity, not a difference. Oh well. Both of these advanced techniques are described in your Mac manuals, more or less. Neither is important except to power-users; most people don't use either one. I'm already sorry I brought it up.)

# Chapter 2
# Doing Windows, Getting Floppy

● ● ● ● ● ● ● ● ● ● ● ● ● ● ● ● ● ● ● ● ● ● ● ● ● ● ● ● ● ● ● ● ● ● ● ● ● ● ● ● ● ● ●

## In This Chapter

▶ All about windows, folders, and icons

▶ Learning keyboard shortcuts

▶ Working with floppy disks

▶ Tips on using windows and floppy disks to raise your social status

● ● ● ● ● ● ● ● ● ● ● ● ● ● ● ● ● ● ● ● ● ● ● ● ● ● ● ● ● ● ● ● ● ● ● ● ● ● ● ● ● ● ●

## Becoming Manipulative

All of the clicking and dragging and window-shoving you learned in Chapter 1 is, in fact, leading up to something useful.

### Foldermania

I've said that your hard disk is like the world's biggest filing cabinet. It's where you store all your stuff. But a filing cabinet without filing *folders* would be about as convenient to handle as an egg without a shell.

The folders on the Mac screen don't occupy any space on your hard drive. They're electronic fictions whose sole purpose is to help you organize your stuff.

Mr. Folder

The Mac provides an infinite supply of them. Want a folder? Do this:

From the File menu, choose New Folder.

Ooh, tricky, this machine! A new folder appears. Note that the Mac gracefully proposes "untitled folder" as its name. (Gotta call it *something*, I suppose.)

Notice something else, though: the name is *highlighted* (black). Remember our earlier lesson? Highlighted = selected = ready for you to *do* something. When *text* is highlighted, the Mac is ready for you to *replace* it with anything you type. In other words, you don't even have to backspace over it. Just type away.

1. Type *USA Folder*. Press the Return key.

   The Return key tells the Mac that your naming spurt is over.

   Now, to see how folders work, create another one.

2. Choose New Folder from the File menu again.

   Another new folder appears, once more waiting for a title.

3. Type *Ohio*. Press Return.

You're going to create one more empty folder. But by this time, your wrist is probably weary from the forlorn trek back and forth to the File menu. Don't you wish there were a faster way to make a folder?

There is.

## Keyboard shortcuts

Pull down the File menu, but don't select any of the commands in it yet. See that weird notation to the right of some of the commands?

```
┌─────────────────────┐
│ File                │
├─────────────────────┤
│ New Folder      ⌘N  │
│ Open            ⌘O  │
│ Print           ⌘P  │
│ Close Window    ⌘W  │
├─────────────────────┤
│ Get Info        ⌘I  │
│ Sharing...          │
│ Duplicate       ⌘D  │
│ Make Alias      ⌘M  │
│ Put Away        ⌘Y  │
├─────────────────────┤
│ Find...         ⌘F  │
│ Find Again      ⌘G  │
├─────────────────────┤
│ Page Setup...       │
│ Print Window...     │
└─────────────────────┘
```

Get used to 'em. They're *keyboard shortcuts,* and they appear in almost every menu you'll ever see. You're by no means obligated to use them, but you should understand that they let you select certain menu items without using the mouse.

## Unimportant sidebar about other menu symbols

Besides the little keyboard-shortcut symbols at the right side of a menu, you'll occasionally run into a little downward-pointing arrow, like this:

**Font**

Avant Garde
Bookman
Chicago
Courier
Futura
Garamond
Geneva
Hartel
Helvetica
Monaco
Palatino
Symbol
▼

That arrow tells you that the menu is so long, it doesn't even fit on the screen. The arrow is implying that there are still more commands in the menu that you're not seeing. To get to them, carefully roll the pointer down the menu all the way to that down-pointing triangle. Don't let it scare you: The menu commands will jump upward, bringing the hidden ones into view.

When you type, you press the Shift key to make a capital letter, right? They call the Shift key a *modifier key* because it turns ordinary, well-behaved citizen keys like 3 and 4 into madcap symbols like # and $. Welcome to the world of computers, where everything is four times more complicated. Instead of having only *one* modifier key, the Mac has *four* of them! Look down next to your spacebar. There they are: in addition to the Shift key, one says Option, one says Control, and another either says Command or has a little ⌘ symbol on it.

It's that little cloverleaf symbol that appears in the File menu. Next to the New Folder command, it's ⌘-N. That means:

1. While pressing the ⌘ key down, press the N key. Then release everything.

   Bam! You've got yourself another folder.

2. Type *Michigan* and press Return.

   You've just named your third folder. So why have you been wasting a perfectly good afternoon (or whatever it is in your time zone) making empty folders? So you can pretend you're getting organized.

3. Drag the Ohio folder on top of the USA Folder.

Michigan

Make sure that the tip of the arrow actually hits the center of the USA Folder so that the folder becomes highlighted. When it turns black, let go of the Ohio folder — and watch it disappear into the USA Folder. (If your aim wasn't good, you'll now see the Ohio folder sitting *next* to the USA Folder; try the last step again.)

4. Put the Michigan folder into the USA Folder in the same way — by dragging it on top of the USA Folder.

As far as you know, though, those state folders have *disappeared*. How can you trust me that they're now neatly filed away?

5. Double-click the USA Folder.

Yep. Opens right up into a window, and there are your two darling states, nestled sweetly where they belong. If you were to double-click one of *them*, you'd open *another* window. (Having a million windows open at once is nothing to be afraid of. If you're a neatness freak, it might make you feel threatened, but it's easy enough to close them — remember the close box in the upper-left corner of each one.)

**Double-click**: *Without moving the mouse, click twice quickly on something, which will open it into a window. Doesn't matter if it's a disk icon, a folder icon, or a document icon.*

OK, so how do you get them *out* again? Do you have to drag them individually? That would certainly be a bummer if you had all 50 folders in the USA Folder.

Turns out there are several ways to select more than one icon at a time.

6. Click above and to the left of the Ohio folder (Example 1, below). Without releasing the mouse, drag down and to the right so that you enclose both folders with a dotted rectangle (Examples 2 and 3).

If you're using System 7, then each icon turns black as the dotted rectangle encloses it. (Otherwise, nothing turns black until you release the mouse.) In any case, release the mouse button when you've got both icons enclosed.

Now that you have several folders selected, you can move them en masse to another location.

Drag the Ohio folder outside of the USA Folder window. The Michigan folder goes along for the ride.

This was a somewhat unproductive exercise, of course, because we were only working with empty folders. It gets much more exciting when you start working with your own documents. All of these techniques work equally well with folders and with documents.

# Eminently skippable trivia

The method of selecting several icons by dragging a rectangle around them is fine if all the icons are next to each other. But how would you select only the icons that begin with the letter A in this picture?

You can't very well enclose the A's by dragging the mouse — you'd also get all the *other* icons within the same rectangle.

The power-user's secret: Click each one *while pressing the Shift key.* As long as you're pressing Shift, you continually add additional, non-adjacent icons to the selection. (And if you Shift-click one by accident, you can *de*select it by Shift-clicking *again.* Try it!)

## *How to trash something*

Here's one more icon-manipulation trick you'll probably find valuable.

1. Close the USA Folder by clicking its close box.

2. Then drag the folder on top of the Trash can in the lower-right corner of the screen.

Don't let go until the Trash can actually turns black (when the tip of the arrow cursor is upon it). When you do let go, notice how the Trash can bulges, a subtle reinforcement of how important it thinks your stuff is. Anyway, that's how you throw things out on the Mac: just drag them on top of the Trash can.

Technically, you've really only put that stuff in Oblivion Waiting Room; it doesn't disappear when it goes into the Trash. It'll sit there forever, in a bulging trash can.

If you need to rescue something, just double-click the Trash to open its window; drag whatever-it-was right back onto the screen.

So if putting something into the Trash doesn't really delete it, how *do* you really delete it? Choose Empty Trash from the Special menu.

## Trash and System 6

If you're using System 6 (that is, if no ⁇ icon appears in the upper-right corner of your screen), then the Trash can *doesn't* sit there, bulging, until you Empty Trash. It gets emptied automatically when you turn off the Mac, and sometimes sooner.

## A truly trivial trash tidbit for techies

Don't tell anybody, but *even after* you've Emptied the Trash, your file *still* isn't really gone forever. There are programs (like Norton Utilities and Complete Undelete) that can unerase a file that's been trashed, as long as you haven't used your Mac much since then. That's useful to remember in case (1) you ever trash something by mistake, or (2) you're a spy.

# *Fun with Floppies*

For our next trick, you're going to need a floppy disk. If you didn't buy a box of blank disks with your Mac, you're going to need some eventually. Call up Mac Connection and order some. They're cheap and you'll have them by tomorrow morning. (Phone number is in the Resource Resource at the back of the book.)

**Disk drive:** *The thin horizontal slot in the front of your Macintosh, where the floppy disk goes. Put the disk in metal-side first, label facing up.*

1. Put the floppy disk into the disk drive slot. The Mac gulps it in with a satisfying *kachunk*. If it's a brand new disk, you see this message:

## A floppy factoid barely worth reading

You know how an audio cassette has that small plastic tab, which you can pry out to prevent your little sister from accidentally recording over the tape?

Well, a floppy has the same thing (a tab, not a sister). In the corner of the disk, on the back, there's a little square sliding tab. On a disk, you don't actually have to pry out the tab (this is progress); you can just slide it back and forth. When you slide the tab so that you can see through the hole, you've *locked* the disk, and you can't erase it or trash any of its contents.

When you slide the tab so that it *covers* the hole, the disk is unlocked, and you can erase it, trash it, or copy new stuff onto it.

Go ahead. Click Initialize. (If you're asked whether you want to make it single-sided [the kind of disk that's way obsolete] or double-sided, select double-sided — unless you're going to be sending this disk to someone who bought a Mac in 1984 and immediately moved to Borneo.) You're then asked to name the disk; type a name, click OK, and then wait about 45 seconds while the Mac prepares the disk for its new life as your data receptacle.

If it's *not* a new disk — for example, if you're using one of the disks that came with your Mac — the floppy-disk icon shows up on the right side, just beneath your hard-disk icon:

To see what's on the disk, double-click the icon. As you've no doubt tired of hearing repeated, a *double-click* on a disk icon *opens* its contents window.

You're about to learn how to copy stuff from your hard drive onto a floppy disk (and vice versa). This is important stuff: In your lifetime, you'll do a lot of copying from floppy disks *to* your hard drive (such as when you buy a new program and want to put it on your hard drive). And if you're smart, you'll also do a lot of copying onto floppies *from* your hard drive (such as when you make a backup copy of all your work, in preparation for the inevitable day when your hard disk calls in sick).

2. Double-click your hard-disk icon.

   If its window was closed, it now opens. If the window was open but hidden behind the floppy-disk window, the hard-disk window now pops to the front.

3. Drag the Ohio folder on top of the floppy-disk icon.

If you already trashed your Ohio folder, no big deal. Choose New Folder from the File menu (or press ⌘-N) to create a new folder. Drag that instead.

## More disk stuff you don't really need to know

The big floppy-disk makers, like Sony and Fuji, churn out disks by the trainload. They have a big market; both Macs and IBM-type computers use these 3½-inch disks.

The thing is, not all computers *format* the floppies in the same ways. Imagine that a little floppy-disk gnome runs around while the disk is being "initialized," making chalk-mark boundaries for the storage of your files. Well, Mac gnomes and IBM gnomes space their disk-surface boundary lines differently — the upshot is that an IBM disk will appear unreadable to a Mac, and vice versa. So Sony and Fuji and the other disk companies don't bother preformatting these disks for you, since they don't know what kind of computer you have, and besides it's too much trouble.

As noted in Chapter 1½, disks come in three capacities, although all the disks look almost alike: the old 400K, or *single-sided* disks; 800K, or *double-sided* disks; and 1.4MB, or *high-density* disks. That is a *lot* of storage for such a little disk; 1.4 megabytes is around 1400K, or 3.5 times as much as the original single-sided disks. High-density disks are marked with the letters CH, for some reason:

Well, OK, it's really supposed to be an upside-down *HD*, for high-density, but the logo designer had a bad night. Anyway, all *recent* Macs can read high-density disks, but there are millions of Mac Pluses and older SE models that can't. So when you exchange disks with somebody, give them 800K (double-sided) disks unless you've made sure they can handle the HD ones.

The point is that, on a Macintosh, making a copy of something is as easy as dragging it to the disk you want it copied onto. You can also drag something into the disk's *window* (instead of onto its *icon*).

Copying something *from* a floppy *to* your hard disk is equally easy. Open the floppy-disk window (by double-clicking the floppy-disk icon). Then drag whatever icons you want from the window onto the hard-disk icon (or into the hard-disk window).

For example, in the illustration below, two files are being copied from a floppy disk — not just into the hard-disk window, but into a *specific folder* on the hard disk:

Rest assured that you can make as many copies of a file as you want without ever experiencing a loss of quality. You're digital now, kids. It's not like copying tapes, where each copy of a copy is a little bit worse than the previous generation. The ten-thousandth copy of your novel will be just as spicy as the first. (That makes software companies nervous; some unscrupulous people make a regular habit of making themselves free copies of their friends' expensive software.)

OK, so you've made a backup copy of your fourth-quarter report, or you've just copied a new program onto your hard disk. Now what? How do you get the disk out?

Well, you wouldn't be alone in guessing that you use the Eject Disk command in the Special menu. But you'd be wrong, more or less. The Eject Disk command does spit out the disk — but it leaves the disk's *icon* on the screen so that the Mac thinks it's still available. The minute you try to go on with your work, the Mac will start displaying messages demanding that you give the disk back to it.

A much better way to get rid of the disk is to select it (noun) and choose *Put Away* (verb) from the File menu. That makes the disk pop out, *and* its image disappears from the screen. (If you care, there's a keyboard shortcut for Put Away: ⌘-Y.)

---

## Dweebs' Corner: Alternative disk tips

Another way to remove a floppy disk is to drag its icon to the Trash can! Yes, yes, I *know* it looks like you're erasing the entire disk. It looks that way to *every* first-time Mac user. But you're not — this action just pops out the disk.

Every now and then, you'll have a situation where a disk won't come out of the drive. If the Mac is still running, hold down the ⌘ and Shift keys together, and press 1. (This works even if you're not at the desktop/Finder.) Even less frequently than that, you'll have a disk in the drive and the Mac will be *off.* In that case, turn on the Mac while pressing the mouse button down continuously until the Trash can appears.

And if *that* doesn't pop the disk out, straighten a paper clip. Push it slowly but firmly into the tiny pinhole to the right of the disk drive slot. That'll shove the disk out.

---

# *Top Ten Window, Disk, and Trash Tips*

"I don't do windows," you say? After reading the following tips, you'll find windows so easy to do that you might even consider defrosting the fridge.

1. To rename an icon or disk, click carefully on its name. Wait for a second or so, until a rectangle appears around the name. That's your cue to type away, giving it a new name. Press Return when you're done.

   It works a little differently in System 6. Just click an icon and start typing. No rectangle, no waiting.

2. If you're looking at a windowful of file icons, you can select one by typing the first couple of letters of its name.

3. Don't forget that you can look at a window's contents in a neat list (choose "by Name" from the View menu). Once in a list view, when a folder is highlighted, you can press ⌘—→ to expand it (as though you'd clicked the triangle to view its contents) and ⌘-← to collapse it again.

4. In System 7, every time you choose Empty Trash from the Special menu, the Mac asks you if you're absolutely sure. If you'd prefer to simply vaporize the Trash contents without asking, select the Trash icon. Choose Get Info from the File menu and click the "Warn before emptying" checkbox so that the X disappears.

5. If you're trying to make a copy of a floppy disk, and you only have one floppy-disk drive, you'll find that the Mac can only copy a little bit at a time. It winds up asking you to insert one disk, then the other; one disk, then the other . . . until your wrists are swollen and bleeding. A better, faster idea: Copy the entire disk to your *hard disk,* eject the floppy, insert the blank floppy, and then copy the stuff from the hard disk to the new floppy. Using the hard disk as an intermediate holding tank in this way eliminates the disk swapping. (Just trash the superfluous copy from your hard disk when it's all over.)

6. If you have a very important document, you can prevent it from getting thrown away by accident. Click its icon. Choose Get Info from the File menu. Select the Locked checkbox. Now, even if you put it in the Trash and try to empty the Trash, the Mac will simply tell you that there's a locked item in the Trash, which it won't get rid of.

7. You already know how to copy a file from one disk to another. You can copy it on the *same* disk, too. Click the icon and choose Duplicate from the File menu. Or, while pressing the Option key, drag the icon onto a new folder.

8. Isn't it frustrating to open a window that's too small to show you all of its contents?

Of course, you could spend a weekend fussing with the scroll bars, trying to crank the other icons into view. Or, using error-and-trial, you could drag the lower-right handle (the resize box) to make the window bigger.

The much quicker solution is to click the *zoom box* in the upper-right corner of the window. The Mac automatically makes the window *exactly* large enough to show all of the icons.

9. You don't have to be content to leave the trash stranded way down there at the bottom of your screen. You can move it anywhere you want, just by dragging it. That's especially handy if you're lucky enough to have one of those screens the size of a Cineplex Odeon and don't feel like packing a week's worth of supplies every time you want to make a Journey to the Trash Corner.

10. You don't have to eject disks and clean up your windows before you shut down the computer. The disks pop out automatically, and the windows will be right where you left them the next time you turn on the Mac.

# Chapter 3
# Actually Getting Some Work Done

• • • • • • • • • • • • • • • • • • • • • • • • • • • • • • • • • • • •

*In This Chapter*

▶ What software is, for those who care

▶ Copying and pasting

▶ Your very first word processing lesson

▶ Saving your work for posterity

▶ Desk accessories and the fruit-shaped menu they're listed in

• • • • • • • • • • • • • • • • • • • • • • • • • • • • • • • • • • • •

*B*uckle your mental seat belts: I'm about to stretch an analogy so far it might pop. Ready?

The Mac is like a VCR. The disks you slide into the Mac are like the tapes you slip into your VCR. Without tapes (disks), the VCR (Mac) is worthless. But with tapes (disks), your VCR (Mac) can take on any personality.

A VCR might let you watch a western one night, home movies another, and a *60 Minutes* exposé about a corrupt Good Humor man another night. In the same way, your Mac can be a typing instructor, a checkbook balancer, or a movie-editing machine, depending on the software you buy. Each piece of software — usually called a program, but sometimes known as an *application* — is like a different GameBoy cartridge: It makes the Mac look, feel, and behave differently. The average Mac user winds up using about six or seven different programs regularly.

## Obsolescence Therapy II

Your relationship with a software company doesn't end when you buy the program. First, the company provides a technical help staff for you to call when things get rocky. Some firms are great about this — it's a toll-free number that's answered immediately by a smart, helpful, customer-oriented technician. More often, though, sending out an SOS is a long-distance call . . . and a long-distance five- or ten-minute wait before somebody can help you. How can you find out how good a company's help line is? By asking around and reading the reviews in *Macworld* and *MacUser* magazines.

## Names and numbers

After you spend a while with Macs, you start to notice some peculiar naming conventions in software. First of all, all programmers must have broken spacebars because you never see spaces between words in the names of programs: PageMaker, MacPaint, WriteNow, and even MyAdvancedLabelMaker (yuck). Today, having a space in your title is like clipping your nails on the bus: it's simply not done by our kind of people.

You learn to tell how recent a program is by the version number after its name. What begins as WordMeister version 1 becomes WordMeister 1.5 when its maker adds a spelling checker to the program, for example. Then they add built-in help messages and call it WordMeister 1.5.2. I don't know where the idea of multiple decimal points came from, but it's pretty dumb. It's only a matter of time before we'll start seeing ads for things like MacFish 2.4.9.6 and PageMan 3.6.5.4.2.1.

Oh, and when a program gets upgraded too many times, the company adds the word Pro to its name.

Like the computers themselves, software applications are continually being improved and enhanced by their manufacturers. Just as in owning a computer, owning a software program isn't a one-time cash outlay; each time the software company comes out with a new version of the program, you'll be offered the chance to get it for a small "upgrade fee" of $25 or $99, for example.

You'd think people would get fed up with this endless treadmill of expenses and just stick with the version they've got, refusing to upgrade to successive versions. Some manage it. Most people, however, succumb to the fear that somehow they'll be left behind by the march of technology, and wind up forking over the upgrade fees once a year or so.

# Credit Card Workout #2: Buying Software

(Credit Card Workout #1, by the way, was buying the computer.)

Unless you actually bought (or received) some software when you got your Mac, you won't be able to do much more than admire the Mac's contribution to the décor. So unless you bought a Performa model, which comes with a handsome bonus gift of software preinstalled on your hard disk, get ready for another buying spree. (Even if you do have a Performa, you've still got to pay if you want the manuals for the free programs.)

Of course, every Mac comes with *some* software. For example, each Mac comes with the System software (usually on white floppy disks) that it needs for its own internal use. It comes with some miniprograms, like the Calculator and the Note Pad, called *desk accessories*. And it comes with HyperCard Player, which is a topic for a later, rainier day (Chapter 5). None of this free software will make you very productive on the day you set up your computer.

Software, for the most part, is expensive. The world's most popular Mac word processing program, for example, is Microsoft Word, and the lowest price I've seen for it is $300. If you plan to do number crunching, over 80 percent of Mac users use the spreadsheet Microsoft Excel (another $300). Want a database for handling order forms, tracking phone calls, and creating merged form letters? Check out the fantastic FileMaker Pro (around $200).

There are lower-priced alternatives, of course. If you really want to do your homework, read a few recent issues of *Macworld* and *MacUser* for some guidance. WriteNow, for example, is a super, fast, easy-to-use word processing program, and it's only $150. It can even exchange files with Microsoft Word. Unfortunately, you may feel a little bit left out with one of the underdog programs, since almost all the talk, help, and articles will be about the big three (Word, Excel, and FileMaker).

If you're on a budget and don't much care about being in the vanguard, you can get a lot of power in the form of an *integrated* program like ClarisWorks (or any other program whose name ends with "Works") — which is the kind of program you get when you buy a Mac Performa. For the cost of a single program, you get several programs mashed into one: word processor, database, spreadsheet, drawing program, and so on. Of course, it doesn't do any one thing as well as a separate program would, but it does everything pretty well.

In any case, you definitely need a word processor. Most people could use an address book program like Super QuickDex and a calendar/reminder program like Now Up-to-Date. And then there are graphics: if you want to draw or paint, read Chapter 5 for some explanations and suggestions.

## El Cheapo software

Once you've read Chapter 7, and you've decided it might be fun to plug your Mac into the telephone line to dial up faraway computers, you may stumble onto another kind of bargain-basement software: *shareware*. These are programs written by individuals, not software companies, who make them freely available on "electronic bulletin boards." You can grab them, via telephone, and bring them to your own Mac. And get this: only the *honor system,* for heaven's sake, compels you to pay the authors the $15 or $20 they're asking for.

Sure, you usually get what you pay for; shareware often has a homemade, not-quite-ready-for-prime-time feel to it. On the other hand, some of it's really terrific: ZTerm, for use with a modem, has won awards; Compact Pro and StuffIt, used to make files take up less space on the disk, are classics; and there are acres and acres of sounds, pictures, and clip art available on dial-up services like America Online and CompuServe.

## Where to get it

There are two places to buy software: via mail order and at a store. At a store, you get to pick up and heft the actual box, tap a live human being on the shoulder to ask questions, ask other customers what they've had luck with, and so on. In some stores you can even try out the software on a real live Mac, so you won't wind up buying something you don't need.

On the other hand, mail-order companies give much bigger discounts; most take returns after you've opened the box; they don't charge sales tax; and, of course, you don't have to fire up the old Volvo. You get your stuff delivered to your door by the next day (the overnight shipping charge is usually $3 per order).

At the risk of sounding like a broken CD, I'm going to direct you to the Mac magazines like *Macworld* and *MacUser* for more info on mail-order companies. They're called things like Mac Connection, Mac Zone, and Mac Warehouse. They all have toll-free phone numbers, and their catalogs and ads all appear in every single issue of those magazines. (Their numbers also appear in Appendix B, the Resource Resource.) Overnight mail-order companies like these are truly one of the bright spots in the Mac world. After being around them awhile, you'll start to wish there were overnight mail-order grocery stores, gas stations, and dentists.

In this chapter, you're going to do some word processing. That's what 90 percent of Mac users do the most of (when they're not hang gliding, housing the homeless, and saving the environment, I mean). I have no way of knowing what software, if any, you bought with your computer. Maybe you already have a word processing program, maybe not. (Look over your pile of boxes. If there's one that says Microsoft Word, WriteNow, WordPerfect, Nisus, or anything that ends with the word *Works,* then you have a word processor.) If you don't have a word processor yet, call up Mac Connection or some other company and order one right now, so you'll be able to work with it tomorrow.

Until Federal Express delivers your new software, however, let me show you some of the basic principles of the computer. To make sure you've got the same thing on your screen that I do, we'll start off by using the built-in programs that came with your Mac.

## Your very first software

There are several menus across the top of the screen (remember these?). As you get to know the Mac, you'll discover that their wording changes from program to program. Right now, they say File, Edit, View, Label, and Special; in a word processor they might say File, Edit, Font, Size, and Format, and so on. The menu names (and the commands listed in those menus) are tailored to the function of the software.

There's one menu that's *always* on your screen, though: the Apple menu, which is the  at the left edge of the menu bar. Among other things, this menu provides immediate access to some useful miniprograms known as *desk accessories*. Desk accessories are sure-fire, nonthreatening, and fun — perfect for your first baby steps into the world of software.

# Desk Accessories

Let's start simple. Move your cursor up to the  menu and choose Calculator. The Calculator pops up in a tiny window of its own.

---

## Desk accessory details you can get by without

The Calculator, along with other miniprograms like the Note Pad, Alarm Clock, and so on (all in the Apple menu), is called a desk accessory. It's always available to you, no matter what Mac activity you're in.

In the olden days of System 6, the Apple menu *only* contained desk accessories. They were small, inexpensive, and cute. One of the new features in System 7, however, is that you can stick anything you want into that Apple menu: full-fledged software applications, a disk icon, a folder, a document you work on a lot, a sound, and so on.

(Some people wind up with *very* long Apple menus.)

Want to know the secret of making your own Apple menu in System 7? Check it out: Point to your hard-drive icon in the upper-right corner of the screen, and double-click. Now double-click your System Folder icon. Inside *that,* you'll find a folder called Apple Menu Items. (Pretty cryptic, I know.) Go ahead and drag any icon into this folder: another folder, a letter, your word processing program, whatever; instantly it appears in the Apple menu for easy access.

## The Calculator

Using the mouse, you can click the little calculator buttons. The Mac will give you the correct mathematical answer, making you the owner of the world's heaviest and most expensive pocket calculator.

What's neat is that you can also type the keys on your *numeric keypad,* the block of number keys off to the right side of your keyboard. As you press these real keys, you can watch the on-screen keys in the Calculator window get punched accordingly. Try it out!

(Of course, a PowerBook doesn't *have* a numeric keypad. Still, the numbers on the top row of regular alphabet keys work just as well.)

Take a moment to reinforce your love of windows: by dragging the *title bar* (where it says "Calculator"), move the Calculator window into a new position. If you were good and tired of looking at it, you could also make the Calculator go away by clicking its close box (in the upper-left corner, like on all windows).

But don't close the Calculator just yet. Leave it open on the screen.

## The Note Pad

Now go to the  menu again, and this time choose Note Pad. Instantly, the world's most frill-free word processor appears on the screen.

You'll learn more about word processing in the next section. For now, we're just going to do some informative goofing around. With the Note Pad open on your screen, type a math problem, like this:

37+8+19*3-100

(In the computer world, the asterisk * means "times," or multiply.) If you make a mistake, press the big Delete key at the upper-right corner of your keyboard. This means "Backspace."

Now, by dragging the Note Pad's title bar, move it so that you can see the Calculator window, too. You're going to use two programs at once, making them cooperate with each other — one of the most remarkable features of the Mac.

## *Selecting text*

This is about to get interesting.

Using the mouse, carefully position the pointer at the left side of your equation (below, top). Press the button and drag, perfectly horizontally, to the right (middle). Release the mouse when you've highlighted the entire equation (bottom).

]37+8+19*3-100

37+8+19*3-100

37+8+19*3-100 ]

You've just *selected* some text. Remember in Chapter 1 when you *selected* an icon — and then used a menu command? Struggling, as always, to come up with a decent analogy, I likened this *select-then-operate* sequence to building a noun-verb sentence.

Well, it works just as well with text as it does with icons. You've now high-lighted, or selected, some text. The Mac now knows what the noun is — what it's supposed to pay attention to. All you have to do is select a verb from one of the menus. And the verb du jour is *Copy*.

## The cornerstone of human endeavor: Copy and Paste

Choose Copy from the Edit menu.

Thunder rolls, lightning flashes, the audience holds its breath . . . and absolutely nothing happens, as far as you can tell.

Behind the scenes, though, something awesomely useful occurred. The Mac looked at the selected equation and memorized it, socking it away into an invisible storage window called the *Clipboard*. The Clipboard is how you transfer stuff from one window into another and from one program into another. (Some programs even have a Show Clipboard command, in which case I take back the statement about the Clipboard being invisible.)

Now then. You can't see the Clipboard at this point, but in a powerful act of faith, you put your trust in me and you believe that it contains the highlighted material (the equation).

## The Application menu

Do you see the tiny Note Pad icon at the right end of your menu bar? It's next to that question mark thing.

(Don't go bug-eyed searching for it. If it's not there, then you probably don't have System 7 installed in your Mac. The Application menu, as well as the question mark icon, are both elements of System 7.)

This icon actually represents a menu — the Application menu. It lists all the programs you have running at once. And at this moment, you have *three* programs running at once: the Note Pad, the Calculator, and the famous Finder (or desktop).

You multitasking maniac, you.

Choose Calculator from the Application menu.

The Calculator window comes to the front, and the icon in the upper right changes to look like a Calculator.

Those of you still awake will, of course, object to using the Application menu to bring the Calculator forward. You remember all too plainly from Chapter 1 that simply *clicking* in a window brings it to the front, which would have required less muscular effort.

Absolutely right! You may now advance to the semifinals. However, learning to use the Application menu was a good exercise. There are going to be many times in your life where the program that's in front covers up the *entire* screen. So *then* how will you bring another program forward, big shot? That's right. You won't be able to *see* any other windows, so you won't be able to click one to make it active. You'll have to use the Application menu.

In any case, the Calculator is now the active application. (*Active* just means it's in front.) Now then: Remember that intricate equation that's still on the Mac Clipboard? Instead of having to type an equation into the Calculator by punching keys, let's just paste it in.

1. Press the Clear key on your Mac keyboard or click the C button on the Calculator.

    You just cleared the display. We wouldn't want your previous diddlings to interfere with this tightly controlled experiment.

2. From the Edit menu, choose Paste. Watch the Calculator!

If you looked in time, you saw the number keys flashing like Las Vegas at midnight. And with a triumphant beep (sometimes), the Mac displays the answer to your math problem. (It should be 92.)

Did you get what just happened? You typed out a math problem in a word processor (the Note Pad), copied it to the Clipboard, and pasted it into a number-cruncher (the Calculator). Much of the miracle of the Mac stems from its capability to mix and match information among multiple programs in this way.

It's a two-way street, too. You can paste this number back into the word processor.

1. From the Edit menu, choose Copy.

   But wait! There was already something on the Clipboard. Where is the Mac supposed to put this *new* copied info?

   On the Clipboard, of course. And whatever was there before (your equation) gets nuked. The Clipboard contains exactly one thing at a time — whatever you copied *most recently*.

2. From the Application menu, choose Note Pad (or just click the Note Pad window).

   The Note Pad is now the active application.

3. Type this:

   *Dear son: You owe me $*

   Stop after the $ sign. Move the mouse up to the Edit menu.

4. From the Edit menu, choose Paste.

Bingo! The Mac pastes in the result from the Calculator (which it had ready on the Clipboard).

Incidentally, whatever's on the Clipboard stays there until you copy something new or until you turn off the machine. In other words, you can paste it over and over again.

5. For a second time, choose Paste from the Edit menu.

Another 92 pops into the window.

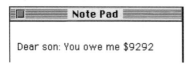

Dear son: You owe me $9292

By now, you're probably cradling your wrist, which no doubt aches from all those trips to the menu. Although what you're about to learn is, technically speaking, a *power-user technique,* it will save you all kinds of time and chiropractor bills.

You don't have to use the menu to issue a command like Copy or Paste. If you wish, you can use a keyboard shortcut to do the same thing. You may remember having used the ⌘ key in Chapter 3 to issue commands without using the mouse.

And how are you supposed to remember which letter key corresponds to which command? Well, usually it's mnemonic: ⌘+P for Print, ⌘+O for Open, and so on. But you can cheat; try it right now. Pull down the Edit menu, but don't let go of the mouse button.

There's your crib sheet, carefully listed down the right side of the menu. Note that the keyboard shortcuts for all four of these important commands (Undo, Cut, Copy, Paste) are adjacent on the keyboard: Z, X, C, V.

C is Copy. And V, right next to it, is Paste. Let go of the mouse button and let's try it.

1. While holding down the ⌘ key, type a V.

Bingo! Another copy of the Clipboard stuff (92) appears in your Note Pad. (In the future, I'll just refer to a keyboard shortcut like this as "⌘-V.")

2. Press ⌘-V again.

   Yep, that kid's debt is really piling up. He now owes you $92,929,292.

   But after all, he's your son. Why not just let him pay 10 percent down on the amount he owes you? In other words, why not *undo* that last 92 pasting?

3. From the Edit menu, choose Undo.

   The most recent thing you did — in this case, pasting the fourth 92 — gets undone.

Rewriting history is addicting, ain't it?

Remember, though, that Undo only reverses your *most recent* action. Suppose you (1) copy something, (2) paste it somewhere else, and then (3) type some more. If you choose Undo, only the typing will be undone (step 3), *not* the pasting (step 2).

There are some other DAs, too. (No, not District Attorneys. Like everything in the Mac world, it's cooler to call something by its initials. DA = desk accessory.) Play around with (and look up in your Macintosh owner's guide) the Puzzle, the Alarm Clock, Key Caps, and all that stuff.

## *Control Panels*

There's one item in your Apple menu that *isn't* a DA. It says Control Panels, and all it does is open up your Control Panels folder. And what exactly is your Control Panels folder? Well, it's a folder that lives inside your System Folder. It contains a bunch of icons, each of which controls some aspect of your Mac. Go ahead and choose Control Panels from the  menu to make this window appear:

Everybody's got a slightly different set of control panels, so your screen may look different. In any case, I'll show you around one control panel, then you can take it from there.

1. Quickly type *GE* on your keyboard.

   Remember this handy trick? You can select one icon in a folder just by typing the first couple of letters of its name. In this case, you get the General Controls window.

   (If your Mac has System 6, you have to scroll through the icons until you see the one you want; the letter-typing business is a perk of System 7.)

2. Double-click General Controls.

   The General Controls window opens. It looks like . . . well, rather like a control panel. These controls govern the way your Mac works; you can customize your working environment, to a certain extent, or change the time, or whatever. (The Performa controls look slightly different.)

The Desktop Pattern is the shading that fills the background, behind the windows and stuff. You can change the design; see Chapter 8 for details.

When you type (as in the Note Pad), the Mac marks your place with a blinking *insertion point*. These buttons control how fast it blinks, in the event that the blinking rate has been triggering those inconvenient seizures.

Click a number to change the time. Usually, when you buy a Mac, it's set to California time, so double-check this.

Click "24 hr." if you are a military-type person who wakes up at 0600 hours each morning.

Click a number to change the date.

When you choose a command from a menu (and release the mouse), the command blinks. This setting controls how many times. How did we *live* before we had this?

All right — close the General Controls window by clicking the close box in the upper-left corner; enough fooling around. Time to get some work done. (Fortunately, *working* on the Mac is almost as much fun as goofing off.)

# *Word Processing 101*

If you have a word processing program, install it onto your hard disk now, if you haven't already done so. You'll find the instructions at the beginning of its manual.

Find the program's icon on your hard disk. It may be inside a folder, which you can open by double-clicking. In any case, after you find the word processing program icon, double-click it; you'll be presented, after a moment, with a blank white screen.

If you don't have a word processor yet, you can use your discount word processor, the Note Pad; choose its name from the  menu.

## *Top three rules of word processing*

The first rules of typing on a computer are going to be tough to learn, especially if you've been typing for years. But they're supercrucial. Here they be:

- ✔ **Don't press the Return key at the end of each line.** I'm dead serious here. When you type your way to the end of a line, the next word will *automatically* jump down to the next line. If you press Return in the middle of a sentence, you'll mess everything up.

- ✔ **Only put ONE space after a period.**

- ✔ **Don't use the L key to make the number 1.** All right, this one's not so crucial to your future happiness. Still, your Mac, unlike the typewriter you grew up with, actually has a *key* dedicated to making the number 1. If you use a lowercase L instead, the 1 will look funny, and your spelling checker will choke on it every time.

If those statements give you uncontrollable muscular facial spasms, I don't blame you. After all, I'm telling you to do something that you were explicitly taught *not* to do by your sharp-tongued high school typing teacher.

Nonetheless, don't put two spaces after a period. Typewriters print letters onto paper by slapping tiny metal blocks against a ribbon, and every block (every letter) is the same width — including the space. But on a Mac, every letter has a different width; look how much wider this W is than this I, for example. On the Mac, a space is *already* extra-wide, thus saving you that precious calorie you would have exerted to press the spacebar a second time.

---

## See here?

There are two spaces after this sentence.  It looks sort of wide.
There's only one space after this one. Looks pretty good.

---

# The point of no returns

Why aren't you supposed to hit Return at the end of each line?

First time in print! An actual example of the kind of mess you can get into by pressing Return after each line of text.

At left: the original passage. Suppose you decide to remove Paulson's title, "Chief Executive Officer," since everybody already knows what kind of guy he is (left). But suppose you'd been foolish enough to press Return after each line of text; if you remove those three highlighted words, the word *Paulson* flops back to the left side of the line, but the rest of the sentence stays where it is, looking dumb (right). On the other hand, if you *hadn't* put Returns into your text, you'd get the figure below, where everything looks peachy.

There are a few other rules, too, but breaking them isn't serious enough to get you fired. So let's dig in. Make sure you have a blank piece of electronic typing paper open in front of you — either a new, untitled word processing screen, or the Note Pad.

You should see a short, blinking, vertical line at the beginning of the typing area. They call this the *insertion point* because it shows you where the letters will appear when you start to type.

Type the passage below. If you make a typo, press the Delete key, just like Backspace on a typewriter. *Don't* press Return when you get to the edge of the window. Just keep typing, and the Mac will create a second line for you. Believe. *Believe.*

> *The screams of the lions burst Rod's eardrums as the motorboat, out of control, exploded through the froth.*

See how the words automatically wrapped around to the second line? They call this feature, with no small originality, *word wrap.*

But suppose, as your novel is going to press, you decide that this sleepy passage really needs some spicing up. You decide to insert the word *speeding* before the word *motorboat.*

Remember the blinking cursor — the insertion point? It's on the screen even now, blinking calmly away at the end of the sentence. If you want to insert text, you have to move the insertion point.

There are two ways to move the insertion point. First, try pressing the arrow keys on your keyboard. You can see that the up-and down-arrow keys move the insertion point from line to line, and the right-and left-arrow keys move the insertion point across the line. Practice moving the insertion point by pressing the arrow keys.

If the passage you want to edit is far away, though (on another page, for example), using the arrow keys to move the cursor is inefficient. Your fingers would be bloody stumps by the time you finished. Instead, use the mouse, like this:

1. Using the mouse, move the cursor (which, when it's near text, looks like this Ɩ) just before the word *motorboat*. Click the mouse.

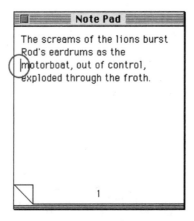

This is as confusing as word processing ever gets — there are *two* little cursors, right? There's the blinking insertion point, and there's this oneɪ, which is called an *I-beam* cursor. In fact, they're quite different. The blinking insertion point is only a *marker,* not a pointer. It always shows you where the next typing will appear. The I-beam, on the other hand, is how you *move* the insertion point to a different location; when you click with the I-beam, you set down the insertion point.

2. Type the word *speeding*.

The insertion point does its deed, and the Mac makes room on the line for the new word. A word or two probably got pushed onto the next line. Isn't word wrap wondrous?

So much for *inserting* text: you click the mouse (to show the Mac *where*) and then type away. But what if you need to delete a bunch of text? What if you decide to edit out the first half of our sample text?

Well, unless you typed the challenging excerpt with no errors, you already know one way to erase text — by pressing the Delete key (which is called Backspace on some keyboards). Delete takes out one letter at a time, just to the left of the insertion point.

That's not much help in this situation, though. Suppose that you decide to take out the first part of the sentence. It wouldn't be horribly efficient to backspace over the entire passage, just so you could work on the beginning.

No, instead you need a way to edit any part of your work, at any time, without disturbing the stuff you want to leave. Once again, the Macintosh method, noun-then-verb, saves the day. Try this:

1. Using the mouse, position the I-beam cursor at the beginning of the sentence.

   This takes a steady hand; stay calm.

2. Click *just* to the left of the first word and keep the mouse button pressed down. Drag the I-beam cursor to the end of the word *as*.

   As you drag, the text gets highlighted, or *selected.* You've done this once before, in your copy-and-paste lesson.

```
The screams of the lions burst Rod's eardrums as the
speeding motorboat, out of control, exploded through
the froth.
```

   If you accidentally drag up or down into the next line of text, the highlighting jumps to include a big chunk of that additional line. Don't panic; without releasing the mouse button, simply move the cursor back down or up onto the original line you were selecting. And this time try to drag more horizontally.

If you're especially clever and forward-thinking, you'll have selected the blank space *after* the word *as,* as well. Take a look at the illustration above.

All right, in typical Mac syntax, you've just specified *what* you want to edit by selecting it (and making it turn black to show it's selected). Now for the verb:

1. Press the Delete key.

   Bam! The selected text is gone. The sentence looks pretty odd, though, since it doesn't begin with a capital letter.

2. Using the mouse, position the cursor just before (or after) the letter *t* that begins the sentence. Drag it sideways across the letter so that it's highlighted.

The speeding motorboat, out of control, exploded
through the froth.

Here comes another ground rule of word processing. See how you've just selected, or highlighted, the letter *t*? The idea here is to capitalize it. Of course, using the methods for wiping out (and inserting) text that you learned earlier, you could simply remove the *t* and type a *T*. But since you've selected the *t* by dragging through it, replacing it is much easier:

3. Type a capital *T*.

The selected text gets replaced by the new stuff you type. That, in fact, is the fourth ground rule: *Selected text gets replaced by the new stuff you type.* As your Macintosh life proceeds, keep that handy fact in mind; it can save you a lot of backspacing. In fact, you can select 40 pages of text so that it's all highlighted and then type one single letter to replace all of it. Or you could select only one letter but replace it with 40 pages of typing.

Take a moment now for some unsupervised free play. Try clicking anywhere in the text (to plant the insertion point). Try dragging through some text: if you drag perfectly horizontally, you select text just on one line (below left). If you drag diagonally, you get everything between your cursor and the original click (below right).

You deselect (or, equally poetically, unhighlight) text by clicking the mouse. Anywhere at all.

Try pointing to a word and then double-clicking the mouse: you've easily selected exactly that word without having to do any dragging.

As you experiment, do anything you want with any combination of drags, clicks, double-clicks, and menu selections. It's nice to know — and you might want to prepare a fine mahogany wall plaque along these lines — that *nothing you do with the mouse or keyboard can physically harm the computer.* Oh, sure, it's possible to erase a disk or wreck one of your documents or something, but none of that requires a visit to a repair shop. You can't *break* the computer by playing around.

## Form and format

For the rest of this lesson, you're going to need a real word processor. Sorry, kids, the Note Pad will only get you so far in life.

One of the most important differences between a typewriter and its replacement — the personal computer — is the sequence of events. When you use a typewriter, you set up all the formatting characteristics *before* you type: the margins, the tab stops, and (for typewriters with interchangeable type heads) the type style.

But the whole point of a word processor is that you can change anything at *any* time. Many people type the text of an entire letter or proposal or memo into the Mac and *then* format it. When you use a typewriter, you might discover, after typing the entire first page, that it's *slightly* too long to fit, and your signature will have to sit awkwardly on a page by itself. With a Mac, you'd see the problem, and nudge the text a little bit higher on the page to compensate.

Word processing has other great advantages: no crossouts; easy corrections that involve no white-out and no retyping; a permanent record of your correspondence that's electronic, not paper, and so it's always easy to find; a selection of striking typefaces — at any size; paste-in graphics, and so on. I think it's safe to say that once you try it, you'll never look back.

## The return of Return

With all the subtlety of a Mack truck, I've taught you that you're forbidden to use the Return key *at the end of a line.* Still, that rectangular Return key on your keyboard *is* important. You press Return at the end of a *paragraph,* and only there.

To the computer, the Return key works just like a letter key — it inserts a *Return character* into the text. It's just like rolling the paper in a typewriter forward by one notch. Hit Return twice, and you leave a blank line.

The point of Return, then, is to move text higher or lower on the page. Check this example, for instance.

Dearest·Todd,¶
¶
I·have·never·loved·so·much·as·I·did·last·
night.·Imagine·my·joy·as·I·watched·you·
plunch·your·shining·scimitar·into·the·
greasy·flesh·of·that—that—hideous·thing·
from·the·deep.¶
¶
Unfortunately,·the·IRS·has·determined·
that·you·failed·to·file·returns·for·the·years·
1982–1986,·They·have·asked·that·I·notify·
you·of·¶

¶
Dearest·Todd,¶
¶
I·have·never·loved·so·much·as·I·did·last·
night.·Imagine·my·joy·as·I·watched·you·
plunch·your·shining·scimitar·into·the·
greasy·flesh·of·that—that—hideous·thing·
from·the·deep.¶
¶
Unfortunately,·the·IRS·has·determined·
that·you·failed·to·file·returns·for·the·years·
1982–1986,·They·have·asked·that·I·notify·
you·of·¶

Return characters move text down on the page. So, if you want to move text up on the page, drag through the blank space so that it's highlighted (above left); of course, what you've really done is to select the usually invisible Return characters. If you delete them, the text slides up the page (right).

Combine this knowledge with your advanced degree in Inserting Text (remember? you click to place the blinking insertion point and then type away), and you can see how you'd make more space between paragraphs or push all the text of a letter down on the page.

## Seeing the unseen

I said that Returns are *usually* invisible. However, every time you press the Return key, the Mac actually does plop down a symbol onto your screen. Same thing with the spacebar. Same with the Tab key.

You'll have to check your own word processor's manual to find out the exact command, but virtually every word processor lets you see these markings. The command may be called Show Invisibles; in Word, the command is called Show ¶. In any case, the result looks something like this:

➔ "Alison—my·god,·not·that!·Anything·but·that!"¶

➔ But·it·was·too·late.·She·had·already·disappeared.¶

## *Appealing characters*

Another big-time difference between word processing and typing is all the great *character formatting* you can do. You can make any piece of text **bold**, *italic*, underlined, all of the above, and more. You also get a selection of great-looking typefaces — only a few of which look like a typewriter. By combining all these styles and fonts randomly, you can make any document look absolutely hideous.

Here's the scheme for changing some text to one of those character formats: noun-verb. Sound familiar? Go for it:

1. Select some text by dragging through it.

   Remember, you can select a single word by double-clicking it; to select a bunch of text, drag the cursor through it so that it turns black. You've just identified *what* you want to change.

   Each word processor keeps its Bold, Italic, and Underline commands in its own specially named menu, but they're definitely there. Drag your cursor through each menu name, reading the commands on each menu as it drops down, until you see the character formats like bold and italic.

2. From the Font menu (or Format menu, or wherever they are in your program), choose Bold.

   Or Shadow or Outline or whatever. You've just specified *how* you want to affect the selected text.

You can apply several of these formats to the same text, too, although you won't win any awards for typographical excellence. Try changing the typeface, also; the various fonts are called things like Chicago, Geneva, Times, and so on. Changing fonts works the same way: Select text and then choose the font. And sizes — same deal: Select some text and then choose a type size from your word processor's menu. (Again, the name of the menu may vary. But for specifics on Microsoft Word and ClarisWorks, see Chapter 5.) The font sizes are measured in points, of which there are 72 per inch. Works out nicely, too — a Mac monitor has 72 *screen* dots per inch, meaning that 12-point type on the screen really is 12-point.

Before you know it, you can whip your document into mighty handsome shape.

## *Getting rid of the black*

Text changes color as you drag across it, right? This is called highlighting.

A panicked phone call from a novice Mac owner recently alerted me to a strange fact: nobody ever tells you *how to make the text white again!* It's not in the manuals, it's not in the books, it's not in the menus.

## The efficiency zealot's guide to power typing

Because you *can* format text after you've typed it doesn't mean you *have* to. Most power-users get used to the keyboard shortcuts for the common style changes, like bold and italic. They're pretty easy to remember: In every word processing program I know of, you get bold by pressing ⌘-B, and italic with ⌘-I.

What's handy is that you can hit this key combo just *before* you type the word. For example, without ever taking your hands off the keyboard, you could type the following:

> He stared at the **Delinquent Birds** folder. No: it *was not* happening!
>        ↑              ↑           ↑   ↑
>      ⌘-B         ⌘-B        ⌘-I  ⌘-I

In other words, you hit ⌘-B once to turn bold *on* for the next burst of typing, and ⌘-B again to turn it off — all without ever having to use a menu.

To make text white again (unselected), *click the mouse* anywhere in the window.

Just click anywhere…          …to get rid of the highlighting.

There. I think I just made the world a better place.

## Formatting paragraphs

Where type styles and sizes can be applied to any amount of text, even a single letter, *paragraph formatting* affects a whole paragraph at once. Usually these styles are easy to apply. To select a paragraph, you don't have to highlight all the text in it. Instead, you can just click anywhere within a paragraph to plant the insertion point. Then, as before, choose the menu command that you want to apply to that entire paragraph.

This figure shows some of the different options every word processor provides for paragraph formatting — left-justified, right-justified, fully justified, centered, and double-spaced.

Her heart pounding, whe looked toward the door. It swung open with a creak. The stench hit her first—an acrid, rotting swamp smell. She covered her mouth with the blood-soaked handkerchief and stepped backward, her naked back pressed hard against the fourposter.

Her heart pounding, whe looked toward the door. It swung open with a creak. The stench hit her first—an acrid, rotting swamp smell. She covered her mouth with the blood-soaked handkerchief and stepped backward, her naked back pressed hard against the fourposter.

Her heart pounding, whe looked toward the door. It swung open with a creak. The stench hit her first—an acrid, rotting swamp smell. She covered her mouth with the blood-soaked handkerchief and stepped backward, her naked back pressed hard against the fourposter.

Her heart pounding, whe looked toward the door. It swung open with a creak. The stench hit her first—an acrid, rotting swamp smell. She covered her mouth with the blood-soaked handkerchief and stepped backward, her naked back pressed hard against the fourposter.

Her heart pounding, whe looked toward the

door. It swung open with a creak. The

stench hit her first—an acrid, rotting

swamp smell. She covered her mouth with

the blood-soaked handkerchief and

stepped backward, her naked back pressed

hard against the fourposter.

There are other ways you can control paragraphs, too. Remember in high school when you were supposed to turn in a 20-page paper, and you'd try to pad your much-too-short assignment by making it two-and-a-half spaced? Well, if you'd had a Mac, you could have been much more sneaky about it. You can make your word processed document single-spaced, double-spaced, quadruple-spaced, or any itty-bitty fraction thereof. You can even control how tightly together the letters are placed, making it easy to stretch or compress your writing into more or fewer pages.

Take this opportunity to toy with your word processor. Go ahead, really muck things up. Make it look like a ransom note with a million different type styles and sizes. Then, when you've got a real masterpiece on the screen, read on.

# Someone Save Me! (Working with Documents)

It might terrify you — and it should — to find out that you've been working on an imaginary document. It's only being preserved by a thin thread of streaming electrical current. It doesn't exist yet, to be perfectly accurate, except in your Mac's *memory*.

You may recall from the notes you took on Chapter 1½ that *memory is fleeting*. (Specifically, I mean computer memory, but if you find a more universal truth in my words, interpret away.) In fact, the memory is wiped away when you turn the Mac off — or when your coworker's trip over the power cord turns it off for you. At that moment, anything that exists on the screen is gone forever.

Therefore, almost every program has a Save command. It's always in the File menu, and its keyboard shortcut is always ⌘-S.

When you save your work, the Mac transfers it from transient, fleeting, electronic memory onto the good, solid, permanent disk. There your work will remain, safely saved. It will still be there tomorrow. It will still be there next week. It will still be there ten years from now, when your computer is so obsolete it's valuable again.

Therefore, let's try an experiment with your ransom note document on the screen.

From the File menu, choose Save.

Uh-oh. Something weird just happened: The Mac presented you with a box full of options. It's called a *dialog box* because the computer needs to have a little chat with you before proceeding. (If you have a Performa, it says "Documents" at the top of this window.)

## OK, OK, not all programs

The occasional program — Word, for example — doesn't propose a title (like "Untitled 1") in the text box of the Save as dialog box. Instead, you just see the little blinking insertion point in the empty blank. The message is the same, though: "Type your title *here.*"

What the Mac mainly wants to know is: "Under what name would you like me to file this precious document, Massssster?"

And how do you know this? Because in the blank where it says "Save as," there's a proposed title that's *highlighted* (selected already). And what do you know about highlighted text? *Anything you start typing will instantly replace it.*

The Mac, in its cute, limited dialog-y way, is trying to tell you that it needs you to type a title. Go ahead, do it: Type *Ransom Note.*

At this point, you could just click the Save button. The Mac would take everything in perilous, fleeting memory and transfer it to the staid, safe hard disk, where it would remain until you're ready to work on it some more.

However, there's a bunch of other stuff in this dialog box. Especially since this is the Numero Uno source of confusion to beginners, I think a tour of the Save File box is in order.

## *Navigating the Save File (and Open File) box*

You've already learned about the way your computer organizes files: with folders and with folders *in* folders. Remember this little exercise?

Well, the point of all the complicated-looking stuff in the Save File box is a miniature version of that same folder-filing system. Suppose you see this when you're trying to save your file:

```
┌─────────────────────────┐
│ 🗁 USA folder ▼          │
├─────────────────────────┤
│ 🗀 Alaska            ⇧   │
│ 🗀 California            │
│ 🗀 Connecticut          │
│ 🗀 Hawaii               │
│                         │
│                     ⇩   │
└─────────────────────────┘
  Save as:
  ┌─────────────────────────┐
  │ Ransom Note             │
  └─────────────────────────┘
```

Look at the open-folder "menu" (in a rectangle above the list). It tells you that you're viewing the contents of the USA folder. (If you have a Performa, you always see the Documents folder at this point.) In other words, if you click the Save button, you'll file your new Ransom Note document in the USA folder, mixed in among the state folders.

But suppose you want to file the Ransom Note document in one of the state folders. You already know how you open a folder — by double-clicking it — so you'd point to Alaska, for example, and double-click.

```
┌─────────────────────────┐
│ 🗁 Alaska ▼              │
├─────────────────────────┤
│ 🗀 Interview        ⇧   │
│ 🗀 Nome                 │
│ 🗀 Politics             │
│ 🗀 Population           │
│ 🗀 Resources        ⇩   │
└─────────────────────────┘
  Save as:
  ┌─────────────────────────┐
  │ Ransom Note             │
  └─────────────────────────┘
```

Now the open folder "menu" above the list says Alaska, and you can see the stuff inside the Alaska folder. Most of their names are dimmed because they're all *documents;* the only things whose names are black in this dialog box are folders. (The Mac wants to know where you want to put your new document. Since you can't very well store one document inside *another* document, the document names are grayed out and unavailable, and only the folder names are black and available.)

OK. So now you're viewing the contents of the Alaska folder. What if you change your mind? What if you decide that the ransom note should really go in the World folder — the one that *contains* the USA folder?

You must retrace your steps. That's what the little open folder menu is all about (the open folder icon is in front of the word *Alaska*). They call this doohickey a *pop-up menu:* it's a menu, but it's not at the top of the screen. The small black triangle beside the name Alaska tells you: "Click me!"

Sure enough, when you click the word Alaska (above left), you see the list of all the nested folders you had to travel through to get here (above right). This is where things get a little weird: The list is *upside-down* from the path you took!

In other words, if you were in the Finder instead of in this Save File dialog box, you started at the Desktop level (gray background). You'd have double-clicked the hard-disk icon to open its window. Then you'd have double-clicked the World folder to open that, and the USA folder inside of that, and finally the Alaska folder. If you look at the menu picture above, you'll see that, sure enough, your entire folder path is listed. You can view the entire hierarchy of folders — as long as you get used to the fact that the list is upside-down, and the outer levels (the hard disk and the Desktop) are listed at the bottom.

Therefore, if you wanted to file the ransom note in the World folder (below right), you'd simply slide down the pop-up menu list and choose World (below left).

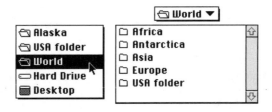

Then, at long last, when you're viewing the contents of the folder you want to save the file in, you can click the Save button.

For the purposes of following along with this exercise, double-click a folder — any folder — to store your file in. And then click Save.

Your file gets snugly tucked away into the folder whose contents you're viewing.

Want proof, O Cynic? All you have to do is choose Finder from the Application menu. Remember, the Application menu is the icon at the upper-right side of the screen. (If you're not using System 7, never mind.) It lists all the programs that are running at once.

When you choose Finder, our friends the folders, windows, and Trash can pop up. If you wanted to make sure your file really exists, and it really got put where you wanted it, you could now double-click your way through folders until you found it. In our example, your ransom note would be in the World folder:

Why are we kicking this absolutely deceased horse? Because the same folder-navigation scheme (where you see an upside-down list of nested folders) is used for *retrieving* files you've already created. You need to know how to climb up and down your folder tree, as you'll see in a moment, if you ever want to find your files again.

## Closing a file, with a sigh

You've created a ransom note. It's got all kinds of text and formatting. You've saved it onto the disk so that it'll be there tomorrow. In a moment, you'll get a chance to prove it to yourself.

Click the close box in the upper-left corner of the window. Once.

In the Mac's universal language of love, clicking the small white square up there means close the window, as you'll recall. If all went well, the window disappears.

## The worrywart's balm

From the way I've described the terrifyingly delicate condition of a document that's on the screen (that you haven't saved to disk yet) — that is, precariously close to oblivion, kept alive only by electric current — you might think that closing a window is a dangerous act. After all, what if you forgot to save some work? Wouldn't closing the window mean losing that critical memo?

Not really — if you try to close a document, the Mac won't *let* you proceed until it asks you if you're *sure* you want to lose all the work you've done. It will say something like:

Click Yes if you do want to save your work. Click No if you were only goofing around or showing off your Mac to somebody and don't want to preserve your labors. Click Cancel if you change your mind completely about closing the document and want to keep working on it.

## *How to find out what the heck you're doing*

This gets sort of metaphysical. Hold onto your brain.

Just because you closed your *document* doesn't mean you've left the *program*. In fact, if you pull down the Application menu at the right side of the screen, you'll see that the word processing program is, in fact, still running. (It's the one with a check mark beside it; your word processing program may be different.)

You could bring the Finder to the front by choosing its name from the Application menu — without exiting the word processor. They both can be running at the same time, but only one can be in front.

In fact, that's the amazing thing about the Mac (using System 7). You can have a bunch of programs all running at once. The more memory your Mac has, the more programs you can run simultaneously.

What gets confusing is that one program (say, your word processor) may be active, but you'll *think* you're in the Finder. After all, you'll see your familiar icons, Trash, folders, and so on. You have to understand that all of this is simply *shining through* the emptiness left by your word processor, which has no windows open at the moment. If a window *were* open, it would cover up the desktop behind it.

Right now, for instance, I realize that it's hard for you to believe that you're using a word processor, when there are no words on the screen. But you have three clues as to what program you're using:

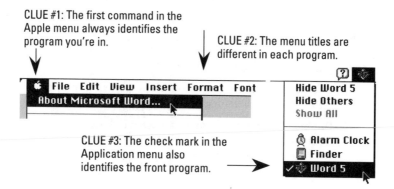

CLUE #1: The first command in the Apple menu always identifies the program you're in.

CLUE #2: The menu titles are different in each program.

CLUE #3: The check mark in the Application menu also identifies the front program.

For the moment, I want you to stay in your word processing program.

## *Those crazy relationships: Parents and children*

OK. You've typed a ransom note. Using the Save command, you turned that typing on your screen into an icon on your hard disk. Now it's time for a concept break.

There are two kinds of files on your hard disk right now: *programs* (sometimes called *applications*) and *documents*. A program never changes; it's like a Cuisinart on your kitchen counter, sitting there day after day. Documents are what you *create* with a program — they're the cole slaw, crushed nuts, and guacamole dip that come out of the Cuisinart. You pay money to buy a program. Once you own it, you can create as many documents as you want, for free.

For example, you could use the Word Proc-S-R program (above top) to create all the different word processing documents below it and thousands more like them. If you love analogies as much as I do, you can think of the application as the mommy and the documents as the kiddies.

Here's what their family relationships are like:

1. Double-click the *program* icon when you want to open a brand new, untitled, clean-slate document.

2. Double-click a *document* icon to open that document. Unbeknownst to you, double-clicking a document simultaneously opens the program you used to create the document.

Double-click a document to open it...

...and the Mac automatically launches the corresponding program that gave it birth, even if it's buried in a folder somewhere.

This may seem unimpressive to you. But in the dark days of DOS and other scary pre-Macintosh computers, there was no such automatic program-launching. You'd have to know what program you used to create the document, launch it first, and *then* retrieve a document. And even then, you'd have to remember what you named it, exactly, and type that name precisely on the screen.

## Orphaned documents

The Mac's ability to launch the mommy program when you double-click a document may occasionally seem not to work. That is, you may double-click a perfectly innocent-looking icon but get a message like this:

> The document "Angela's Recipe" could not be opened, because the application program that created it could not be found.
>
> OK

In its adorably inarticulate way, your computer is trying to tell you that it can't *find* the mommy program. You may have taken the application off your hard disk. You may have received the document from a friend, and you don't even own the program that created it. (If your friend gives you a music document, but all you own is a word processor, you're out of luck.) Then, too, some icons — mainly stuff in the System Folder — aren't *meant* to be opened. They're just helper files for programs or System features, and you're not supposed to mess with them.

This weirdness is described in greater detail in Chapters 6 and 9.

## *Fetch: How to retrieve a document*

Let's return to our increasingly fruitful exercise with the ransom note, shall we?

Let's pretend it's tomorrow. Yawn, stretch, fluff your hair (if any). You find out that the person you've kidnapped actually comes from a wealthy Rhode Island family, and so you can demand much more ransom money. Fortunately, you created your ransom note on the Mac, so you don't have to retype anything; you can just change the amount you're demanding and print it out again.

But if you've been following the steps in this chapter, then there's *no* document on the screen. You're still *in* your word processing program, though (or should be; look for the check mark in the Application menu). So how do you get your ransom note file back?

Like this:

   1. Choose Open from the File menu.

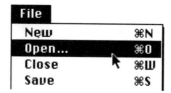

A dialog box appears.

You probably remember dialog boxes — in fact, you probably remember this one. It looks just like the Save dialog box, where you were asked to give your document a title. This one, navigationally speaking, works exactly the same way.

Double-click a folder to see what's in it.

Use this pop-up menu to see what folder *this* folder is inside of.

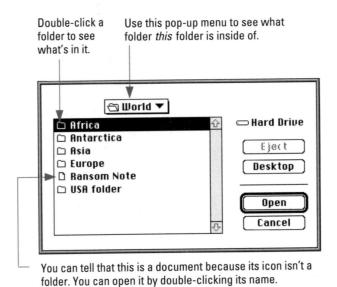

You can tell that this is a document because its icon isn't a folder. You can open it by double-clicking its name.

Unfortunately for my efforts to make this as instructional as possible, if you've been following these steps, your ransom note is staring you in the face right now. It's in whichever folder you saved it into. The Mac is nice that way — it remembers the most recent folder you stashed something in and shows you that location the next time you try to save or open something. (Unless you have a Performa, which shows you the Documents folder, no matter what.)

If you want to emerge from this experience a better person, pretend you can't find your ransom note. Pull down the pop-up menu and jump to your hard-disk level:

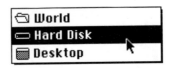

Now the display changes to show you the contents of your hard disk:

And from here, you know how to get back into the World folder, don't you? Correct — double-click the World folder, and you're right back where you started.

2. Double-click the ransom note.

This is what you've been working up to all this time. The ransom note appears on your screen in its entirety. Now, at last, you can edit it to your heart's content.

# Save Me Again!

To continue this experiment, make some changes to your document. Once again, you have to worry about the fact that your precious work only exists in a fragile world of bouncing electrons. Once again, turning the Mac off right now means you'll lose the *new* work you've done. (The original ransom note, without changes, is still safe on your disk.)

Therefore, you have to use that trusty Save command each time you make changes that are worth keeping. (For you desk potatoes out there, remember that ⌘-S is the keyboard shortcut, which saves you an exhausting trip to the menu.) The Save dialog box will *not* appear on the screen each time you use the Save command (like it did the first time). Only the very first time you save a document does the Mac ask for a title (and a folder location).

As mentioned in Chapter 1½, you've probably heard horror stories about people who've lost hours of work when some glitch made their computers crash. Well, usually it's their own darned fault for ignoring the two most important rules of computing:

> **Rule 1. Save your work often.**

> **Rule 2. See Rule 1.**

"Often" may mean every five minutes. It may mean after every paragraph. The point is to do it a lot. Get to know that ⌘-S shortcut, and type it reflexively after every tiny burst of inspiration.

Ever notice how you can control the weather? If you haul around an umbrella all day, it won't rain. If you forget the umbrella, it's Noah's flood.

It's precisely the same with computers. If you save your work often, you'll wonder why you bother; nothing will ever go wrong. The day — no, the *minute* you forget to save something you've typed, you'll get something called a system crash and lose your entire document into the electronic ether.

## Learning to be a quitter

Now you know how to start a new document, edit it, save it onto the disk, reopen it later, and save your additional changes.

You know how to launch (open, or run) a program — by double-clicking its icon or by choosing its name from the  menu. You've discovered the fact that you can have more than one program open at once, which can be handy when you need to copy numbers from the Note Pad and paste them into the Calculator (for example).

But now you have to learn to get out of a program when you're finished for the day. It's not terribly difficult: Choose Quit from the File menu.

If the word processor was the only program you were running, then you return to the Finder. If you were running some other programs, then you just drop down into the next program. It's as though the programs are stacked on top of each other; take away the top one, and you drop into the next one down.

## The other most important rule of computing

Duty compels me to keep this chapter going just long enough to preach one other famous word of advice to you: Back up.

To *back up,* or to *make a backup,* means to make a safety copy of your work.

When you're in the Finder, the documents you've worked on appear as icons on the hard disk. Your hard disk is like a giant-sized floppy disk. Like any of us, these disks occasionally have bad hair days, go through moody spells, or die. On days like those, you'll wish you had made a *copy* of the stuff on the hard disk, so your life won't grind to a halt while the hard disk is being repaired.

Remember the cruel gods that make the computer crash when you don't save your work frequently? Those same deities have equal powers over your hard disk, and an equal taste for irony. That is, if you don't back up, your hard disk will *certainly* croak. On the other hand, if you back up your work at the end of every day or every week, nothing will ever go wrong with your hard disk, and you'll mumble to yourself that you're wasting your time.

Life's just like that.

## The idiot-proof guide to backing up

Put a blank floppy disk in the disk drive. (If it's a brand new disk, you'll be asked to *initialize* it [prepare it for use by a Mac]; do it.)

Now select the icons of the documents you want to back up. Drag them, together or one by one, onto the floppy disk icon. If the floppy fills up, insert another one and continue. Label the floppy disks *Backup* (and note the date). Keep them away from magnets and telephones.

If you're a business person, you might even want to invest in a backup *program,* which essentially backs up automatically. DiskFit, Redux, and Retrospect are some popular backup programs. If you have a Performa, you already own a backup program, you lucky dog, called Apple Backup.

# *Top Ten Word Processing Tips*

1. Select a word by double-clicking — and then, if you keep the mouse down on the second click and drag sideways, you select additional text in complete one-word increments.

2. Never, never, never line up text using the spacebar. It may have worked in the typewriter days, but not anymore. For example, you may get things lined up like this on the screen:

   **1963      1992                  2001**
   Born      Elected President   Graduated college

   Yet, sure as death or taxes, you'll get this when you print:

   1963   1992                2001
   Born   Elected President   Graduated college

   So instead of using spaces to line up columns, use *tab stops* instead. Learn how your word processor does tabs, and use 'em!

3. You can select all the text in your document at once by using the Select All command (to change the font for the whole thing, for example). Its keyboard equivalent is almost always ⌘-A.

4. Aesthetics Rule of Thumb: Don't use more than two fonts within a document. (Bold, italic, and normal versions of a font only count as one.) Talk about ransom notes!

5. Don't use underlining for emphasis. You're a typesetter now, babe. You've got *italics!* Underlining is a cop-out for typewriter people.

6. The white box in the scroll bar at the right side of the window tells you, at a glance, where you are in your document:

The position of the white box in the scroll bar tells you whether you are at the beginning...   ...the middle ...   ... or the end of your document.

By dragging that white box, you can jump anywhere in the document.

There are two other ways to move around:

Click in the gray area above or below the scroll box to jump *one screenful* up or down.

Click (or hold down the button on) the up or down arrow to move up or down in your document a line at a time.

7. You've already learned how to *copy* some text to the Clipboard, ready to paste into another place. Another useful technique is to *cut* text to the Clipboard. Cut works just like Copy, except it snips the selected text out of the original document. (Cut-and-paste is how you *move* text from one place to another.)

8. It's considered uncouth to use "straight quotes" and 'straight apostrophes.' They hearken back to the days of yore (the days of your typewriter, that is). Instead, use "curly double quotes" and 'curly single quotes' like these. (See the difference?)

   You can produce curly double quotes by pressing Option-[ (left bracket) and Shift-Option-[ (right bracket) for the left and right ones, respectively. The single quotes (or apostrophes) are Option-] and Shift-Option-], for the left and right single quotes, respectively.

   But good heavens — who can remember all that? That's why every word processor I've ever heard of (like ClarisWorks or Word) has an *automatic* curly quote feature, which is a much better solution.

9. If there's an element you want to appear at the top of every page, like the page number or the date or *The Mister Rogers Story, Part VII: The Early Years,* don't try to type it onto each page. Not only is that a waste of effort, but the minute you add or delete text from somewhere else, this top-of-the-page information will become middle-of-the-page information.

   Instead, use your word processor's *running header* feature — it's a little window, into which you can type whatever you want. The program automatically displays this info at the top of each page, no matter how much text you add or take away. (There's also such a thing as a *running footer,* which appears at the *bottom* of the page, as well as a *running politician,* which you want to avoid at all costs.)

10. Be painfully aware that what you see on the screen isn't always what prints out. The number one source of rude surprises happens when you write with a Mac connected to *one* printer (like a StyleWriter) but print on a different one (like a laser printer). Since the typefaces are handled differently for these different printers, you'll discover that sentences, lines, and pages end in different places in the printout than they did on the screen.

    The solution is simple. Before you print, trick the Mac into thinking it's got that laser printer already attached, so you can see what it's about to do to you. From the Apple menu, select Chooser. (You'll read more about this fascinating Stone Age relic in Chapter 4.) You should see the name of several printers there, like StyleWriter or LaserWriter (which is used for *all* brands of laser printer). Click the one you *plan* to print on, even if it's not currently connected.

    If you don't see more than one printer icon in the Chooser, you have to reinstall it from your System or printer disks. (In the System 7 disk set, these little icons are on the disk called Printing.)

# Chapter 4
# A Quiet Talk About
# Printers, Printing, and Fonts

### In This Chapter

▶ What the different kinds of printers are and how much they cost

▶ How to hook up and start printing

▶ More than you ever wanted to know about PostScript and TrueType (and other words with no spaces in the middle)

▶ Why printouts sometimes look horrible

*I* hope you're seated for this chapter. In fact, I hope you're leaning way back with your feet up and a daiquiri in your hand.

Because there's no greater source of confusion and irritation for the beginning Mac user than understanding printers and fonts, and how to get the best of the latter from the former. After dropping $1,000 on a laser printer, some people still get jaggedy, irregular type in their printouts. Others aren't able to print at all — they get error messages. And still others have been printing their correspondence for years, in happy ignorance, using the Chicago font — the heavy black type style that's used in the Mac menus.

It's time to make some sense of it all. If possible.

# Credit Card Workout #3: A Printer Primer

Printers come in all kinds of configurations and prices. You can spend next to nothing and get a dot-matrix printer whose printouts are so jagged that they look like Dante's *Inferno* written in Braille. Or you can spend a thousand clams or so and get a printer whose printouts look like they were typeset.

*Dot matrix: A printer named for the way it produces type on the paper — as a pattern of dots. (Matrix is computerese for pattern.) As the little printing head glides back and forth across the page, tiny metal pins shoot out against the ribbon, pressing it against the paper at specific moments. All of this happens really fast, and with very precise pin choreography. But dot-matrix printouts look like dot-matrices — you can actually see the little dots that constitute each character.*

## Low-cost, low-quality

I'm talking about the Apple ImageWriter II. It's called a *dot-matrix* printer because it prints by firing little pins against a ribbon that strikes the paper. The resulting collection of dots form the letters.

The ImageWriter is slowish and so noisy that people regularly buy *mufflers* for them. The print quality isn't anything to write home about (and it's only barely good enough for letters home. See the print samples below). Unless you regularly need to print onto multiple-page forms (like Fed Ex labels), let this dinosaur lie.

# ImageWriter
# StyleWriter
# LaserWriter

## Low-cost, high-quality, low-speed

Yes, Virginia, there *is* a high-quality printer that won't bleed you dry: the Apple StyleWriter II. Its quality almost matches a laser printer's. It's very small, very lightweight, and almost silent. You can feed all kinds of nonliving things through it: tagboard, envelopes, sheet metal, whatever. And it costs less than $350.

So what's the catch? Well, for people who are used to laser printers, the StyleWriter II's speed — two pages per minute — seems pretty slow. (They shouldn't complain; the original StyleWriter only printed half a page per minute!) Still, the StyleWriter II is so compact, quiet, and inexpensive — and it prints grays (such as photographs) so beautifully — that it's hard to resist.

Both the StyleWriter II and its popular $400 rival, the Hewlett-Packard DeskWriter, are *inkjet* printers. They create a printed image by spraying a mist of ink. Note, therefore, that the printing isn't laser-crisp if your stationery is even slightly absorbent. Note, too, that inkjet-printed pages smear if they ever get the least bit damp, making them poor candidates for use during yacht races.

## PostScript printers

If you can afford to pay something like $1,000 for a printer, though, some real magic awaits you: *PostScript laser printers.* Don't worry about the word PostScript for now. Just look for the word PostScript in the printer's description, as though it's some kind of seal of approval.

A PostScript printer, like most of Apple's LaserWriter models, can print any text, in any style, at any size, and at any angle, and everything looks terrific. PostScript laser printers can also print phenomenal-looking graphics, like all the diagrams in Macintosh magazines. They're quick, quiet, and hassle-free; most can print envelopes, mailing labels, and paper up to legal-size (but not tagboard).

Remember the old saying, "The power of the press is limited to those who have one"? Well, the combination of a Mac and a laser printer is what put the Mac on the map because it turns anybody into a self-publisher. If you can afford a PostScript printer, get it. If you're a small-time operation — a home business, for example — get the cheapest PostScript laser printer you can find. Almost all laser printers between $900 and $1,500 have exactly the same quality printouts. If you're going to print mainly normal-looking text without fancy graphics, you can save some bucks by getting one of the LaserWriter printers that *isn't* PostScript, such as the LaserWriter Select 300.

# How to Print

Bet you haven't had a lesson with *that* title since about first grade. Anyway, I'm going to assume that you've happily purchased a printer. If it's already hooked up, and you've made some successful printouts already, fast-forward to the end of this section.

## Plugging in a 'Writer

If you bought an ImageWriter, StyleWriter, or other 'Writer, a cable (printer-to-Mac) probably came with the printer. It's a no-brainer to connect them; there's only one possible place to plug the cable into the printer. The other end goes into the back of the Mac; there's a little round jack with a printer icon. (Be careful not to plug it into the nearly identical jack next to it, which is marked with a telephone icon.) Of course, you also need to plug your new appliance into the wall.

## Plugging in a laser printer

If you bought a laser printer, believe it or not, you probably did *not* get a cable with it. Like anything precious in the computer jungle, it'll take some bushwacking through the technical underbrush to get at the explanation.

When Apple invented the LaserWriter — the very first PostScript laser printer — they charitably recognized that not every company could afford a $6,000 printer to sit beside each desk. They had a great idea, though: Invent a system where several Macs could all plug into the *same* printer.

Ladies and gentlemen, I hereby introduce you to the word *network*.

The wires and connectors that attach these Macs to a single shared printer (and which, by the way, can also connect Macs to each *other*) are called LocalTalk. These connectors aren't cheap — last I looked, a pair of connectors (what you need for *one* Mac and *one* printer) was about $100.

Soon thereafter, competitors got into the act, with rival connectors called things like PhoneNet and ModuNet. There are two brilliant concepts behind these rival wiring systems. First, they're much less expensive than Apple's product; second, they use ordinary phone wire to connect the connectors. (Apple's LocalTalk requires special cables.) If you decide to move your printer into the next room, no big deal — just buy a longer piece of phone wire from Radio Shack.

This is all relevant only if you believe that you *must* have a network in order to plug a Mac into a laser printer. And, in fact, that's exactly what the salespeople would like you to believe.

But here's another money-saving *Macs For Dummies* secret: You only need all that fancy wiring *if* you plan to share your laser printer with other Macs.

If it's just you, your Mac, and a cup of coffee on the desk, get a plain old ImageWriter II cable for $15. After all, one Mac and one printer hardly qualify as a *network*. Put the other $85 into a skiing weekend or something.

Anyway, if you do get the more expensive connectors, plug one connector into the back of the printer and the other into the printer jack in the back of the Mac. Then connect the connectors using LocalTalk cable or phone wire, as appropriate. And if you're just going to use an ImageWriter cable, "Plugging in a 'Writer."

## *The Chooser: Where Mac meets printer*

The hardest part of printing on a Mac comes at the very beginning — an unfortunate fact for the novice who simply wants to get going. You have to take this step no matter what brand or kind of printer you've just connected.

When you first plug a printer into the Mac, it's not smart enough to notice that it's got a new friend. Therefore, after the Mac is connected to the printer, turn on both machines. Now choose Chooser from the  menu. You should see something like this:

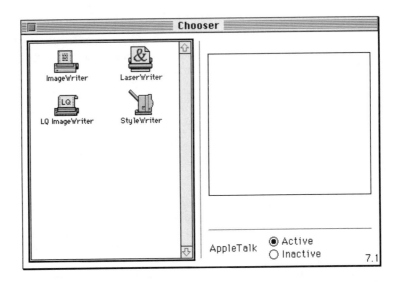

Your screen may look different, of course. The icons that appear in the left half of the window depend upon which *printer drivers* have been placed in your System Folder. A printer driver is a little piece of software that teaches the Mac how to communicate with a specific printer. Its name and its icon match the printer itself, as you can tell, sort of, from the figure above.

If you see a printer driver icon in the Chooser window that matches your printer, you're in luck! Click it. You should see your actual printer's name show up in the *right* side of the Chooser window (if it's turned on), as shown here:

Good going! Everything's coming up roses. If the names of *several* printers show up on the right, then you're either part of an office network with several printers, or you're an unexpectedly wealthy individual. Congratulations. Click the one you want to print on.

If you don't see *any* icons in the left half of the Chooser window, then nobody bothered to install them. (Or, more likely, since the System 7 installer *automatically* places the printer drivers into your System Folder, somebody's taken them out.) No matter — you'll find all these icons on the original white Apple software disk called Printing. Find the one that matches your printer, and drag it on top of your System Folder icon. (If you have a laser printer and System 6, you also need the Laser Prep icon.) Don't worry if your laser printer isn't made by Apple — use the LaserWriter driver for any brand of laser printer. The Mac will install it automatically. Now you can repeat this Chooser business, and everything should go fine.

If you see *some* printer driver icons in the Chooser window, but none of them matches your printer, here again you need to copy the appropriate driver icon into your System Folder from the original Apple disk.

If things *still* aren't going well — for example, if you click the driver icon, but your printer's name doesn't show up in the right side of the window — then see Chapter 11.

Anyway, once you click a printer driver icon, a couple of things happen. If you're selecting a laser printer, you'll be told to turn on *AppleTalk*. AppleTalk is related to LocalTalk, the networking system described earlier; remember that if you have a laser printer, you're supposedly part of a network even if just one Mac is attached to it. So make sure the little AppleTalk setting (in the lower-right corner of the dialog box) is Active if you have a laser printer.

When you close the Chooser, you get a soon-to-be-annoying alert message:

You have changed your current printer. Please choose "Page Setup..." in all of the open applications.

OK

It tells you (as if you didn't know) that you've just changed to a new printer. Its advice, though, is sound. After you select a printer driver, choose Page Setup from your File menu. A dialog box appears. Don't *do* anything in this box; just click OK.

You've just introduced the Mac to its new printer. All of this is a one-time operation, by the way; unless you have to switch printers or something, you'll never have to touch the Chooser again.

## Why the Chooser exists

You're entitled to wonder why you have to go through this Chooser business just to get a darned printout.

Imagine that you work in a big office; you have three different kinds of printers and a dozen Macs, and they're all wired together into a giant network. You want to print something. You have to be able to tell the Mac (1) what *kind* of printer you want to use (laser, StyleWriter, whatever), and, if there's more than one of each connected to the network, (2) which *one.*

That long-winded scenario was supposed to help you understand why there's a Chooser. It's designed to let you specify which printer you want to use.

If you're a one-person operation, of course, the Chooser is utterly superfluous. But you have to go through it anyway (only once, at the beginning of your computing career). What the heck — maybe it'll give you some healthy sympathy for people who work in offices.

## Background printing

In the Dark Ages of the 1980s, when you printed something, the printer's soul took over your Mac's body. You couldn't type, you couldn't work, you couldn't do anything but stare at the sign on the screen that said "Now printing." It was a dark and stormy era, a time of wild and rampant coffee breaks. Only when the paper came out of the printer were you allowed to use your computer again.

Since then, some clever engineer at Apple figured out how to allow *background printing.* When you use this handy feature, the Mac sends all the printing information, at a million miles per hour, into a *file* on your hard disk. It then immediately returns its attention to you and your personal needs.

Then, quietly, behind the scenes, the Mac shoots a little bit of that file to your printer at a time. It all happens during the microseconds between your keystrokes and mouse clicks, making it seem as though the Mac is printing in the background. In time, the printer receives all the information it needs to print, the paper comes gliding out, and you've been able to keep working the whole time.

In practice, there are a few chilly background printing realities to consider. First, a document takes much *longer* to print in the background than it would if the Mac devoted all of its brainpower to printing. Similarly, making your Mac concentrate on two things at once also bogs down what *you're* doing; while something's being printed in the background, you can outtype your word processor, windows seem to take longer to open, and so on. Finally, background printing isn't available for ImageWriters (unless you buy a program, called a *spooler*, especially designed for the ImageWriter).

Turning the Background Printing feature on and off is easy. Select Chooser from the ⌘ menu. In the lower-right side of the box, you'll see the On/Off buttons. Go for it.

I mention this tidbit so that you'll remember it when you're in a serious hurry for a printout. When it's 2 a.m. and your novel is due on the publisher's desk by 9 a.m. Or it's 1:55 p.m. and the meeting is at 2:00. Or you're leaving the house anyway and want to make sure your printout is ready when you get back. In all of these cases, it would be wise to turn *off* background printing to ensure that you get your printout as fast as possible.

## *After all that: How you actually print*

OK. Suppose that your printer is finally plugged in and, via the Chooser, has been introduced to the Mac. The moment has arrived: you'd actually like to *print* the thing.

Choose Print from the File menu. This dialog box appears; it looks different depending on your printer, but the one pictured below is what you see if you have a laser printer:

```
┌─────────────────────────────────────────────────────────────────┐
│ LaserWriter "Silentwriter 95"              7.1.1   ┌─ Print ─┐   │
│ Copies:[1]      Pages: ◉ All ○ From:[   ] To:[   ] └─Cancel─┘    │
│ Cover Page:   ◉ No ○ First Page ○ Last Page                     │
│ Paper Source: ◉ Paper Cassette ○ Manual Feed                    │
│ Print:        ◉ Black & White   ○ Color/Grayscale               │
│ Destination:  ◉ Printer         ○ PostScript® File              │
└─────────────────────────────────────────────────────────────────┘
```

The main thing you do in this dialog box is tell the Mac which pages of your document you want it to print. If you just want page 1, type a *1* into *both* the From and To boxes. If you want page 2 to the end, type *2* into the From box and leave the To box empty.

Specify how many copies you want by clicking and typing a number in the Copies box.

## Using the Tab key in dialog boxes

Now would be a good time, I suppose, to mention what the Tab key does in dialog boxes. Suppose that you want to print *two* copies of page 3. Instead of using the mouse to click in each number box on the screen, you can just press Tab to jump from box to box.

Therefore, you'd just type *2* (in the Copies box); press Tab, type *3* (in the From box); press Tab, type *3* again (in the To box). And the mouse just sits there gathering dust.

Anyway, after you're done filling out the options in this box, you can either click the Print button *or* press the Return key. (Pressing Return is always the same as clicking the outlined button.) The Mac should whir for a moment, and pretty soon the printout will come slithering out of your printer.

If you can't get anything to work right, check Chapter 11 for trouble-sleuthing tips.

## Canceling printing

If you want to interrupt the printing process, ⌘-period does the trick — that is, while pressing the ⌘ key, type a period. Several times, actually. Even then, your printer will take a moment (or page) or two to respond to you.

# A Guide to Jagged Printouts

This is really going to be "A Guide to *Avoiding* Jagged Printouts." Just wanted to grab your attention.

But listen: if your printouts look great, you're done. Outta here. Finito. Go on to the next chapter. This section gets a little dense, and it's only here if you need it or, God forbid, if you *want* to know what's going on behind the scenes.

You see, to understand why lettering sometimes prints out jaggedly, you must suffer through a description of the three different font formats that may lurk inside your Mac.

## Font format 1: Bitmapped fonts

When the Mac first appeared, every typeface (which Apple calls a *font*) was formed of dots in a particular arrangement. It was a "map" of dots, if you will (and even if you won't). It was therefore called a *bitmapped* font. (So why don't they call it a *dotmap?* You kidding? That'd be too easy to understand.)

These fonts were named after cities: New York, Geneva, Athens, and so on.

---

### The ten great city fonts

All of the original Mac bitmapped fonts are still around. If you're a System 7 user, you probably only see a few of them in your font menus — the Installer doesn't automatically give you all of them. (The remaining fonts are tucked away on your Fonts disk; drag them onto your System Folder to install them.)

Here, for the sake of history, are the city-named, non-PostScript fonts. Note the little jaggies at the edges, even though they've been printed by the most expensive printer in the world. (The picture font is Cairo.)

New York     San Francisco     Athens
London     Venice
Monaco     Chicago
Geneva     Los Angeles

---

The Mac screen, then and now, has 72 tiny square dots per inch. (To make sure as many people as possible are left in the dark, everybody abbreviates "dots per inch" as *dpi.*) This screen resolution worked out incredibly well: the only Mac printer — the ImageWriter — *also* printed 72 dots per inch. In other words, each dot you saw on the screen produced a corresponding dot on the page. For the first time in the history of computers, you got a printout that looked *exactly* like what you saw on the screen.

In an inspired burst of cuteness, the term *WYSIWYG* was born, which supposedly is pronounced wizzy-wig and stands for "what you see is what you get."

There are two drawbacks to bitmapped fonts. First, 72 dots per inch may sound, at first, like a plethora of dots … dots aplenty … a veritable dotfest. But believe it or not, 72 dpi is still too coarse to produce smooth printouts. You can still see the chunky square dots that compose each letter.

Second, if you think about it, you'll realize that a bitmapped font can only be printed clearly at a single size — the size at which its designer arranged the dots to look good. True, each bitmapped font usually comes in a *selection* of different sizes, each painstakingly mapped to screen dots — usually 10-point, 12-point, 14-point, 18-point, and 24-point sizes. But if you try to select an in-between type size, you get pretty gross-looking results.

For example, 12- and 24-point below looks fine, but no 17-point New York font bitmap comes with your Mac, as evidenced by the chunky example in the middle:

New York at 12-point size

**New York at 17-point size**

New York at 24-point size

## Which sizes are in stock?

After reading the discussion of bitmapped fonts, you may wonder how you can tell for sure which bitmapped font sizes have been included in a set. Just consult the Font Size menu in one of your programs, as shown at right.

If a point size number is hollow, you've got it. If it's black, you don't, and the type will look squashed and blocky on the screen.

| Size |
| --- |
| 6 Point |
| 9 Point |
| ✓10 Point |
| 12 Point |
| 14 Point |
| 18 Point |
| 20 Point |
| 24 Point |
| 36 Point |

**The 5th Wave** **By Rich Tennant**

"WELL, MR. BOND, I GUESS THIS IS FAREWELL. LOWER...THE...LASER...PRINTER!"

Therefore, if you're getting crummy-looking text in your printouts, the first possibility is that you've used a bitmapped font — one with a city name — in your document. (And if it looks *really* wretched, you're probably using it at a non-predesigned point size.) For example, London, Venice, and Los Angeles are the names of fonts that come on the Fonts disk with every Mac. But they're destined to be forever jagged. Change the font to a non-city–named font, and read on.

# Font format #2: PostScript fonts

The world changed when Apple created the LaserWriter printer. Its resolution was *300* dots per inch — over four times sharper than the ImageWriter.

The main thing about the LaserWriter, though, was the new technology called PostScript that was built into it. They call PostScript a "page description language." It was invented by a little California company called Adobe. Once Apple saw how cool PostScript was, they struck a deal with Adobe to build PostScript technology into each laser printer. (By the way, there is such a thing as a *non-PostScript* laser printer. There are even a couple *nonlaser* PostScript printers. But in *general,* and in this chapter, "PostScript printer" = "laser printer.")

You can read all kinds of things about how PostScript works. But all *you* need to know is that:

- ✔ A PostScript laser printer means the end of jaggies. It can create extremely sharp, clear printouts that look published.

- ✔ To print sharp text on a PostScript laser printer, you have to use special fonts. (They're called, of course, *PostScript* fonts).

- ✔ PostScript fonts can be printed at any size or angle — no matter how big, small, or absurdly stretched — with equal clarity.

*PostScript* fonts, unlike bitmapped ones, don't print text by specifying the placement of each dot on the page (below, left). Instead, the Mac thinks of each letter in a PostScript font as a hollow outline. The printer fills in that outline with solid black (below, right). Since a PostScript printer thinks of fonts by their shapes, it's simple to tell the printer "Make this bigger"; it just multiplies the outline-shape by a point size number you specify. Printouts of 12-point, 35.8-point, and 128-point type all look equally sharp on a PostScript printer.

Unfortunately, there are *two parts* to each PostScript font. There's a regular bitmapped font, with all the usual problems of ugliness-at-strange-sizes, for use on the screen. (It's sometimes, therefore, called a *screen font.*) And there's a separate file, called a *printer font,* that you put in your System Folder.

The printer fonts have the same names as the screen fonts, with the last letters lopped off. In your word processor's Font menu you might see Palatino Roman — but in your System Folder, there'll be a printer-font file called PalatRom. (If there's a Fonts folder *inside* your System Folder, then *that's* where you'll find these printer files.) For *each* type family, like Futura, you need a whole rat's nest of printer-font files in your System Folder: one each for **bold,** *italic,* ***bold italic,*** and so on. In the following figure, you can see a suitcase icon (which contains the screen fonts) and its associated printer fonts.

Anyway, this is all leading up to explaining a second (and more common) cause of jagged type. If you've used PostScript (non-city-named) fonts in the document you're printing, and they're not looking terrific in the printout, then the appropriate printer-font file is missing or in the wrong place (i.e., not in the System Folder).

"And where," I can almost hear you asking, "am I supposed to *get* this piece of font that you claim I'm missing?"

"Well," you can almost hear me replying, "no PostScript fonts *come with* your Mac! So if you have a PostScript font, either you or somebody else *bought* it (or, um, copied it from somebody) and installed it on your Mac." Therefore, seek the missing printer-font file on the original font disk.

## *Font format #2½: Adobe Type Manager (ATM)*

As I mentioned, PostScript fonts look stunning in your laser printouts. But text on your *screen* still looks horrible if you use oddball sizes, like 17-point type, because you're still looking at a plain, old bitmapped font. Then, too, you only get this gorgeous print if you use a *PostScript laser printer.* If you tried to save some diñero by buying, say, a StyleWriter printer, then PostScript fonts gain you absolutely nothing. It's Jagged-Edgeville all over again.

So Adobe, the company that dreamed up PostScript, introduced a clever little gizmo called Adobe Type Manager, or ATM. (At last you know that Mac people don't actually go to cash machines a lot. Half the time they say "ATM" they're *not* talking about automated teller machines.)

ATM makes type on the *screen* look sharp at any size, just the way a PostScript printer does. The secret: It consults the printer font in your System Folder, decides what each letter should look like based on its *outline,* and draws it on the screen. Better yet, ATM works the same magic for nonlaser printers like the StyleWriter. ATM makes PostScript fonts print sharp, clear, and terrific at any size on those printers, too.

The price: ATM takes up a good chunk of memory, and it slows down the screen display a bit. Still, at $99 per copy, Adobe sold a gazillion copies of ATM, and then promptly bought the state of Nevada for its employee parking lot.

Fortunately, Apple eventually persuaded Adobe to *give away* ATM. Unfortunately for everybody who'd paid $99 for it, you can now get ATM for a mere $7.50 shipping charge. (Call 800-776-2333.)

## For would-be weenies only

If you really, really give a darn about how ATM gives you great-looking type on nonlaser and non-PostScript printers, I'll indulge you. But please remember that there's not a reason in the world for you to actually know this info.

Even in the early days of Mac (1984), printouts on the trusty ImageWriter weren't quite as jagged-looking as text on the screen. The ImageWriter has a little bit of smarts; it gives you a choice of three print qualities — Draft, Faster, and Best. If you choose Faster, then you indeed get a printout with precisely the quality you see on the screen — one printed dot for every black dot on your screen.

If you choose Best quality, though, a clever thing happens. The ImageWriter can actually print 144 dots per inch. (Those of you handy with a calculator may note that 144 is exactly double the 72-dpi resolution of the Mac screen.) When you print a document containing (for example) 12-point New York type, and you choose Best quality, the printer ransacks your System file, looking for *24-point* New York. If its search is successful, the ImageWriter actually prints your document in 24-point New York but packs the dots onto the page twice as densely.

The result of these shenanigans: You get type that's 12-point *size* but twice as crisp. It's the same effect as using a photocopier with a reduction feature — the resulting copy is finer and crisper than the original.

Subsequent generations of non-PostScript and nonlaser printers have taken this theme and run with it. The ImageWriter LQ, for example, is capable of printing with a resolution of 270 dpi. So if you want a printout at 12-point size, you need a *triple*-sized font installed in your System to get the highest quality printout. The printer does the same trick as the original ImageWriter — it consults that 36-point font and prints it at one-third the size (and triple the crispness of the screen display).

The best-selling Hewlett-Packard DeskWriter came along next, with a super-crisp resolution of 300 dpi. Now you were supposed to have a *quadruple*-sized bitmapped font installed in your System Folder to get that juicy resolution.

As you can imagine, these higher resolution printers started requiring whopping System Folders, creaking at the seams with these jumbo fonts. To have a selection of 10-, 12-, 18-, or 24-point sizes, you'd have to have the 40-, 48-, 72-, and 96-point sizes installed — each of which takes up a good chunk of your hard disk space — *per type style*.

When the 360-dpi Apple StyleWriter came along, which would have required *quintuple*-size fonts, no wonder people welcomed TrueType and ATM, which eliminate all that math and inconvenience. Since TrueType and ATM can scale any font of its type to any size, you simply need the TrueType font file (or the PostScript printer-font file) in your System Folder — a single smallish file — instead of the zillions of jumbo bitmapped screen fonts.

Aren't you glad you asked?

I mention ATM so that you'll know what it is, of course. But I also want you to know what to do if a PostScript font, *even* with ATM, *still* looks lousy on the screen. If that happens, it's the same problem as jagged PostScript printouts: you're missing the printer-font file for the typeface in question.

Here's where things get hairy. It turns out that there usually *are no* printer-font files for the standard ten PostScript fonts (Times, Helvetica, Helvetica Narrow, Palatino, Avant Garde, Bookman, New Century Schoolbook, Courier, Symbol, or Zapf Chancery). Because these are so standard, their printer-font information comes *built into* virtually every laser printer made. Of course, that doesn't do ATM much good. It needs *printer fonts,* man, *printer fonts.* And it needs them in the System Folder. And guess what else? The version of ATM that Adobe so sanguinely sells you for $7.50 *doesn't include* printer-font files for that basic set!

Therefore, if you want smooth text on the screen (or on your nonlaser printer), you have three choices:

1) Get the $7.50 version of ATM and buy some fonts to go with it (or get some fonts from a user group, as described later).

2) Get the package called Adobe Type Basics, which contains ATM, the printer files for those 35 built-in fonts, and a handful of bonus fonts, for about $130.

3) Bail out of PostScript fonts altogether, and consider TrueType fonts instead (read on).

## Font format 3: TrueType fonts

I'll mention this third font format only to avoid negligence suits. I mean, it *is* a font format — in fact, it's the one you most likely have — but you cannot *possibly* get jagged type from it, either on paper or on the screen.

It's TrueType. It's a special kind of font that Apple invented relatively recently. It has all the advantages of PostScript fonts (smooth type at any size). Yet it eliminates the problems associated with the PostScript scheme. Instead of having two separate files — one for the printer and one for the screen — TrueType fonts are self-contained. Likewise, instead of cluttering up your life with a separate font for each style variation (bold, italic, and so on), all the styles in a TrueType font are built into that one font suitcase file. And finally, instead of needing ATM for crisp, on-screen type at any size — a potentially costly add-on — TrueType fonts always look good on the screen automatically.

A TrueType font, therefore, *never* looks or prints jagged.

Incidentally, when TrueType appeared, everybody said "Ooh, font fight!" Everybody geared up for a big tragic rivalry between TrueType and PostScript. People also expected all kinds of system crashes and goofy-looking printouts if both font types were installed at once.

None of it happened. The two technologies coexist just fine.

Yet despite its convenience, TrueType didn't blow the world away, for two reasons.

✔ *There aren't many fonts in this new format.* Apple provides a half dozen with every System 7 Mac, and you can buy hundreds of others from font companies. But by the time TrueType was invented, people had invested thousands of dollars in PostScript typefaces. Most people muttered that they couldn't afford to build a type library from scratch again.

✔ *TrueType is only a font technology.* PostScript, on the other hand, is a *graphics* technology. It can do much more than manipulate text. It can also create lines, circles, patterns, wild shadings, and three-dimensional re-creations of Marilyn Monroe standing over an air shaft. Indeed, two of the most famous professional graphics programs of all time, Illustrator and FreeHand, are PostScript drawing programs. TrueType, which deals only with type, can't possibly replace all the flexibility of PostScript.

This is all going to get much easier — or much more complicated, depending on your point of view — in the next couple of years. Apple has finally conceded that PostScript and ATM are here to stay. So in some future version of the System software (see Chapter 6), they're going to have TrueType *and* PostScript *and* ATM all built right in, so you don't have to worry about all those nutty files in all their preassigned places. Code word for this technology: *QuickDraw GX.* Be the first in your computer group to pronounce it!

# ID'ing a font

So: there are *three* kinds of fonts: bitmapped, PostScript, and TrueType. In your quest to understand what you've got on your computer, and to straighten out whatever jagged-printout problems you might be having, here's your own personal Guide to Font Identification.

# If you have System 7

If your Mac uses System 7, and you haven't added any new fonts yourself, then everything's TrueType. On a new System 7 Mac, even the city-named fonts (like Chicago, Geneva, and New York), which are usually presumed to be bitmapped fonts, are actually TrueType ones. No matter *what* kind of printer you own, TrueType fonts look great when printed, and you don't have to worry about point sizes, or printer-font files, or any of that jazz.

You can prove this to yourself by opening your System Folder and double-clicking the System file itself (or your Fonts folder if you have one). If you choose By Icon from the View menu, you'll see TrueType fonts displayed with this special icon (see all those little A's?):

New York

Now, it's remotely possible that you or somebody you love has enhanced your Mac with additional fonts. Here are the fonts that come with a System 7 Mac: Times, Helvetica, Helvetica Narrow, Monaco, Chicago, Geneva, Palatino, Avant Garde, New Century Schoolbook, Bookman, Courier, Symbol, Zapf Chancery, Zapf Dingbats.

If you have any fonts not in this list, then it's a sure thing you've got extra fonts. If they have a city name (like Los Angeles), they're bitmapped fonts, and they'll look cruddy no matter what kind of printer you use.

If you have extra fonts that *don't* have city names, they're either PostScript or TrueType fonts. Open your System file (or Fonts folder), as I mentioned a moment ago, and decide for yourself by looking at each font's icon.

Just remember that if the font is a PostScript font, it'll only look terrific when you print *if* you also have the corresponding printer-font files in your System or Fonts folder.

There are 35 exceptions to that generalization — the 35 type styles *built into* your laser printer. These fonts *don't* need printer files in your System Folder. (Although *Oblique* and *Demi* may sound like part of a sleazy trapeze act, they are in fact the trendy words for *Italic* and *Bold,* respectively.) Here's the list:

| | | |
|---|---|---|
| Times Roman | New Century Schoolbook | Helvetica Roman |
| **Times Bold** | Roman | **Helvetica Bold** |
| *Times Italic* | **New Century Schoolbook** | *Helvetica Oblique* |
| ***Times Bold Italic*** | **Bold** | ***Helvetica Bold Oblique*** |
| | *New Century Schoolbook* | |
| Avant Garde Roman | *Italic* | Helvetica Narrow Roman |
| **Avant Garde Demi** | ***New Century Schoolbook*** | **Helvetica Narrow Bold** |
| *Avant Garde Italic* | ***Bold Italic*** | *Helvetica Narrow Oblique* |
| ***Avant Garde Demi Italic*** | | ***Helvetica Narrow Bold Oblique*** |
| | Palatino Roman | |
| Bookman Roman | **Palatino Bold** | *Zapf Chancery* |
| **Bookman Demi** | *Palatino Italic* | |
| *Bookman Italic* | ***Palatino Bold Italic*** | αβχδεφγηιφκ (Symbol) |
| ***Bookman Demi Italic*** | | |
| | Courier   Roman | ❂❂✳✳✳✳ (Zapf Dingbats) |
| | **Courier   Bold** | |
| | *Courier   Italic* | |
| | ***Courier   Bold   Italic*** | |

If there's a font in your font menu that doesn't appear in this list (other than city-named fonts), then it didn't come with the Mac. You're going to need the printer-font file equivalent of it in your System Folder.

One more word of advice, ye lucky laser printer user: Nobody's ever gone to hell for this, but it's a good idea not to let the TrueType and PostScript versions of the *same* font coexist on your system. Times, Helvetica, Courier, and Symbol are the fonts in question here. Make a decision to go with the TrueType versions or the PostScript versions, and stand by it — and remove the duplicates.

# *If you have System 6*

First of all, it's extremely unlikely that you have any TrueType fonts. You *can't* use TrueType fonts, in fact, unless you've put a special file, called the *TrueType init,* into your System Folder, which you'd probably remember doing.

Therefore, it's very simple. If your font has a city name, it's not going to win any awards when printed on a laser printer or StyleWriter. Avoid it.

And if the font *doesn't* have a city name, it's a PostScript font. It'll look great when printed on a laser printer *if* (1) it's one of the Built-In 35 or (2) you have the corresponding printer-font files installed.

## *The output upshot*

If you just bought a new Mac, you have nothing to worry about. Whether you know it or not, *all* of your fonts are TrueType fonts, which do their elfin-magic behind the scenes. And no matter what printer you own, you can rest easy knowing that TrueType will give you the highest quality printouts it's capable of. End of story.

Things only get more complicated if you (1) crave more variety, (2) find fonts in your font menu that *you* didn't put there, or (3) have a Mac running System 6.

If any of those conditions are true for you, use this table to help you figure life out.

| Your Mac | Your printer | Use TrueType fonts? | Use PostScript fonts? | Use city-named fonts? |
|---|---|---|---|---|
| System 7 | PostScript laser | Sure | Yes, with ATM and the printer-font files in your System Folder | Yup (cause they're really TrueType) |
| System 7 | StyleWriter, DeskWriter, non-PostScript laser | You betcha | Yes, with ATM and the printer-font files in your System Folder | Go for it ('cause they're really TrueType) |
| System 6 | PostScript laser | No* | Yes, with ATM and the printer-font files in your System Folder | No way |
| System 6 | StyleWriter, DeskWriter, non-PostScript laser | No* | Yes, with ATM and the printer-font files in your System Folder | Only if you have the appropriate point size installed (see the sidebar on page 96) |

*Unless you have System 6.0.7 *and* the TrueType INIT, as described earlier.

# A Veritable Font-u-copia

You actually get more fonts with your Mac than you think — the Installer program, which you (or your dealer or your local computer whiz) used to set up your hard disk, only installs a handful of basic ones. As you go on through life, you may (and can and should) want to add new typefaces to your Mac or trash some of the ones you've already been given.

So where do you get additional fonts? The universal response to that kind of question is, of course: Buy them. Those on a budget, however, can still get tons of great fonts. On your white Fonts disk that came with your Mac, for example, there are about a dozen interesting extra ones. (Alas, they're all the bitmapped kind.)

**User group:** *A Macintosh computer club in your area. Call Apple at 800-538-9696 to find out the nearest one. You can also get disks from most user groups by mail.*

Or you can call up your local user group and pay about $5 for a disk full of new fonts. Or if you have a modem (as described in Chapter 7), you can dial up America Online or another on-line service and help yourself to as many fonts as your typographical taste buds can tolerate.

## How to install a font in System 7

Quit all your programs (if you're running any) before trying this.

Drag the font file icon on top of the System Folder icon. That goes for both printer-font files and screen font files, if it's a PostScript font you're installing. (Do *not* drag them into the open System Folder *window.* Do not drag them to the Trash can. Do not collect $200.)

You'll see a message alerting you that the Mac is going to install the font for you. Just smile, wave, and click OK.

## How to install a font in System 6

If you're using System 6, installing fonts is much uglier and more difficult. I'll make the effort, but you should feel free to consult your Mac manuals for more patient instructions.

Find the program called Font/DA Mover. It's either on your hard disk someplace or still on the white Apple disks that came with your Mac. Double-click the icon. You'll see two lists. One side lists all the fonts you *already* have in your System. The other side is probably empty.

Click the Open button on the empty side, and navigate your way to the font you want to install. Double-click its name; you return to the main Font/DA Mover window. Drag through the names of the fonts you want to install and then click the Copy button. (To remove fonts from your system, drag through their names on the System side of the list and click Remove.) And then think about getting System 7, where installing fonts isn't such a pain.

## *How to remove a font*

First of all, choose About This Macintosh from the  menu; read the little message that appears. If it says you've got System 7.1 or 7.1p, open your System Folder and then open the Fonts folder therein.

If you've got any other edition of System 7, open the System Folder and then double-click the System *file* icon itself.

In any case, you'll now see a list of your fonts in a window:

| System | | |
|---|---|---|
| 61 items | 34 MB in disk | 4 MB available |
| Name | Size | Kind |
| Geneva 18 | 5K | font |
| Geneva 20 | 7K | font |
| Geneva 24 | 9K | font |
| Helvetica | 60K | font |
| Helvetica 9 | 11K | font |
| Helvetica (bold) | 58K | font |
| Helvetica 10 | 10K | font |
| Helvetica 12 | 11K | font |
| Helvetica 14 | 11K | font |

To see what a font looks like, double-click it; a little window opens, displaying a line from classical literature, displayed in the font you're investigating.

To remove a font, just drag it out of the window. Put it onto the desktop or in some other folder or right into the Trash can.

## For technology lovers only

When you look through your System file (or your Fonts folder), you may discover a bunch of icons that would seem to disprove what I just told you about fonts. That is, you'll see a TrueType font icon (like New York) all right, but you'll *also* see icons for a bunch of bitmapped fonts in specific sizes (New York 10, New York 12, and so on).

Don't freak — what I told you is still true. But remember when ATM came out and made everything slow on the screen? That's because it had to consult the printer-font file to learn how to draw each letter. Apple didn't want TrueType technol-ogy to give you the same problems, so along with each TrueType font, you also get a bunch of ready-made bitmapped screen fonts in common sizes. Any time you format a document in one of these fonts and sizes, the Mac doesn't have to consult the TrueType font file at all since you've already got that point size installed as a bitmap. The result — faster screen display. You *could,* if you wanted to, throw away these specific point size files, leaving only the numberless TrueType font icon, and everything would still work OK... just a little bit slower.

# *Top Ten Free Fun Font Factoids*

1. Every Mac comes installed with Times, Helvetica, Courier (which looks like an electric typewriter), Symbol (a bunch of Greek symbols), New York, Chicago (the font used for menu names), Geneva (the font used for icon names in the Finder), and Monaco (a really ugly *monospaced* font, where every letter is exactly the same width). The Mac won't let you remove the last three; it uses them for various things on the screen.

2. Some of the bitmapped fonts that come with the Mac correspond to PostScript fonts. New York is pretty much like Times; Geneva is sort of like Helvetica; and Monaco is a lot like Courier (they're both monospaced).

   If you have a non-System 7 Mac, and you try to print a document prepared in New York, Geneva, or Monaco, the Mac will, at your request, *substitute* the PostScript equivalents (Times, Helvetica, Courier) automatically. ("At your request" means that, when you choose Page Setup from the File menu and encounter a dialog box, you make sure that Font Substitution is selected.)

   However, you're much better off not using this feature. When the Mac does this font substitution for city-named fonts, it doesn't account for the fact that New York and Times (for example) have different *letter widths.* So you get really weird word spacing in the printout because the Mac tries to *position* every word in the same place (following page, right) as it's shown on the screen (following page, left).

| "Agatha!" I screamed, my lungs bleeding and raw from the violent pounding of the vicious surf spray. | "Agatha!"    I screamed,    my lungs bleeding    and raw   from   the violent    pounding    of the vicious surf    spray. |

Much better idea: Format your documents with laser fonts to begin with! Unless you like the look of free-floating words in space, keep Font Substitution clicked off.

3. Ten font families are built into most PostScript laser printers. They are, as you'll recall, Times, Helvetica, Helvetica Narrow, Avant Garde, Palatino, Bookman, New Century Schoolbook, Symbol, Zapf Chancery, and Zapf Dingbats.

   Any PostScript font that doesn't appear on this list has to be *downloaded* (transferred) to the printer each time you turn on the printer and try to print. As such, they're called *downloadable* fonts. That's why their printer-font files have to sit in your System Folder, where the Mac will know where to find them.

   Downloadable fonts impact your life in several ways. First, you have to buy them. Second, documents that use downloadable fonts take more time to print; the Mac has to teach the printer what each character looks like.

   Third, if you use several downloadable fonts in a document, it may not print at all. The printer's memory will get filled up with font information even before the Mac starts to send the document. The result: The printer keeps saying "Wait, wait, I'm not ready yet . . ." to the Mac, and the Mac keeps saying "Ready? Ready? Here it comes . . .", until you get disgusted and flip one of them off. (Marriage counseling for computer equipment is not yet available outside California.)

   The solution, of course, is to reformat your document using the built-in fonts (Times, Helvetica, and so on) instead of downloadable ones — or to install more memory into your printer. (You'll find more nitty-gritty on this topic in Chapter 11.)

4. Choose Page Setup from the File menu. The Page Setup dialog box has a handful of very useful options — what paper size you plan to use, for example, or how much you want your document enlarged or reduced.

   In the upper-right corner, though, there's a nifty Options button (if you have a laser printer). Click it. Up comes a dialog box:

## The Dogcow

No Mac book would be complete without at least a passing acknowledgment of the Dogcow.

His name, need I point out, stems from the fact that nobody can precisely figure out what kind of animal he is. In the inner sanctum of Apple Computer Corporation, it is said that, late at night, you can hear the sound made by the Dogcow: Moof!

To get a little preview of each option, click the appropriate checkbox and watch the helpful Dogcow illustrate the effect on your printout.

Most noteworthy, though, is the item called Larger Print Area. The average laser printer can only print to within ¼ inch of the page edge. Select Larger Print Area, though, and you gain ⅛ inch all the way around — a very useful gain for graphics, music, page layout, and other kinds of printing.

5. Suppose that you select some text and make it bold. Then you try to print, but the text keeps coming out as *non*bold on the printed page.

   The problem is that some PostScript typefaces, notably Zapf Chancery, *don't have* a bold version. (Zapf Chancery doesn't even have an italic style since it's already sort of italic.)

6. Adobe's PostScript typefaces each include a complete bitmapped screen font for each type style — bold, italic, and so on. Unfortunately, each style name appears in your Font menu prefaced by an initial: "I Times Italic, B Times Bold, BI Times Bold Italic," and so on.

   Who came up with this dumb idea, I can't tell you. But I do know that your font menu lists fonts alphabetically. The result is that each typeface's style variations aren't listed together — they're scattered all over the darned menu, as shown on the left on the following page. Your only chance of getting things into shape is to buy a utility program that combines them into family groups on your menu, with the style variations listed in a submenu (right):

One such utility is sold by (guess who?) Adobe. Because they probably concocted the inconvenient font-naming scheme just so they could sell their utility program to correct it, I'm not going to play along by telling you what the thing is called. Instead, I'm going to recommend WYSIWYG Menus, an even better utility. It's part of the Now Utilities package (see Appendix B, the Resource Resource).

7. In MacWrite II and some other word processing programs, you can actually see the names of the fonts in your font menu *in* those typefaces, like this:

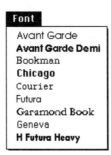

There are a few other ways to get this feature, all of which involve spending some money. Suitcase II, Now Utilities, and MenuFonts are a few programs that add this feature to any program you own.

8. When you first buy your laser printer, you may have noticed (and sworn at) the fact that it spits out a "startup page" every time you turn it on. This startup page contains a host of extremely unimportant information, like the number of pages you've printed in the printer's lifetime (including the useless startup page in your hand). Meanwhile, the Brazilian rain forests keep getting smaller.

   You can tell the printer not to waste that paper and ink, if you want. Use the little program called LaserWriter Font Utility; it's on the Tidbits disk that comes with System 7. Double-click it, and choose Start Page Options from the Utilities menu. Click Off, and savor the fact that you made the world a better place for your grandchildren.

9. If you have something important to print, keep in mind that you don't actually have to *own* a laser printer to get that professional look. Even if you use an ImageWriter or other 'Writer at home, you can always take your disk in to an "output bureau" (a high-tech copy shop) and pay a certain amount per page for laser-printed (or even higher quality) printouts. But if you do so, just remember the golden rules of which fonts to use, as described earlier in this section.

10. Want to look good the next time you're hanging out with a bunch of type geeks? Then learn to bandy about the terms *serif* (pronounced SAIR-iff) and *sans serif* (SANNZ sair-iff).

    A serif is the little protruding line built onto the edges of the letters in certain typefaces. In the *serif font* pictured in the top example here, I've drawn little circles around some of the serifs:

# Terrif serifs
# Sans-serif

A *sans serif* font, on the other hand, has no little protuberances, as you can see by their absence in the little squares (in the lower example above). Times, Palatino, and the font you're reading are all serif fonts. Helvetica, Geneva, and the headlines in most newspapers are sans serif fonts.

And that information, plus 29¢, will buy you a first-class postage stamp in the United States.

# Part II

## Increasing Your Coolness Quotient

**The 5th Wave** By Rich Tennant

"WELL, RIGHT OFF, THE RESPONSE TIME SEEMS A BIT SLOW."

# In this part...

**E**ither you've faithfully plowed through the personally-enriching material so far, nursing your inner child (the one that always wanted to use a computer), and are now ready for more . . .

. . . or you've just skipped over a lot of stuff to get here. Either way, you won't be disappointed: the mind-blowing *Faking Your Way Through the Top Ten Programs* will be your survival guide for maintaining status in the office, and *More Stuff to Buy and Plug In* will help you unleash your Mac's potential (and unload your wallet).

# Chapter 5
# Faking Your Way Through the Top Ten Programs

● ● ● ● ● ● ● ● ● ● ● ● ● ● ● ● ● ● ● ● ● ● ● ● ● ● ● ● ● ● ● ● ● ● ● ● ● ● ● ● ● ● ● ●

## In This Chapter

▶ Faking your way through ClarisWorks

▶ Faking your way through graphics programs like MacPaint, MacDraw, and Canvas

▶ Faking your way through word/page processing programs like Word, PageMaker, and QuarkXPress

▶ Faking your way through famous number/data crunchers like Excel and FileMaker

▶ Plus excellent productivity-enhancers like QuicKeys and Apple File Exchange

● ● ● ● ● ● ● ● ● ● ● ● ● ● ● ● ● ● ● ● ● ● ● ● ● ● ● ● ● ● ● ● ● ● ● ● ● ● ● ● ● ● ● ●

*T*his chapter is a survival guide for stranded-on-a-desert-island, filling-in-for Mr.-Big, my-son's-at-school-but-I-need-to-print-out-something, the-computer-just-arrived-but-the-board-meeting-is-in-two-hours, in-a-computer-store-to-try-something-but-don't-know-how-it-works situations.

I'm going to assume that you know the basics by now. If you ever were a dummy to begin with, at this point you're only a *demi*-dummy: you already know how to save files and retrieve them (from Chapter 3) and how to use fonts and print (from Chapter 4). And if you want to do something fancier than what I'll be showing you, I'm assuming that you do have access to either (a) the manuals or (b) whoever got you into this mess to begin with.

Macintosh users are notorious for not reading their software manuals. They're actually belligerently *proud* of the fact that they never read manuals. Of course, two years down the line, one user will look at another user's techniques and intone, astounded, "I never knew it could do *that!*"

You're welcome to join this cult of instant gratification, with this chapter as your guide — but at least read the manual for your word processor (or what-ever program you spend the most time in).

The one thing this section *isn't* for is to help you use an illegal copy of one of these programs. Humor me on this; living in New York City is dangerous enough without worrying that some scary-looking goons in trench coats and dark glasses are gonna show up at my apartment accusing me of encouraging software piracy.

# HyperCard ... not!

In earlier printings of *Macs For Dummies,* this chapter started with HyperCard because HyperCard used to come free with every Mac. HyperCard is often described as a "software Erector set" because you could create lots of neat things with it: an address book, a planning calendar, a recipe book, and so on.

At the time, you could also buy HyperCard from Claris Corporation — for $200. I guess not too many people were buying, though. Why would they, when they already had a free copy of the program?

So a funny thing happened near the end of 1992: without saying a word to anyone, Apple stopped giving away HyperCard with each Mac. Instead, you now get a stripped-down doodad they call HyperCard Player. You can't use it to design your own cool miniprograms. All the Player can do is open *other* people's HyperCard files.

Since HyperCard was yanked out of the Software Top Ten, I'm going to spend the following pages teaching you about a much more popular program: ClarisWorks. If you bought a Performa Mac, ClarisWorks probably came already installed on your hard disk. It's definitely one of the top ten programs, and it's a durned fine program.

# ClarisWorks

ClarisWorks is Swiss Army Knife software. Just look at all you get, even if you don't know what they are yet: a word processor, a database, and a spreadsheet. *Now* how much would you pay? But wait: you also get a graphics program that can even serve as a basic page-layout system. And if you order now, you even get a little communications program (to use if you own a *modem* — a phone hookup for your Mac).

All of these modules are neatly bundled into a single integrated program. You can write a letter and put a graphic in it; or design a flyer that has a little spreadsheet in it; and so on. This section will be worth reading even if you don't own this particular software because ClarisWorks works exactly like most other Mac programs.

And listen up, Performa users. You smug, lucky so-and-so: you probably got ClarisWorks for free, preinstalled on your Mac, right? Yeah. Except unless Apple got a lot more generous between the time I wrote this sentence and the time you're reading it, you didn't get any *manuals* with it. (They want you to send in some money if you want the manuals. This chapter may save you the trouble.) Also, they may have given you an out-of-date version, and they want you to send in some money if you want the latest. *That* money is well spent. Most of the following stuff applies equally well to versions 1.0 and 2.0 of ClarisWorks; the stuff near the end, however, is only in version 2.0.

## *Launching ClarisWorks*

Double-click the ClarisWorks icon.

After the Claris logo disappears, you're asked to decide what you want to accomplish. Because you'll face this decision every time you use this program, a run-down may be in order here.

*Word Processing:* You know what a word processing document is: something you type. A memo, a novel, a ransom note.

*Drawing:* This is ClarisWorks' version of MacDraw (more later in this chapter). In this kind of document, you toy around with lines, shapes, and colors to produce logos, maps, Hangman diagrams, and other important visuals.

*Painting:* This is ClarisWorks' version of MacPaint or Photoshop (more on these later in this chapter, too). Painting is another way of making graphics. Unlike the Drawing mode, where you can only create distinct circles, lines, and squares, the Painting tools let you create shading, freeform spatters, and much more textured artwork.

*Database:* An electronic index-card file, very much like FileMaker (see later in this chapter). You type in your lists — household expenditures; record collections; subscriber list to *Regis & Kathie Lee!* magazine — and the program sorts them, prints them, finds certain pieces of info instantly, and so on.

*Spreadsheet:* A computerized ledger sheet, almost exactly like Excel (also coming up later). Crunches numbers: calculates your car's mileage per gallon, your bank account, how much of the phone bill your teenage daughter owes, that kind of thing.

*Communications:* You need this kind of program if you want to use your modem for dialing up (1) local "electronic bulletin boards," (2) a pay-by-the-hour information service like CompuServe, or (3) your local school's computer system.

To make ClarisWorks strut its stuff, I'll show you how to create a thank-you letter. But not just any thank-you letter — this is going to be the world's most beautiful and personalized *form letter.* You're going to merge a list of addresses into a piece of mail, creating what appear to be individually composed letters; thus, the technoid term for what you're about to do is *mail merge.*

Yeah, yeah, I hear ya: form letters aren't exactly what you bought a computer to do. Follow along anyway; this exercise will take you through most of ClarisWorks, and you'll brush up against some features that *will* be useful to you.

## *Your first database*

Suppose you just got married. You were showered with lovely gifts. And now it's your task to write charming thank-you notes to each of 100 people. You'll begin by typing a list of the gift givers. The ideal software for organizing this kind of information is a *database.*

Therefore, double-click the Database button.

> **New Document**
>
> ○ Word Processing    ○ Spreadsheet
> ○ Drawing            ● Database
> ○ Painting           ○ Communications
>
> Stationery [None ▼]
>
> [ Cancel ]    [   OK   ]

Don't be alarmed. The screen that now appears may look complicated, but it's actually not so bad — it simply wants to know what blanks you'll be wanting to fill in for each person in your list (name, address, gift type, and so on).

You're about to type names for these blanks (which the program calls *fields*). As always, if you make a typo, just press the Delete key to backspace over it. Here we go:

1. Type *First Name.* Press the Return key. (Pressing Return is the same as clicking the Create button.)

2. Type *Last Name.* Press Return.

3. Type *Address.* Press Return. (See how you're building a list?)

4. Type *Gift.* Press Return.

5. Type *Adjective.* Press Return. (In this blank, you'll eventually type a word that describes the glorious present this person gave you.)

6. Finally, type *Part of House.* (You'll see why in a moment). Press Return.

Your masterpiece should look something like this

7. Click the Done button in the lower-right corner. The dialog box goes away.

When you see what you've created, things should make a little bit more sense. You've just created the blanks (oh, all right, *fields*) to be filled in for each person in your list.

| | |
|---|---|
| **First Name** | |
| **Last Name** | |
| **Address** | |
| **Gift** | |
| **Adjective** | |
| **Part of** | |

## Data entry time

This is important: To fill in the fields of a database (like this one), just type normally. To advance from one field to the next — from "First Name" to "Last Name," for example — press the Tab key. (You can also move to a new field by clicking in it, but the Tab key is quicker.) So here goes:

1. Make sure you can see a dotted-line rectangle for each field, like the ones in the figure above. If not, press the Tab key. The little blinking cursor should be in the "First Name" blank. (If it's not, click there.)

2. Type *Josephine*. Press the Tab key to jump to the "Last Name" field.

3. Type *Flombébé*. (See "Accent Heaven" on the next page.) Again, press Tab. Now you're in the Address blank.

4. Type *200 West 15th Street*. Now press Return. Note that you don't advance to the next blank; instead, the program thoughtfully makes *this* box bigger, so there's room for another line of address.

| | |
|---|---|
| **First Name** | Josephine |
| **Last Name** | Flombébé |
| **Address** | 200 West 15th Street |
| **Gift** | New York, NY 10010 |
| **Adjective** | |
| **Part of** | |

5. Go ahead and type *New York, NY 10010*. Then press Tab. (And don't worry that the second line of the address immediately gets hidden. The information you typed is still there.)

6. Type *acrylic sofa cover* (and press Tab); *practical* (and press Tab); *living room* (and stop).

# Accent heaven

Ah, mais oui, mon ami. C'est vrai, c'est la vie, c'est la résumé.

I know what you're thinking: *What a smooth, sophisticated guy to be able to speak French like that!* Thank you.

But you're also thinking: How did he get those cool accent marks? Very easily—and you, having been smart enough to choose a Mac over all its inferior competitors, can do it too.

The Mac has a ton of these special characters. Look at your keyboard—I bet you don't see ©, or ™, or •, or ¢, or any other useful symbols Mac people use all the time. That's because they're hidden. The secret that unlocks them is . . . the Option key.

It works like the Shift key: while pressing Option, you type a key. Here are some popular ones:

| To get this . . . | Press Option and type this . . . |
| --- | --- |
| © | g |
| ™ | 2 |
| ç | c |
| ¢ | 4 |
| ¡ | 1 |
| £ | 3 |
| • | 8 |
| ® | r |
| † | t |

Anyway, there are dozens of these things. What's nice to know is that you have a complete built-in cheat sheet that shows their locations on the keyboard. It's the Key Caps desk accessory, which is in your    menu.

Open it up and take a look. Now try pressing the Option key.

So *that's* where all those little critters live!

Anyway, there's one more wrinkle to all this. A few symbols, called *diacritical marks* (that's not a computer term, it's a proofreading one, I think) can be placed over *any* letter. They include the markings over this ü, this é, this è, and so förth. Since the Mac doesn't know ahead of time which vowel you're going to type, creating these is a two-step process:

1. While pressing Option, type the key as shown here:

| To get this . . . | Press Option and type this . . . |
| --- | --- |
| é | e |
| ü | u |
| è | ' |
| ñ | n |
| î | i |

When you do this, *nothing will happen.* In other words, no marking appears on the screen — until you do step two.

2. Type the letter you want to appear under the diacritical marking.

Only now does the entire thing — letter and marking — appear on the screen. So if you think about it, typing the six-letter word *résumé* requires eight keystrokes. *C'est formidable, ça!*

You've just filled in the information for your first gift sender. So that this won't take all day, let's pretend that it was a *very* small wedding, and you only received gifts from three people.

But let's see, we need a new set of fields, don't we? Come to think of it, wouldn't life be sweeter if there were a computer term for "set of fields"? By gumbo, there is! A set of fields is called a *record*.

I wouldn't bother with that term if it didn't crop up in the next set of instructions.

1. From the Edit menu, choose New Record.

2. A new record appears, and you're ready to type the second person's information. Type anything you want, or copy the example below, but remember to press Tab at the end of each piece of information. (Oh, and if you want a second line for the address, remember to press Return. Make up a town and state; you're a creative soul.)

| First Name | Ginnie |
|---|---|
| Last Name | May |
| Address | 42 Pocono La. |
| Gift | air conditioner w/ remote |
| Adjective | high-tech |
| Part of | bedroom |

3. Once again, choose New Record from the Edit menu. Type a third set of information, perhaps along these lines:

| First Name | Suzie |
|---|---|
| Last Name | Khiou |
| Address | 1 Doormouse Ave. |
| Gift | Harley |
| Adjective | expensive |
| Part of | garage |

4. Fabulous! You're really cooking now. As a final wise step, choose Save from the File menu. Type *Gift List* as the name of your database.

5. Click Save to preserve your database on the hard disk.

You've just created your first database. Having gone through the tedium of typing in each little scrap of information the way the Mac wants it, you can now perform some stunts with it that'd make your grandparents' jaws drop. You can ask it to show you only the names of your friends whose last names begin with Z. Or only those who live in Texas. Or only those whose gifts you've categorized as *fabulous.*

For instructions on finding, showing these lists, and sorting your database, read the section on FileMaker later in this chapter.

## Forming the form letter

Next, you're going to write the thank-you note. At each place where you want to use somebody's name (or other gift-related information), you'll ask ClarisWorks to slap in the appropriate info.

1. Choose New from the File menu. (Once again, you're asked to choose the kind of document you want.)

2. Double-click Word Processing.

   Now you get a sparkling new sheet of electronic typing paper.

This area represents the margins of the page. You can't type here.

Do your typing here. Press the Delete key to fix a typo.

Incidentally, if you have a small-screen Mac like a Classic or a PowerBook, you probably don't want all that margin area eating up your screen. You can hide it easily enough: choose Document from the Edit menu. A dialog box appears; click the Show Margins checkbox to deselect it. And then click OK. Now your whole screen is filled with typeable area.

Now then — on with the form letter. You'll start the letter with the address, of course. Yet the address will be *different* on each letter! This is where mail-merging is handy:

3. From the File menu, choose Mail Merge. When the little window appears, you'll see your database name, "Gift List," prominently displayed.

4. Click OK (to tell ClarisWorks that Gift List is the database you want to work with).

Now a strange-looking window appears:

In the scrolling list you see the *field names* from your database. Here's how it works:

5. Point to *First Name* and double-click.

See what happened? The program popped a placeholder for the First Name right into your letter. When you print, instead of <<*First Name,*>> it will say *Josephine*.

6. Type a space. In the Mail Merge window, point to *Last Name* and double-click. Press Return; then point to the Mail Merge window again and double-click *Address*.

Before you continue typing, you may want to drag the little Mail Merge window off to the side of your screen as best you can. (To move the window, drag its title bar.) You're going to want to see both it and your typing simultaneously.

7. Press Return a couple of times. Type *Dear,* followed by a space.

8. Point to the words *First Name* in the Mail Merge window, as you did a moment ago. Double-click. Type a comma. Your letter should look something like this:

```
«First Name» «Last Name»
«Address»

Dear «First Name»,
```

9. This is where it gets good. Press Return a couple of returns. Type *I nearly cried when I unwrapped the incredible,* followed by a space.

10. Double-click the word *Gift* in the Mail Merge window.

11. Continue typing: *you gave me for my wedding. It is far and away the most* (and now double-click *Adjective* in the Mail Merge window) *gift I will ever receive.*

```
«First Name» «Last Name»
«Address»


Dear «First Name»,

I nearly cried when I unwrapped the incredible «Gift» you gave me for my wedding. It
is far and away the most «Adjective» gift I will ever receive.
```

Are you getting the hang of this? At each place where you want ClarisWorks to substitute a piece of information from your Gift List database, you insert a little <<placeholder>>.

To see the last field name, *Part of House,* you have to use the Mail Merge window's scroll bar. Then finish the letter as follows:

12. Type *It will look sensational in the* (double-click *Part of House* in the Mail Merge window) *of our new home.*

13. Press the Return key twice and finish up like this: *I had to write this personal note to you and you alone, so you'd know how much I treasure your gift above all the others. Love, Marge.*

```
«First Name» «Last Name»
«Address»


Dear «First Name»,

I nearly cried when I unwrapped the incredible «Gift» you gave me for my wedding. It
is far and away the most «Adjective» gift I will ever receive.

It will look sensational in the «Part of House» of our new home.

I had to write this personal note to you and you alone, so you'd know how much I
treasure your gift above all the others.

Love, Marge.
```

Naturally, Emily Post would go instantly bald in horror if she thought you were about to send out a letter that says *Dear First Name.* But through the miracle of computers, when these letters are printed, it'll be impossible to tell that each one wasn't typed separately.

Anyway, go ahead and choose Save from the File menu. Type *Thank-you letter,* and click Save.

## The graphics zone: Designing a letterhead

You'll read a lot more about graphics programs in the next couple of sections. But just to show you how you can tie everything together, let's whip up a quick letterhead in the Graphics module.

Choose New from the File menu. Our friend, the New Document dialog box, appears. This time you should double-click the Drawing button.

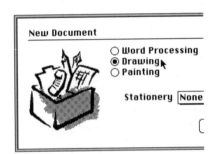

Claris Works shows you its drawing window. The grid of dotted lines is there to give things a nice architectural look; it won't appear in the finished printout.

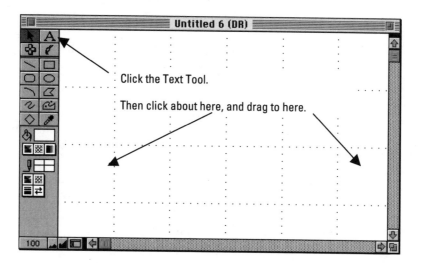

See the tool icons on the left side of your screen? They're pretty much covered in the section on MacDraw, later in this chapter. Now then:

1. Click the text tool (it looks like a letter A). Drag across the screen, as shown in the figure above.

2. Use the Font menu; choose Times. Use the Size menu; choose 24 Point.

3. Type three spaces; then a long dash. (To make a long dash, hold down the Shift and Option keys, and type a hyphen.) Type *A Very Personal Note*. Type another long dash and then three more spaces.

> —A Very Personal Note—

4. Press the Enter key so that handles appear around your text. Using the Alignment submenu of the Format menu, choose Center.

5. Finally, you'll add that elegant white-lettering-against-black look that shows up on so many corporate annual reports. At the left side of your screen, there's a set of odd-looking icons. Find the one immediately below the tiny pouring paint can icon, as shown by the following arrow:

This icon is actually a pop-out palette. Click the icon, but keep the mouse button pressed so that the palette appears. Drag carefully to the right until the pointer is on the solid black square, as shown at right (above). (If you have a black-and-white Mac, choose the *word* "Black.") Release the mouse.

You've just used the Fill palette to color in the entire text block with black. Which is just great, except that now the text is a solid black rectangle! To fix the problem, you need to make the *text white*.

6. From the Text Color submenu of the Format menu, choose White. Ta-da!

## *The return of Copy and Paste*

All that remains is for you to slap this letterhead into your mail-merge letter.

1. From the Edit menu, choose Copy.

2. Now you have to return to your word processing document. Here's a quick way to pull it to the front: From the Window menu, choose Thank-You Letter (WP). (WP stands for Word Processing document, DB stands for Database, DR stands for Drawing, and PT stands for Painting. GR, if you have ClarisWorks 1.0, stands for graphics, which is the same as Drawing.)

   Your letter springs to the fore.

3. From the Format menu, choose Insert Header. (A *header* is an area at the top of every page, above whatever text you've typed. In this case, it looks like an empty text area.)

4. From the Edit menu, choose Paste.

   *Et voilà* . . . your graphic pops neatly into the header.

# For control freaks only: The View buttons

Before you leave the drawing window, cast your eyes upon the lower-left corner of the screen. There you'll find this odd-looking array of controls:

Pop-up menu     Hide palette

Zoom in; Zoom out     Split the screen

As you can tell, ClarisWorks makes it extremely easy to blow up your work. (Obviously I mean *magnify* it; *destroying* it is up to you.) A quick click on either of those little mountain buttons makes the artwork smaller or larger. Or jump directly to a more convenient degree of magnification by using the percentage pop-up menu (where it says 100 in the figure above). You're not changing the actual printed size — only how it's displayed on the screen.

If you're on a small-screen Mac, you can hide that inch-wide strip of tools at the left side of the window by clicking the palette-hiding button, as shown above. Finally, you can see two widely separated parts of the drawing simultaneously by dragging the fat little black strip, indicated by the words "Split the screen" in the figure above, to the right. Now you've got two distinct panes of your masterpiece, which you can scroll independently.

You've actually done it: combined a database, a word processor, and a drawing program in a single project! For a real kick, choose Print from the File menu and watch how the program automatically replaces actual names for the <<place-holders>> on the screen.

---

### —A Very Personal Note—

Suzie Khiou
1 Doormouse La.
San Francisco, CA  94108


Dear Suzie,

I nearly cried when I unwrapped the incredible Harley  you gave me for my wedding. It is far and away the most expensive gift I will ever receive.

It will look sensational in the garage of our new home.

I had to write this personal note to you and you alone, so you'd know how much I treasure your gift above all the others.

Love, Marge.

---

# For pixel-painting landscapes

Don't know about you, but when I first installed ClarisWorks and then tried to paint, it opened up a little-bitty square of white (for me to paint on). And it gave me an error message that said:

> 🖳 **The document size has been reduced to fit the available memory.**
>
> [ OK ]

Nice, huh?

Anyway, the solution to this problem — and many other Disrespectful-Software Behaviors — is to give the program more memory. This process is explained in excruciating detail in Chapter 11. In the meantime, here's the scoop:

Quit ClarisWorks. Highlight its icon. Choose Get Info from the File menu. In the Size box at the bottom of the Get Info window, you'll see a number (probably something like 900 or 950). Change this number to, say, 1400, and you'll finally be able to paint more than miniatures.

---

## *A little paint*

There are two excellent features of ClarisWorks I feel it's my duty to mention.

First, there's the Painting window (which isn't in ClarisWorks version 1.0). By this time, I trust you know how to get there: choose New from the File menu and then double-click the Painting button.

Suddenly you're in a pixel-blitzing wonderland, where you can create all kinds of "painted" artwork. As you'll discover when you read ahead to the MacPaint section, this kind of artwork has pros and cons. The pro is that you can change the color of *every single dot* on the screen (instead of just drawing circles, lines, and rectangles, which is all you can do in the Drawing window). The con is that you can't move or resize something in a painting after you've laid down the "paint" (which you *can* do in the Drawing window).

## *A little outline*

This is a *really* great feature of ClarisWorks 2.0 and later.

Open a new word processor document. From the Outline menu, choose Outline View.

Now start typing an outline. When you want to create a new indented level, choose New Topic Right from the Outline menu, or press the keyboard shortcut instead. Alternatively, begin by just pressing Return at the end of every line so that your outline looks like the following illustration:

◇ Major Achievements
◇ Fifth-grade basketball tournament
◇ Getting hired by the MTA
◇ Purchase of Nintendo stock in 1970
◇ Major Gaffes
◇ Senior Prom—enough said
◇ Being the last one chosen in kickball
◇ Discuss the psychological and emotional scars
◇ Burning the wedding cake
◇ It really wasn't my fault
◇ Anyway Mom said "Leave it in another 10 minutes"

. . . and then click each individual heading and choose Move Right or Move Left from the Outline menu to whip the outline into shape:

◆ Major Achievements
    ◇ Fifth-grade basketball tournament
    ◇ Getting hired by the MTA
    ◇ Purchase of Nintendo stock in 1970
◆ Major Gaffes
    ◇ Senior Prom—enough said
    ◆ Being the last one chosen in kickball
        ◇ Discuss the psychological and emotional scars
    ◆ Burning the wedding cake
        ◇ It really wasn't my fault
        ◇ Anyway Mom said "Leave it in another 10 minutes"

Anyway, the beauty of all this is that you can *rearrange* the little topics so easily! Just click one of those little diamonds (or to the *left* of one) and drag it up or down to any other location in the outline!

Don't pooh-pooh this feature just because you don't write doctoral theses very much. By highlighting some of your outline and using the Outline Format command (in the Outline menu), you can transform your outline into a shopping list, a daily calendar, your financial priorities for the month, or even a to-do list with checkboxes you can tick off as you progress:

◆ By next week
    ☑ Replace missing front door
    ☑ Bathe at least once
    ☐ Consider career overhaul
◆ By the time I'm married
    ☐ Increase income above poverty level
    ☑ Hone interpersonal skills
    ☐ Meet suitable potential spouse

Spend at least 15 minutes playing with this highly useful organizational tool.

### *That's not all there is*

The only parts of ClarisWorks we've left unexplored are the spreadsheet (which I couldn't figure out how to tie in to a thank-you letter) and the Communications module. Spreadsheets are covered under Excel later in this chapter. And if you have a modem and want to learn about the Communications program, then the little extra ClarisWorks manual does a nice job of explaining how to make your phone line a highway to the world of information. Or, if it's worth spending some bucks on, buy *More Macs For Dummies* (coming in the spring of '94 to a bookstore near you), where the whole distinctly not-for-beginners world of modem-dialing is covered with astonishing clarity, brilliance, and modesty.

## *MacDraw, Canvas, SuperPaint*

All of these programs, and a healthy helping of others, work essentially alike. They're called *drawing programs.* As much as that sounds like they'd be the same things as *painting programs,* they're not.

Painting programs create art called *bitmapped* graphics. When you lay down some "paint," it's stored as a bunch of dots. You can erase them, but you can't change the original shape you painted — a circle, say, or a letter of the alphabet — because the Mac no longer thinks of them as a circle or a letter. It just thinks of them as a bunch of painted little dots. The advantage: You have control over each individual dot, and you have dot-manipulation tools like the Spray Can. In the figure below, note (1) the speckled effect, and (2) the fact that you can drag a chunk of circle out of the original collection of dots:

Drawing programs, on the other hand, create *object-oriented* graphics. When you draw a circle, the Mac doesn't store it as a map of black dots. It remembers that you drew a *circle* of a fixed shading and size. That means that you could never speckle it, and you could certainly never erase (or remove) a chunk of it.

But the advantage of drawing programs is that, later, you can return to that circle and move it by dragging it. Or you can overlap another object on top of it — and later change your mind. Or you can change a circle's shading long after you drew it. Or, as shown in the next figure, you can tug a circle's handles to stretch it.

## A high-end sidebar barely worth a glance

There's yet a *third* type of graphics program. Ever read *USA Today?* How about *Time* magazine? Well, then, surely you've seen Sunday newspaper Stop-N-Shop ad inserts showing little line drawings of Clorox and Fig Newtons?

The drawings and diagrams in all of these fine publications are typically produced with either FreeHand or Illustrator, called *PostScript* graphics programs. Printouts from these programs are incredibly smooth and high quality. When used with a color printer, these illustration programs can be (and are) used for package designs, brochures, maps, you name it. These two professional programs may be in the top ten, but they sure ain't in the *beginner's* top ten, so I'm not even gonna touch them—but their operation has much in common with the drawing-type programs described here.

Drawing programs tend to print out with much sharper quality than painting programs.

## *Concepts*

The palette in all of these drawing programs contains the same basic tools. Here's the *Reader's Digest* condensed version:

Text Tool: Lets you add type to your artwork. You can edit this text later.

Hand (or Grabber): Slides the drawing around on your screen, giving access to offscreen areas.

Rounded Rectangle Tool: Creates rectangles with rounded corners.

Line Tool: Draws straight lines—or, with Shift pressed, draws perfectly horizontal or vertical (or 45-degree) lines.

Polygon Tool: Creates multisided shapes; click at each corner, and double-click to finish the shape.

Arrow Tool: Selects objects, grabs their handles for stretching.

Magnifying glass: Enlarges the display, or "zooms in," for detail work.

Rectangle Tool: Creates rectangles—or, with Shift pressed, creates squares.

Ellipse Tool: Creates ovals—or, with Shift pressed, creates circles.

Arc Tool—Draws a quarter-circle.

Each program has a few goodies of its own, too, but these basics are always included.

To draw something, click the tool (and release the button), move to a blank part of the screen where you want to place the object, hold down the mouse button, and drag. When you let go, you'll see the new line or shape enclosed by small black *handles*. Using the arrow tool, you can drag these handles to stretch or resize the object you just drew. Or click in the middle of it to drag the object to a new location.

Or just click an object to make its handles show. After they appear — letting you know that the object is selected — you can use the menus to change the object's appearance. For example, suppose you draw a thin line (below left). While it's selected, you can choose a new line thickness (below middle) from the line thickness palette (every program has one). The result: The same line has a different thickness (below right).

Using the palette of colors (or of patterns), you can change the color (or pattern) that fills the inside of a shape the same way: select, and then apply.

When you press the Shift key while you draw something, the Mac constrains the movement of your mouse to flat or symmetrical movements. For instance, press Shift when you draw a line, and the line will be perfectly horizontal, vertical, or 45-degree diagonal. Press Shift while you draw a rectangle, and it will be a perfect square. And so on.

## *Selecting and grouping multiple objects*

In the Finder, after you click one icon, you can select additional icons by Shift-clicking them (that is, clicking them while pressing the Shift key). In a word processor, if you have selected a word, you can extend the selection by Shift-clicking some place later in the paragraph.

Yes, indeed, Mr. Watson, there is a pattern here. This Shift-click-to-extend-a-selection deal is a common Mac technique. Same thing in drawing programs: click to select one object, Shift-click to select others.

After you've got a bunch of objects selected, you can *group* them — combine them into a single new object — using (what else?) the Group command. You can even group groups. You may want to group objects in this way just to make sure their alignment to each other doesn't get disturbed.

Handiest yet, you can *un*group a group, or even ungroup a grouped group of groups. (I'll give you a moment to work on that.) Drawing programs ungroup objects in the same order in which they were grouped. So imagine that you group objects A and B together, and then group object C to the first group. The first time you use the Ungroup command, you'll wind up with the A/B group and the C object loose; apply Ungroup a second time to split up A and B.

## Text FX

One of the nicest things about drawing programs is that text is text, and text it remains. Text in a bitmapped program (like MacPaint), on the other hand, turns into a text-shaped collection of painted *dots* instantly. You can't edit the text or change the font or correct a typo, once you're done typing. And the printout looks exactly as jagged as it does on the screen:

> # A Green Onion

In a drawing program, though, each piece of text remains editable inside its little boundary rectangle. You can change the font or the size of the text or the dimensions of this rectangle at any time. And because the Mac still thinks of it as text (and not dots), it prints out at full text sharpness on a laser printer or StyleWriter:

> # A Green Onion

After you create a text block, you can paste it into a word processor and drag those little corner boxes. The word processor thinks it's just a plain old graphic and proceeds to squish it any way you like. The result is fantastic text effects you couldn't create in a word processor alone:

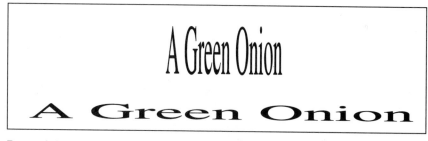

Beyond these concepts, a drawing program really doesn't require a degree in rocket science. I now release you to your creative juices.

# MacPaint, SuperPaint, UltraPaint, Studio/1, and Others

There's about a dozen of these programs, all of which (except for Studio/1) end with the word *paint*. Most of them work alike — only the frills differ from program to program. Super-, Ultra-, and PixelPaint work in color (so do the expensive pro-level painting programs like Photoshop, ColorStudio, and Studio/32). The rest are black and white.

They're called *painting* programs because they produce *bitmapped* artwork. (For a discussion of what that means, see the introduction to the MacDraw section.) Printouts from bitmapped programs tend to be a little bit jagged since the Mac is reproducing the Mac screen when it prints out.

There's not much mystical hidden knowledge to be unearthed in paint programs. Once you've used a tool, you've pretty much mastered it for life. Here, then, is a typical Tool palette. You click a tool (and release), move the cursor to the page, and then drag across your white screen. With this guide — and the all-important Undo command in the Edit menu — you're well on your way to the world's toniest art galleries.

| | | |
|---:|:---:|:---|
| Marquee | ▢ ⌇ | Lasso |
| Pencil | ✎ A | Text Tool |
| Spray can | 🖌 🖌 | Paint brush |
| Paint bucket | 🪣 ⌫ | Eraser |
| Line Tool | ╲ ▭ | Rectangle |
| Rounded rectangle | ▢ ◯ | Ellipse |
| Polygon Tool | ◁ ⌐ | Arc Tool |
| Hand grabber | ✋ 🔍 | Magnifying glass |

## Impossibly trivial info about dots per inch

The Mac screen has 72 dots per inch. (In elite computing circles, this is abbreviated *72 dpi.*) A laser printer's printouts look much sharper because it crams in 300 dpi. Therefore, when you print a MacPaint document on a laser printer (or a StyleWriter), the results appear especially jagged.

There are two exceptions to this rule-o'-thumb. First of all, some programs — like SuperPaint, Studio/1, and ArtWorks — let you *edit* your painting at 300 dpi, the same as the laser. That way you have the best of both worlds: You get high-resolution printouts (typical of a drawing program), but you get the fine control over every dot (as in a painting program). The downside is that 300 dpi editing makes your Mac work harder. It takes more memory, more disk space, and more time to process each editing move you make.

The other exception to the Jaggy-Printout Law is the Graphics Smoothing option. Before you print, choose Page Setup from the File menu (doesn't matter what program you're in — every program has this command). Make sure the Graphics Smoothing option is selected. When you print this way, the Mac's internal graphics gnomes run around with sandpaper and smooth out the rough edges of your graphics (see below for a before-and-after example). It's not quite as sharp-looking as the 300 dpi editing mode, but it's fine for flyers and stuff — and besides, the jagginess is actually a "look" that certain Greenwich Village artists I know think is kinda neat.

*Jaggies*

*Smoothies*

## *Marquee and Lasso*

These tools don't create any marks on the artwork. Instead, they're *selection* tools. They draw a dotted, shimmering line as you drag the mouse; you're creating an enclosure. Anything within the enclosure — the selected area — will be affected by your next move. For example, you can click within the selection to drag that chunk into a new position. Or press the Delete key to erase it. You can also apply special effects to the selected region, such as Invert (which swaps white areas for black, and vice versa) and Trace Edges (a bizarre one; try it).

There are two important differences between the Marquee and the Lasso. The Marquee always creates rectangular selected areas, *including whatever white space* is inside the rectangle. In the following illustration, you can see that when you drag a rectangular selection on top of a dark object (left), the white part of the selection remains opaque (right):

The Lasso, on the other hand, requires you to draw a circle all the way around the image you're trying to select. When you let go of the mouse, the dotted line snaps like a rubber band inward, enclosing only black regions of your artwork (below left). Therefore, when the selected part is dragged on top of a dark object, the latter shows through the former (below right):

# Pencil

The Pencil is pretty tame. Drag across the white area to draw a one-dot-thick line.

There's only one trick to it. If you begin your line by clicking in a *dark* spot, the line you draw will be white, even if you cross over into a white area.

# Text Tool

Not much to this one: click in a blank area and start typing. While you're typing, you can press Delete (or Backspace) to fix a typo; in some programs you can even use the mouse to drag through stretches of text for editing. But beware! The instant you click the mouse outside of the text box, your text freezes into a noneditable clump of dots (yes, a *bitmap*).

In most programs, you can double-click the Text Tool icon to set the font and size for your type (before you do the typing). Obviously, after you click the mouse outside the text box (and freeze the text into a bitmap), it's too late to change type characteristics. You have to delete the whole thing if you want to change it.

That's such a bummer that some programs, like Studio/1 and SuperPaint, have a separate transparent layer where you can type real, editable, word-processable text that never turns into a bitmap. Of course, bitmaps have some advantages; after selecting one with the Lasso or Marquee, you can apply any *transformation* commands to it (found in a menu): Stretch, Distort, Slant, whatever. See here:

## Spray can

Painting at its finest. Drag it across the painting area to create a fine mist of dots, just like an airbrush or spray paint can. Dawdle over an area to make it darker; hurry across the screen for a lighter mist. The color (or pattern) of the spray is whatever color (or pattern) you've selected from the color (or pattern) pop-up menu. In some programs, you can double-click the Spray can icon to produce a dialog box, where you can adjust the rate and size of the spray. For post-pubescent thrills, try drawing a subway car and then spraypaint your name across it.

## Eraser

Pretty basic. Drag across dark areas to erase them. Don't forget to zoom in (enlarge the screen image, using the Magnifying Glass) for detail work. For more mature thrills, draw your ex-spouse on the screen and then erase his/her head.

## Line Tool

Choose a line thickness (there's usually a pop-up menu for this purpose) before you draw. Then drag to create a straight line. If you want a perfectly horizontal, vertical, or 45-degree line, press Shift while you drag. Some programs also let you specify the color or pattern of the line.

## Rectangle, Rounded rectangle, Ellipse, Polygon, Arc

These shape tools pretty much work alike: drag diagonally to produce the shape. (The Polygon Tool works differently — click once for each corner point of your multisided shape; then double-click to finish the shape.)

In any case, you can usually control both the color (or pattern) of the *interior* of the shape as well as that of the *outline* of the shape by using pop-up color (or pattern) menus. The Line Thickness pop-up menu governs the thickness of the outline. As before, the Shift key is the great constrainer: press it to create a perfect square (with the Rectangle Tool), circle (with the Ellipse Tool), and so on.

## Hand grabber

Unless you have a large monitor, you usually can't see a full page of art at once. You can always use the scroll bars to slide your image up or down on your screen. But the Hand grabber is much more direct — just drag in the direction you want to shift the painting.

Each program has its own keyboard shortcut for this handy tool; usually it's the spacebar or the Option key. When this special key is pressed, your cursor turns into the Hand grabber; when you release the key, you return to whatever tool you had previously selected.

## Magnifying glass

Click this tool; then click the painting to zoom in and/or enlarge the display for detail work. Of course, you're not actually making anything bigger (in terms of its printout); you're really just magnifying the *screen* image to get more control over those pesky dots. Keep zooming in until you get an idea of how those little dots make up your painting. You can use the Pencil to click the dots either black or white.

To zoom out again or return to normal size, you usually press Option while clicking the painting.

# Microsoft Word

Q: Where does an 800-pound gorilla sit?

A: Anywhere it wants.

Refer to this age-old discourse the next time somebody asks you why Microsoft Word, a program with numerous flaws and irritations, is the best-selling Macintosh program of all time. Microsoft is a gargantuan software company in Washington state. They sell so much software that the founder/owner (Bill Gates) is the youngest multibillionaire in history. Probably because of Microsoft's huge presence in the IBM-PC world, it's the 800-pound gorilla in the Mac world, too.

Of course, Microsoft Word isn't *bad*. In fact, it's got some truly wonderful features, one of which is that *everybody* uses Word. (Well, the vast majority does.) That means that when you hand your letter (on a disk) to a friend, you usually don't have to worry whether or not she's got the software needed to read it.

Anyway, you've already absorbed most of the basics of word processing (in Chapter 3). Word has a few fancy features worth learning, though (and does some basic features in interesting ways).

# Views

To start a new document, double-click the Word icon. You arrive at a blank screen. Go ahead and start typing your Oscar-winning screenplay. Use the usual word processing techniques (Delete to backspace, drag through text to select it, use the Edit menu to copy and paste, and so on) to whip it into shape.

You'll discover, though, that your piece of paper appears to be endless, as though it's delivered on a never-ending roll of Bounty. That's because you're in Normal view, where you never see a page end. (The end of a page is symbolized by a thin dotted line, but you sort of have to watch for it.) In Normal view, you don't get to see page-related elements like page numbers, either. They're hidden until you go to another view.

If you want to see a more accurate display of what you'll get when you print, choose Page Layout from the View menu. Things start to bog down in Page Layout view — that is, it takes longer to scroll around and visit different corners of your document. But you clearly see where each page ends, and you get to see things like page numbers and multiple columns.

There's also an Outline view, which is pretty bizarre. I'll let you cuddle up to the manual for that one.

Finally, there's Print Preview, an absolutely vital and useful view. (Just to make sure the program isn't too easy to use, they've put the Print Preview command in the *File* menu, not the View menu with the others.) In Print Preview you get to see the entire page — in fact, two side-by-side pages — no matter what size monitor you have.

# To change the margins

Print Preview also provides the easiest way to adjust the margins. Just drag the small black handles; remember that you're adjusting the margins for *all* the pages when you do this.

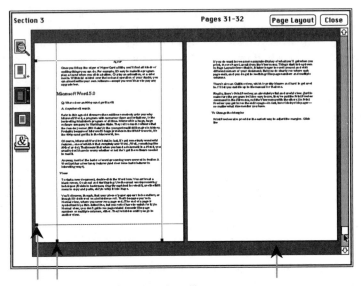

Drag these black handles (and the others like them) to adjust the margins...

...and then click the gray background to see the changes.

To return to Normal view from Print Preview, click Close.

## *The unbearable lightness of interface*

In their efforts to make Word user-friendlier, Word's designers went, methinks, a tad overboard in the visual-interface department. When you launch Word for the first time, you get not one, not two, but *four* different strips of icons and buttons! I mean, come on. Look at this picture and tell me that you'd know how to work this program on your first time at bat:

I'll do what I can to clear this up. I'll take each strip of cryptic controls and decipher them for you.

But let me make this clear: here I am, a Board-Certified Power-User, and I have most of these things *hidden*. Oh, yes, it's true: you don't have to have these things cluttering up your screen. As we go, I'll mention how you can nuke each of these examples of graphic-interface-run-amok. There are thousands of people who have *all* of these icon strips turned off. Without these strips, using Word is almost exactly like using a typewriter, and that's 100% OK.

## *The Toolbar*

What's the difference between Word 5.1 and previous versions? The primary addition is the Toolbar: a bunch of icon buttons, each of which does exactly the same thing as one of the menu commands. For example, if you click the very first button on the toolbar, you get a new blank empty document. It's exactly the same as choosing New from the File menu.

Here's what the buttons do. (If you have a big screen, you'll see a few additional buttons.)

If you're the kind of person who enjoys dismantling the car and then reassembling it from memory, you can, if you wish, rearrange the buttons, or create a different set, using the Customize command on the Toolbar menu (the button indicated in the figure above).

If, however, your main objective is to have as long and happy a life as possible, you may wish to do away with the Toolbar entirely. There are three degrees of non-Toolbar presence. First, you can rotate it 90 degrees, so that instead of taking up a valuable half-inch across the *top* of your screen, it's running down the *side*. To do this, pull down the Toolbar button/menu (as pictured above), and choose Left.

Second, you can get rid of the Toolbar just for today. To do this, choose Toolbar from the View menu.

Finally, you can request that you never again be tormented with the existence of these enigmatic icons. From the Tools menu, choose Preferences. Scroll down until you see Toolbar. Click the icon. At long last, deselect the View Toolbar checkbox. You shan't see the Toolbar again.

## The Ribbon: Quick word formatting

When you're in Normal or Page Layout view editing text, there are two information strips across the top of the window. The Ribbon is the top one; the Ruler is below it. (If you don't see these strips, somebody must have hidden them. Choose their names from the View menu.)

For the most part, the Ribbon controls *character formatting:* the size of type, the style (bold or italic), and the font. To make it work, you *first* have to select some text you've already typed — by dragging through it. Of course, you can also make some of these settings just *before* you begin to type.

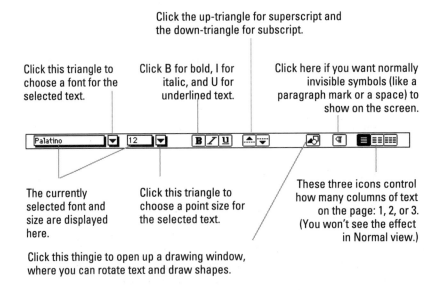

Click the up-triangle for superscript and the down-triangle for subscript.

Click this triangle to choose a font for the selected text.

Click B for bold, I for italic, and U for underlined text.

Click here if you want normally invisible symbols (like a paragraph mark or a space) to show on the screen.

The currently selected font and size are displayed here.

Click this triangle to choose a point size for the selected text.

These three icons control how many columns of text on the page: 1, 2, or 3. (You won't see the effect in Normal view.)

Click this thingie to open up a drawing window, where you can rotate text and draw shapes.

If you ask me, the most useful are the B, I, and U buttons in the middle (for Bold, Italic, and Underline). You can glance at them and know immediately what formatting your next typing will have.

The font and size controls (at the left side) are useful, too, once you figure out that you have to click on the *downward-pointing triangle* to change the setting.

# The Ruler: Quick paragraph formatting

Below the Ribbon is the Ruler. These icons make changes to an entire *paragraph* at a time — and remember, a "paragraph" is anything you've typed that ends with a Return. Before you can use the ruler, you must first *select the paragraphs you want to change!*

Nine out of ten novices surveyed find this concept hard to get used to. If you want to indent *one* paragraph, just click anywhere in it, so that the insertion point is blinking within it — and then use the Ruler's margin control. If you want to change your *entire document,* like making it double-spaced, start by selecting *everything* (the Select All command in the Edit menu is a quick way to do so) — and then use the Ruler.

If you want to affect several paragraphs, but not the whole memo, drag through them — and then use the Ruler.

The point is to remember the Macintosh mantra: Select, then apply. Select, then apply. . . .

Click one of these 3 icons to make the selected paragraphs single-spaced, one-and-a-half, or double-spaced, respectively.

These are 5 "tab wells." Click for a left, centered, right, decimal, or vertical-rule tab; then click it into place on the ruler to make a tab stop.

Click this triangle to choose a Style for the selected paragraphs.

These 3 icons help you format table margins, if you use Word's Table feature.

Click one of these 4 icons to make the paragraph left-aligned, centered, right-aligned, or fully justified.

The first icon means no blank lines between paragraphs; the second icon means Open spacing (an automatic blank line between paragraphs).

Drag the triangle to change the right margin, just for the selected paragraphs.

Drag the top *half* of this marker to set the first-line indent for the paragraph; drag the lower half to set the overall left margin.

# *Be careful on the strip*

And here you thought we'd finished talking about all Word's strips. No such luck.

Word's most hazardous feature, as far as you, Most Honorable Newcomer, are concerned, is its *selection bar*. This is a very, very skinny invisible stripe up the left side of the window. You'll know when your cursor has inadvertently wandered in there because your arrow pointer will suddenly start pointing to the *right* instead of left.

You may find this impossible to believe, but Word's left-margin strip was not, in fact, designed out of pure foaming malice toward new Mac users. It's actually supposed to make editing your work easier by providing some text-selecting shortcuts. Here are a few favorites.

Shortcut 1: Select one line of text by clicking in the selection strip.

> Linda choked back the sobs as the explosions shook the scarred earth around her. She fingered the ashy remnants of the glider.
> "Happy...happy Groundhog Day, Harry," she murmured noiselessly.

Shortcut 2: To select a paragraph instantly, double-click in the selection strip. (Or triple-click anywhere inside a paragraph.)

> Linda choked back the sobs as the explosions shook the scarred earth around her. She fingered the ashy remnants of the glider.
> "Happy...happy Groundhog Day, Harry," she murmured noiselessly.

Shortcut 3: To select the entire document, triple-click in the selection strip. (Do this when you want to change the font for the entire memo, for example.)

> Linda choked back the sobs as the explosions shook the scarred earth around her. She fingered the ashy remnants of the glider.
> "Happy...happy Groundhog Day, Harry," she murmured noiselessly.

As a matter of fact, as long as we're covering different ways to highlight text, here are a couple as free bonuses:

Shortcut 4: Select a certain stretch of text by clicking at the beginning of the part you want then pressing *Shift* and clicking the end point, even if it is pages and pages away.

> Linda choked back the sobs as the explosions shook the scarred earth around her. She fingered the ashy remnants of the glider.
> "Happy...happy Groundhog Day, Harry," she murmured noiselessly.

Shortcut 5: Select one sentence by Command-clicking in it (in other words, click while pressing the ⌘ key).

> Linda choked back the sobs as the explosions shook the scarred earth around her. She fingered the ashy remnants of the glider.
> "Happy...happy Groundhog Day, Harry," she murmured noiselessly.

## *Moving text by dragging it*

One of the coolest features in Word 5 — a feature no other word processor has — is "drag-and-drop" text manipulation. You can highlight some text and simply drag it into a new position without doing the tawdry cut-and-paste routine.

For example, in the sentence below, you select the word *miserable* by double-clicking it. Then point the cursor at the highlighted portion, and drag it carefully into a new position and let go. The result is shown in the lower example.

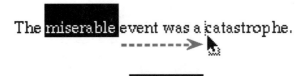

(If the drag-and-drop deal doesn't work, some vandal probably turned this feature off. Choose Preferences from the Tools menu and turn it back on.)

## *Page numbers, headers, date-stamping*

Suppose there's something you want to appear at the top (or bottom) of every single page (like *TOP SECRET: Destroy this document after Xeroxing*). Go to Normal view. From the View menu, choose Header (or Footer for the bottom of the page). A new window opens. Anything you type in here will conveniently appear at the top of every page.

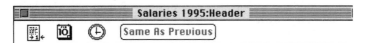

If you click the little page number icon, Word will put a page number (at the insertion point) on every page. Click the middle icon, which is supposed to look like a calendar, to pop the date into this header. And click the clock to insert the time. Go ahead and use all the normal formatting controls — fonts, sizes, styles — to touch up the header text. If you want to see how it looks, choose Page Layout from the View menu.

## *Raw power: Style sheets*

In this book, you see the same kinds of styles used over and over again. For example, this paragraph has specific margins and type characteristics, but the subhead ("Raw power: Style sheets") looks different. Yet I didn't have to reset all those margins and type styles for every appearance of a subhead. I just used styles.

You can read the manual for the full spiel on styles. But here's the easy way to do it.

Type some text. Format the heck out of it. Fiddle with the indents (see the Ruler diagram). Change the type style. Make it double-spaced or whatever. Adjust the tab stops.

Finally, when it's good and ready, click the Style Name box and give this formatting a style name. Go ahead, just type it. Call it Subhead.

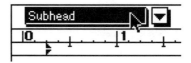

When you press Return, Word will ask you to confirm that you want to create a new Style called Subhead. Click OK.

Now the *next* time you need to format a paragraph this way, don't bother doing all that formatting. Just plop the insertion point anywhere in the paragraph; then, using the small black triangle to the right of the Style name box (on the Ruler), choose Subhead. You've just changed all the formatting characteristics at once.

Now here's the beauty part. Let's say you've got 12,029 subheads in your document. (No *wonder* your editors say you're long-winded.) And now you decide that you want to change the font. For all 12,029 of them.

Fortunately, it's incredibly easy since you assigned them all to one style. Just triple-click *one* subhead to select it. (Triple-clicking highlights the entire paragraph.) Change the font (or make any other changes you want to make). Now, using the Style pop-up menu (that old black triangle again), choose the *same* Style name — Subhead.

Word will ask you what you're doing. Click "Redefine the style based on selection" and then click OK. In the blink of an eye, all 12,029 occurrences of this style change.

## *Checking your spelling*

Click at the beginning of the document. Choose Spelling from the Tools menu. A dialog box appears, in which Word will display each spelling error it finds; click Suggest to see some guesses as to what word you intended. Double-click one to replace the misspelled word in the document.

If none of this happens, and you get some kind of message telling you that the Spelling command isn't installed, then, by gum, the Spelling command isn't installed. (When you first install Word, you're given the choice of which features to include. Thesaurus, Grammar, Hyphenation, and the drawing module are some of the others available. You can install them later, as long as you have the original Word floppy disks.)

## How to kill the summary box

One of the most irritating aspects of Word is that stupid Summary Information box that comes up every darned time you save a document. (You don't mind if I vent a little, do you?)

Before you put your fist through the screen, try this. Choose Preferences from the Tools menu. Click the third icon, the one that says Open and Save.

In the main window, click Prompt for Summary Info to deselect it. That's it!

## How to kill superfluous commands

While I'm going with my flow of hostility, may I point out how many menu commands Word has that nobody ever uses? *TOC Entry? Link Options? Revert to Style?* Let's be real here.

Fortunately, you don't have to live with them. Unless you're trying to crank out the next Sears catalog on your Mac Plus or something, chances are good you won't be needing indexing and auto-hyphenation features, for example.

Removing a command you never use is incredibly easy. While pressing ⌘ and Option together, press the minus (hyphen) key. Your cursor turns into a big fat minus sign! Handle your mouse with care, now — it's a loaded weapon. Any menu command you touch will *disappear from the menu!*

Here's a partial listing of the commands I nuked from my Word menus. Depending on how far you intend to let Word take you, you may want to augment this list (or leave some of these alone):

- ✔ **File menu:** Summary Info, Print Merge.
- ✔ **Edit menu:** Paste Special, Go To, Create Publisher, Subscribe To, Link Options, Edit Object.
- ✔ **View menu:** Print Merge Helper, Annotations, Voice Annotations, Play Movie.
- ✔ **Insert menu:** Section Break, Voice Annotation, Addresses, Index Entry, Index, TOC Entry, Table of Contents, Frame, Object, Movie.
- ✔ **Format menu:** Section, Frame, Revert to Style.

And, by the way, you're not removing these commands from the *program* — you're simply removing them from the *menu listings*. If you ever want to restore Word's menus to their original condition, choose Commands from the Tools menu. Click the Reset button in the lower-right corner of the window that appears.

# PageMaker

The idea of *page layout* software is amazingly simple. You see a blank page. You dump different kinds of page elements onto it: text, graphics, straight lines, photos, whatever. Then you drag them around like tiles on the page until they're in an attractive arrangement. This, kids, is page layout. Without a single union laborer being paid $180 per hour to paste waxed paper strips onto dummy pages (which is how they used to do page layout), you can publish and distribute your very own *Neighborhood Anarchist Weekly* — you can become a "desktop publisher." And since the Macintosh brought this fun new pastime into people's homes and offices, every magazine, brochure, newsletter, flyer, and newspaper from *USA Today* to *Time* is designed this way.

## Starting a new document

Double-click the PageMaker icon. You get a dialog box that asks what size paper you want to use: Letter (8½-inch × 11-inch), Legal (8½-inch × 14-inch), or Tabloid (11-inch × 17-inch), which is what the *National Enquirer* uses.

## The Master Pages

Some elements of your publication are probably going to appear on every page: the logo, the page number, the issue date. Instead of making you retype *Bathroom Fixture Journal* at the top of every page, you can just type it once — on the Master Pages. To get to the Master Pages, you click the little dog-eared page icons in the far lower left of the window:

Now you see two blank pages — the Right and Left Master Pages (if your document has facing pages), whose image lurks behind every individual page of your publication. This is where the logo, the page number (which you create using the Text Tool by holding down ⌘-Option and typing a P), the chapter head, or whatever.

When you're done working with the Master Pages, click one of the individual page icons (each corresponds to a page of your document) to return to one-page-at-a-time editing.

## Adding text

Ideally, you're supposed to write the articles for your newsletter (or whatever) in a word processor like Word. Then go to PageMaker and choose Place from the File menu. A list box appears; find your word-processed article, double-click it, and finally click the mouse (or drag to create a rectangle) on the appropriate starting page. The article spills onto the page, stretching from margin to margin (or filling the rectangle). Now, by grabbing the corner handles, you can resize or reshape the article's layout on the page:

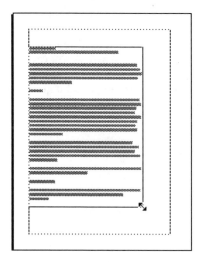

You can also shorten the article's length by dragging the little window shade handle at the bottom, as in the following figure:

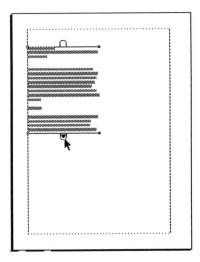

Of course, if you're thinking that an article needs shortening, window-shading it into a shorter *box* is only wishful thinking. All you've done is to place *less* of the article on the page — the rest of it is chopped off but needs to go someplace.

To specify where the rest of the article should go (as in, "continued on page C4"), ⌘-click the "windowshade handle" at the bottom of the text block. The cursor turns into a "loaded text" icon, telling you that the program is ready to pour the remainder of the article wherever your little heart desires. If you *click* someplace, PageMaker will dump the remainder of the article from margin to margin. If you *drag* to create a rectangle, the article will only fill that rectangle, as shown here.

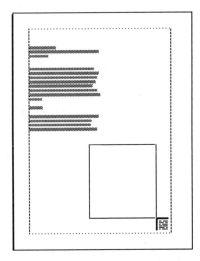

The neatest part of *flowing* text from box to box like this is that if you later have to cut some material from the beginning of the article, the text will flow, snake-like, through every text box it's been poured into. You'll never lose a single precious word.

If you could use some guidance in drawing text boxes, place your pointer in the ruler at the side (or top) of the screen and drag onto the page. A thin "guide" line comes with the pointer, which you can drag into position. (Hint: For consistent pages, place some guides on the *Master Pages,* so they'll be in the same place on every page.) These guides don't print; they're simply straight edges to help you align things, as you can see in the example below.

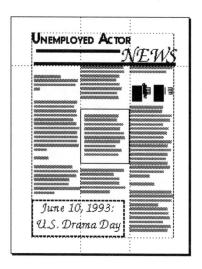

## *Tweaking to perfection*

You can zoom in or out by using the Page menu commands and change the text style by selecting text (with the Text Tool, which looks like an A) and applying fonts, styles, and other attributes using the Type menu. For heavy-duty text editing, you'll want to use the built-in word processor, the Story Editor (choose Edit Story from the Edit menu).

Add straight lines, boxes, and other graphic accents using the appropriate tools on the PageMaker Tool palette; the Element menu controls line thickness and so on. You can either paste in graphics or import them using the Place command in the File menu.

Just remember that the Pointer Tool is what you need to draw, move, resize, delete, shorten, and lengthen text blocks. But you need the Text Tool to do everything that pertains to type, including changing fonts, sizes, styles, line spacing, and so on.

After you become a power-user publishing mogul (God forbid), you may appreciate the Styles palette, which gives you a list of predefined paragraph and text formatting attributes. (See the description of Word to get an idea of why these are useful and how to use them.)

And if you're using PageMaker 5.0 or later, you'll get a kick out of the Control Palette, a veritable carbon copy of the QuarkXPress Measurements Palette (read on!).

# QuarkXPress

QuarkXPress is PageMaker's rival. Both have ardent supporters. (In fact, if you're ever on a blind date with a Mac person, it's a sure conversation starter: "So which do you like — Quark or PageMaker?") The differences are getting smaller and smaller, as each company comes out with an update that duplicates the features of the other.

Anyway, this is not the book to solve the great debate. This *is* the book to help you muddle through a few basic tasks when they're thrown at you.

## The basics

Quark (for some reason, everybody refers to this program by the name of its company) does pretty much the same thing as PageMaker, but the methods are different. The Tool palette looks like this:

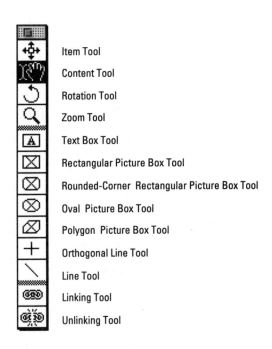

Item Tool

Content Tool

Rotation Tool

Zoom Tool

Text Box Tool

Rectangular Picture Box Tool

Rounded-Corner Rectangular Picture Box Tool

Oval Picture Box Tool

Polygon Picture Box Tool

Orthogonal Line Tool

Line Tool

Linking Tool

Unlinking Tool

The rules of thumb: Use the Item Tool to delete, move, and copy *boxes* (text and picture boxes), but use the Content Tool to resize or edit the *text and pictures themselves*. You can actually leave the Content Tool selected all the time since it's what you use for typing, editing, adjusting text box corner handles, cropping pictures, and so on — and whenever you need to move something, press the ⌘ key and drag. (The ⌘ key switches you temporarily to the Item Tool.)

To create a document, double-click the QuarkXPress icon and then choose New from the File menu. A dialog box appears, where you specify the page size and margins you want; then click OK.

To import some text, click the Text Box Tool and *draw a rectangle.* (You can't paste or import text or graphics in Quark without first drawing a box to contain it.) Quark switches back to the Content Tool automatically; from the File menu, choose Get Text and select the word processing document you want to import. It appears in the selected text box automatically. As in PageMaker, you can now edit the text, drag the text box's corners to adjust its dimensions, and so on.

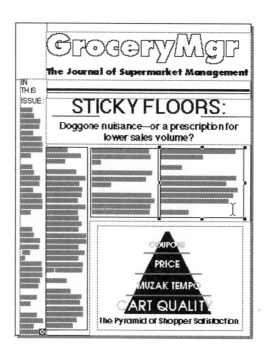

## Linking to page C4

Quark's method of breaking a story up into separate text boxes requires the use of its Linking Tool. First, make sure you've actually drawn both text boxes on the screen, using the Text Block Tool. Now click the Linking Tool. Click the *first* text box and then the *second* text box — that's all there is to it. The text now flows freely from one to the other, even if you edit the text in either box.

What's especially useful about this method of linking is that you can *pre*link text boxes that you've drawn on a Master Page. If you produce a newsletter, for example, that has roughly the same layout month after month, you could design an empty template containing ready-to-go, prelinked, empty text boxes. When those lazy-slob writers are finally ready to turn in their stories, one Get Text command suffices to pour an article into your waiting Quark layout, and all flowing happens instantly.

## Master Pages; Rearranging pages

Quark's Document Layout palette shows a thumbnail view of all pages in your document, including any Master Pages. (You can have up to 127 *different* Master Pages, in case each section of your magazine has different common background elements.)

Master page icons

Document page icons

This Document Layout palette serves a number of useful functions:

- ✔ Double-click a page icon to make the document window jump to that page.
- ✔ Drag a page icon into a new position to rearrange your pages.
- ✔ Drag a Master page icon onto a Document page icon to change its background (master) elements.
- ✔ Double-click a Master page icon to edit that Master page.
- ✔ Drag a blank page (top left of the palette) or a Master page icon in between two existing Document page icons to insert a new page.

There's a bunch of other stuff the Document Layout window does, but this should get you started, and you can always use the QuarkXPress Help feature to read up on the other features.

## Measurement Palette

Choose Measurement Palette from the View menu to see this useful little floating window full of precise numerical controls over the selected object. Click any of these numbers to change them. Try changing the angle for a text box — it's fun!

# Excel

Excel is the best-selling Macintosh spreadsheet program. Well, "best-selling" is about the understatement of the decade. (A recent Excel ad headline said, "99 out of 100 spreadsheet users use Excel. What are we doing wrong?")

If you're not familiar with a *spreadsheet,* get psyched — even if you only use 1 percent of its features, Excel can really be a godsend. It's for math, finances, figuring out which of two mortgage plans is more favorable in the long run, charting the growth of your basement gambling operation, and other number-crunchy stuff.

## Starting up

Double-click the Excel icon. A blank spreadsheet appears on your screen. It's a bunch of rows and columns, like a ledger book. The columns have letters and the rows are numbered. Each little rectangular cell is called, well, a *cell.* It's referred to by its letter and number: A1, for example.

To type a number into a cell, click the cell with the mouse and begin typing. Note that you don't do your typing (and editing) in the cell itself. Instead, all the action is in the editing strip at the top of the window. When you're done typing or editing, press Enter.

## Formatting numbers and text

As you enter numbers, don't bother to format them with dollar signs, decimal points, and all that jazz. Formatting can be applied later. For instance, you could enter the following numbers, each of which has a different number of decimal places:

```
          546
        213.5
       645.88
      987.556
```

Now drag vertically through them with the pointer.

```
          546
        213.5
       645.88
      987.556
```

By now you can probably say it in your sleep: *In the world of Mac, you select something first and then act on it . . . Select, then apply. . . .* After the numbers are selected, you can format them all with dollar amounts in one fell swoop. See the little tiny pop-up menu at the upper-left corner of the screen? Choose Currency from this list.

Instantly Excel formats all the selected numbers as dollar amounts. Note how it adds zeros (or rounds off excess decimal places) as necessary.

```
      $546.00
      $213.50
      $645.88
      $987.56
```

## *Spreading the sheet*

Now it gets good. If you've been fooling around so far, erase everything you've done. Drag the cursor diagonally through it and then choose Clear from the Edit menu. We're gonna start you off fresh-like.

Click in cell B3 (that's column B, row 3; a spreadsheet is like a good game of Battleship). Type in *1963.*

To jump into the next cell to the right, press Tab. Or press the right-arrow key. (You move to the *left* by pressing Shift-Tab — or the left-arrow key.) In any case, enter *1973.* Repeat until you've filled in the years as shown below.

You move *down* a row by pressing Return or the down-arrow key. Shift-Return moves you up a row, and so does the up-arrow key. (There's a certain twisted logic to this, isn't there?)

You can also jump to any cell by clicking in it, of course. Now then: Go wild. With these navigational commands under your belt, type in the text and numbers as shown below. (Frankly, it doesn't make any difference *what* numbers you type. I made them all up anyway.)

| | A | B | C | D | E | F |
|---|---|---|---|---|---|---|
| 1 | | | | | | |
| 2 | | | | | | |
| 3 | | 1963 | 1973 | 1983 | 1993 | |
| 4 | Quarter 1 | 1234 | 2435 | 3466 | 8453 | |
| 5 | Quarter 2 | 3123 | 2396 | 3536 | 3488 | |
| 6 | Quarter 3 | 120 | 1589 | 6455 | 122 | |
| 7 | Quarter 4 | 2000 | 3235 | 5353 | 8441 | |
| 8 | | | | | | |
| 9 | TOTALS: | | | | | |
| 10 | | | | | | |
| 11 | | | | | | |
| 12 | | | | | | |
| 13 | | | | | | |
| 14 | | | | | | |
| 15 | | | | | | |
| 16 | | | | | | |
| 17 | | | | | | |
| 18 | | | | | | |

Worksheet1

Want to make the top row boldface, as shown above? Drag the cursor through the years. (Sounds like a high-tech country song, don't it?) Now click the B button in the ribbon at the top of the screen.

If you haven't guessed, **B** means **Bold**, and *I* means *italic.* (And I mean italic!)

# *Creating automatically calculating cells*

Here comes the juicy part. Click in the Totals row, under the 1963 column of numbers. Click the funny $\Sigma$ button on the ribbon. It's the Sum button, and it's some button.

In the formula bar at the top of the screen, you'll see that Excel has entered "=SUM(B3:B8)."

In English, the program is trying to say: "The number I'll enter into the cell you clicked (Total) is going to be the sum of . . . well, I suppose you mean the numbers directly *above* the cell you clicked — cells B3 down to B8." Isn't it smart to guess what you mean?

| | B3 | X | ✓ | =SUM(B3:B8) | |
|---|---|---|---|---|---|
| | | | | | Fina |
| | | **A** | **B** | **C** | |
| 1 | | | | | |
| 2 | | | | | |
| 3 | | | 1963 | 1973 | |
| 4 | Quarter 1 | | $1,234.00 | $2,435.00 | |
| 5 | Quarter 2 | | $3,123.00 | $2,396.00 | |
| 6 | Quarter 3 | | $120.00 | $1,589.00 | |
| 7 | Quarter 4 | | $2,000.00 | $3,235.00 | |
| 8 | | | | | |
| 9 | TOTALS: | | =SUM(B3:B8) | | |
| 10 | | | | | |

Well, smart, but not quite smart enough. Because you *don't* want the number 1963 included in the total! So you can override Excel's guess by showing it which numbers you *do* want totaled . . . by dragging through them. Try it. While the dotted-line rectangle is still twinkling, drag vertically through the four cells *below* 1963. Then press Enter.

| | B9 | | =SUM(B4:B7) | | |
|---|---|---|---|---|---|
| | | | | | |
| | | **A** | **B** | **C** | |
| 1 | | | | | |
| 2 | | | | | |
| 3 | | | 1963 | 1' | |
| 4 | Quarter 1 | | $1,234.00 | $2,435 | |
| 5 | Quarter 2 | | $3,123.00 | $2,396 | |
| 6 | Quarter 3 | | $120.00 | $1,589 | |
| 7 | Quarter 4 | | $2,000.00 | $3,235 | |
| 8 | | | | | |
| 9 | TOTALS: | | 6477 | | |
| 10 | | | | | |

Neat, huh? Excel automatically totals the four numbers you selected. But that's only the half of it. Now click one of the cells below the 1963 heading — and *change the number.* That's right, type a totally different number. (And press Enter when you're done typing. You always have to press Enter to tell Excel you're done working in a cell.) Voilà — the total *changed* automatically!

This is the origin of the phrase "What-if scenario." You can sit here all day, fiddling with the numbers in the 1963 column. As soon as you change a number and press Enter, the total will update itself. That's why it's so easy to compute a mortgage at 10 percent for five years and see if it's better than one at 8 percent for seven years (or whatever).

## Fill right, feel right

Now then. You have three other columns to contend with. Do you have to redo the $\Sigma$ business each time? Nope. You've already explained to Excel how the Total row should work: it should add up the four numbers above it, *not* including the year at the top of the column.

So just take that magic total cell (B9 in the preceding picture) and *copy it* into the three cells to its right. Excel is smart enough to add up the right numbers in each column (no, it won't put the *1963* total into each cell).

Of course, you could use the regular Copy and Paste commands — but that's too tedious. Use the Fill Right command instead. Drag through the Totals row, starting with the 1963 total and extending through the three other years' total cells.

Then, from the Edit menu, choose Fill Right (or press ⌘-R). Bingo! Excel intelligently copies the *formula* from the first cell and copies it into the other cells, totaling each column automatically. You may as well know that there's also a Fill Down command, used when you want to copy a formula to a series of cells *below* the one that contains it.

## From here to infinity

Using the standard math symbols (+, –, / for division, and * for multiplication), you can build much more complicated auto-calculating cells than the simple SUM function described above. For example, you can use nested parentheses and the whole works. To make a cell calculate how many hours there are in ten years, for example, you'd click on it. Then, in the formula bar at the top of the screen, you'd type *=(24\*365)\*10* and press Enter. The formula always has to begin with the equal sign, but otherwise your equations can be as complicated as you want.

You can have formula cells that work with numbers from *other* formula cells, too — in the example above, you could create a Grand Total cell that would sum up the 1963, 1973, 1983, and 1993 totals automatically. There are even a few dozen more complex formula elements — financial, statistical, math, and time functions — listed in the Paste Function command (Edit menu), if you're into that kinky stuff.

## Making a chart

There are a zillion options for charting, too, but here's the quick-and-dirty approach.

Drag through the table you created earlier — just the data part, not the totals in the bottom row. After this section is highlighted, click the Chart Wizard button on the ribbon, as shown here:

Now the cursor turns into a skinny little crosshair. Excel is waiting for you to show it where, and how big, to make the chart. Drag diagonally across the screen, either below the numbers (if your screen is big enough) or — what the heck — right on top of them. When you let go, a charming little chart pops up. (If a charming little *dialog box* appears instead, click the >> button.) Double-click the chart and then double-click an individual bar to adjust the colors and styles used in the chart.

There are also outlining, drawing tools, macros, a database function, and probably a convenient toaster-oven . . . but this was supposed to be a crash course. If you want those frills, you'll have to actually put your nose in the manual.

# FileMaker Pro

FileMaker is the king, queen, and princess of *database* programs. A database is just what it sounds like: a base of data — a pile of it, if you will — that you can view in a million different ways. Stop me if you've heard this one. Suppose that you have a mailing list, and you want to know how many people in ZIP code 44122 have last names beginning with M. Or you have a list of 2,000 books and want to sort them by author's name or print a list only showing hardcover volumes, or find out the publisher of a book of which you know only one word of the title. For all these tasks, a database is the way to go.

The really far-out feature of FileMaker is that you can set up several different *views* of the information. Suppose you have a mailing list for a party. You could set up your Data Entry view with great big 18-point bold type, which makes it easier for you to type in those names without your glasses. You'd also want a Mailing Label layout, though, which neatly arranges the addresses side-by-side across the page, in a much smaller type size, so that you can print and mail the invitations. Yet a third layout could be the Name-Tag view; it would place only the person's name (and not the address) in a cute font, preceded by the words "Hello! My name is:". Using these different layouts — of the same information — really lets you put the data to work without having to do any retyping.

## Step 1: Starting a file

Double-click the FileMaker icon. A dialog box appears, where you're either supposed to open an existing data file or create a new one; click New. In the next dialog box, type a name for your file and click New again.

## No Save command!?

Why the heck do you have to name your file *before* you type any information into it? Isn't that exactly opposite from the way most programs work, where you type some stuff and *then* choose Save (and give the file a name)?

Yup.

In FileMaker, though, you'll actually come to like this feature—the program saves your data *automatically*, without your having to remember. The result: Your data is always up to date, even when something goes wrong.

Before you know it, a dialog box appears. Brace yourself for a couple more terms. (If you read about ClarisWorks earlier in this chapter, then you'll be on familiar turf here.)

As you design your database, there are two units of information you'll be creating. First of all, there are the individual blanks: the name, the ZIP code, and the state. These are called *fields*. (The International Council of Nerds evidently felt that calling them *blanks* wouldn't have confused people enough.)

A set of fields constitutes one *record*. A record might be a complete name-street-city-state-ZIP set for a mailing list; if there are three people's addresses, there are three records in the database. Still with us?

OK then. In the dialog box now staring you in the face, you're being asked to create the *fields* (the blanks). First type the name of the field; it might be First Name or Last Name or Street or Account Number or Date or Eyebrow Thickness or whatever. Now tell FileMaker what *kind* of data is going to be in this blank, as shown in Table 5-1.

For each field you'll want on the screen, then, type a name and select a data type, and click Create. Repeat for the other fields. (If you want FileMaker to automatically enter data, like today's date, then click Options just after creating a field.)

Anyway, after you're done defining every blank you'll want to use, click Done. You've just finished Step 1.

## A calculated maneuver

If you created a Calculation field, a dialog box will appear as soon as you click Create. In this box, you can build the equation you want FileMaker to use. It usually involves other fields — which are listed at the upper left — combined with the +, −, / (divided by), and * (times) symbols. For example, if you're crazy enough to live in New York City, you would define the Sales Tax field as *Purchase Amount * 1.0825* (8.25 percent is the sales tax rate).

| Table 5-1: | Data Types and Their Consequences |
|---|---|
| *If you select this data type . . .* | *Then this will happen . . .* |
| Text | You can enter any kind of typed data. |
| Number | FileMaker won't let you type letters of the alphabet —only digits. |
| Date, Time | FileMaker will only accept dates or times in any format. |
| Picture | You can't type anything into this field, but you can paste a picture. |
| Calculation | You can't paste or type anything. FileMaker will fill in this field automatically by performing math on other fields, like adding up the Amount and Tax fields. |
| Summary | You can't paste or type anything. FileMaker will fill in this field automatically by performing global math on other fields, like adding them up, counting them, or giving you a running total. |

# Step 2: Data entry

At this point, you can start typing away to input data. The rules are simple: It's just like a word processor, so you use the Delete key to backspace over a typo, cut, copy, and paste selected text, and so on. To advance to the next field, press Tab. To jump back to the previous field, press Shift-Tab. To create a new, blank record (for a new person's address, say), choose New Record from the Edit menu. (Again, for a complete illustrated tour of this process, see the ClarisWorks section a few pages back.)

As you create more records, the little open book icon at the upper left will indicate that it has more and more "pages," each of which is a record.

Click the upper page to see the previous record or the lower page to see the next one or use the slider to the right to jump to any record. Needless to say, if there are too many records to fit on one screen, use the vertical scroll bar to move through your records.

If your goal, in reading this section, is to perform the joyous task of entering data, this may be all the info you'll need. Put down this book and get busy. If, on the other hand, you want to create a database of your own, or if you're supposed to modify an existing database, you may want to learn Step 3.

## *Step 3: Designing a layout*

When you first create a new FileMaker file and define some fields, the program creates a simple default arrangement of the blanks so that you can type in some data. The default arrangement looks like this:

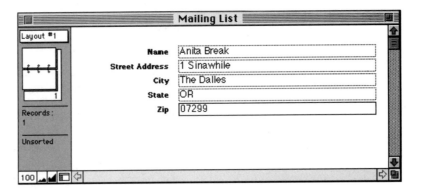

But suppose you want those same fields arranged in a more mailing-labelish layout, like this:

To accomplish this, you must enter the Layout Zone. Choose Layout from the Select menu. You enter a view that looks a lot like MacDraw (or any other drawing program). And, in fact, all the tools (line, rectangle, blah blah blah) work exactly as they do in a graphics program.

So, click the Arrow Tool. Drag the fields around (make sure you can tell the difference between a field and its *label,* which you may or may not want to appear on the screen). Or click a field and then change its type style from the Format menu.

Since you can have as many different arrangements of your information as you want, use this pop-up menu to select the Layout you want to edit.

These are field labels. They don't have to appear in a layout if you don't want them to.

These boxes represent the fields themselves. To re-size one, click, and then drag a corner handle. To move one, drag it by its center.

If you want to see more than one record at a time (when you're in data entry mode), drag the little Body tag upward until it's just below your fields, and choose View as List from the Select menu.

Remember, too, that you can *delete* a field from a particular layout. For example, if you're creating "Hello! My name is:" stickers, you certainly don't need each person's phone number to appear on his or her badge (unless it's *that* kind of party). So you can delete the phone number field from the layout; you do *not* lose any data you've typed in. The phone number field still *exists* — just not in this layout. Using the New Layout command in the Edit menu, you can create another layout . . . and another . . . and so on, until you've had your fill of data rearrangement.

When you're finished designing layouts, return to data entry mode by choosing Browse from the Select menu.

# *Finding*

Once you've got some data typed in, you can manipulate it in all kinds of fun and exciting ways. Choose Find from the Select menu to get what appears to be a blank layout. Type what you're looking for into the appropriate blanks. For example, if you're trying to find everybody who lives in ZIP code 90210, you'd fill out the Find dialog box this way:

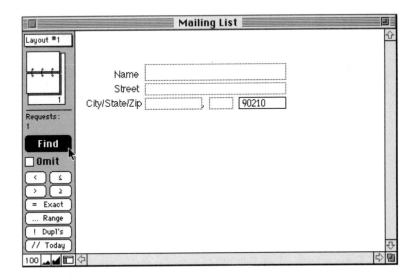

Then click the Find button. After about one second, you'll be returned to
Browse (data entry) view, where you'll see the results of your search. This is
important — FileMaker is *hiding* the records that *didn't* match your search
requirements. You haven't lost them; they're just out of sight until you choose
Find All from the Select menu. You can prove this to yourself by consulting the
little book at the left side of the screen. It will say "Records: 194, Found: 22."
That means FileMaker still knows there are 194 addresses in your mailing list,
but only 22 have ZIP code 90210 (and they're all attractive teenage models on a
major TV show).

## Sorting

To sort your records, choose Sort from the Select menu. FileMaker needs to
know how you want to sort your records: by first name, ZIP code, nose length,
or what? On the left side, you see a list of all the fields in your database; just
double-click the one by which you want to sort. (If you want to sort by last
name and then sort by first name *within* each common last name, double-click
First Name.) Finally, click Sort.

Sorting is the one major drag with FileMaker, by the way. As you're about to
discover, FileMaker doesn't *keep* your stuff in the sorted order! Every time you
add a record or search for something, all your records jump back into the order
in which you first entered them! You have to use the Sort command over again
every time you want things sorted again.

## *Other steps*

There's a million other cool things FileMaker can do. For example, it can look up a piece of info (like a phone number) from *another* FileMaker file and copy it into the appropriate place in *this* file. FileMaker also has a powerful Scripts command, which works a lot like a macro program (see "QuicKeys," following). In other words, you can make the program find all names added since last week, sort them by last name, switch to the Mailing Label layout, and print them — all with a single command from the Scripts menu. These rarefied pleasures are not, however, for the unenlightened. Grab whichever is closest — the manual or your resident computer guru person.

# *QuicKeys*

QuicKeys is a *macro program.* (Bet you'd been hankering for some more lingo, hadn't you?)

A macro is an automated series of mouse or keyboard steps, which you'd otherwise have to perform manually. It's a shortcut, bub. Mouse and keyboard tasks aren't particularly strenuous, of course, except that sometimes you can get tired of performing them, especially if you have to repeat the same steps over and over again.

Typical examples: You have to type a password into some program every day. Or you're asked to open each of 1,000 documents, change the font to Times 96-point bold, print, and save. Or you always sign your letters "With fondest and most lingering feelings of warmth and mutual support, Ingrid." All of these tedious and repetitive tasks can be automated using a macro program like QuicKeys so that only a *single keystroke* (of your choosing) triggers the Mac to do the chore itself.

QuicKeys is the easiest System 7-compatible macro program, and it can perform some amazing stunts. For example, you can make it open up a certain program or document with the touch of a key. It can type out the time or the date when you press another key. And so on. Here be the basics.

## *Teaching by example*

The easiest way to create a macro is the voyeur method: You do whatever-it-is *manually,* while QuicKeys watches.

For example, if you've just installed QuicKeys, you should see "QuicKeys" listed in your ⌘ menu. When your pointer reaches those words, a *submenu* pops out to the right; choose Record Sequence from that submenu.

(These figures illustrate version 3.0 of QuicKeys. Other versions look similar enough for you to figure out what's happening, I'm guessing.)

Suddenly, a little blinking microphone appears where the    normally is. This is QuicKeys's signal to you that it's paying attention. While you have such an attentive student, perform the task, or series of tasks, you'd like it to learn. Some examples:

✔ Type your return address.

✔ Empty the Trash can.

✔ Print, then Save, and then Quit.

✔ Choose Bold, then Italic, and then 12-point from the font menus.

✔ Open the Calculator desk accessory, choose a menu command, flap your arms, or whatever.

As you teach QuicKeys what you want it to do, there's just one caveat: If you want it to click something, make sure that whatever-it-is will always be in the *same place* on the screen. Suppose that you drag an icon to the Trash can. When QuicKeys later tries to repeat what you did, it will click futilely in empty space and drag *nothing* to the Trash can — because that icon is no longer there. Good bets for macros that involve clicking, therefore, are menus, desk accessories, and Tool palette icons — all of which are always in the same screen location.

Anyway, when you're done doing the task yourself, go back to the QuicKeys menu item in your  menu and choose Stop Recording from the submenu. The following box (or something like it) appears:

In the Name box, type a short description of what this macro is supposed to do. Press Tab to jump to the Keystroke box.

Then press the key (or keys) on your keyboard that you want to be the *trigger*. A great choice for a trigger key, by the way, is one of those otherwise useless function keys (F1, F2, and so on) that the IBM world is so bonkers about. If your keyboard has them, they're at the top of your keyboard. Another idea: Use the otherwise useless *Control* key, which you've probably never even noticed. For example, you might make Control-Q save your document and then quit. Or Control-R could type your return address.

In the lower-left quadrant of the screen, you can see QuicKeys's list of the individual steps that constituted this macro. Each type of action — a mouse click, text typed on the keyboard, a menu item selected — is represented by a different icon. You can cut, copy, paste, or delete these, but that's really a topic for your pal, the manual, to cover.

When you're done setting up the name and trigger key for this macro, click OK twice, and you're in business. Whenever you press the trigger key you specified, QuicKeys will perform that series of tasks by itself in very frantic succession. It's really something to see, too — you'll think your Mac has been inhabited by a ghost who's had way too much coffee.

## Opening QuicKeys

For more specific, or more complex tasks, you may want to program macros manually (and not by example). For this, you can create a macro in the QuicKeys control panel.

There are several ways to bring up this panel. First, choose QuicKeys from your ⬤ menu and then choose QuicKeys from the submenu. Alternatively, you can choose Control Panels from the ⬤ menu, double-click the QuicKeys icon, and then click Open. Either way, you wind up facing a screen like this:

The key to creating a macro manually is the Define menu that appears within this panel. It lists 13 kinds of macros, as follows.

An *Alias Keystroke* is a letter substitution. You type a W, but a P appears on the screen. That's a dumb example, of course, but that's the idea. A more useful use: Get QuicKeys to type a *period* instead of a > symbol every time you press Shift-period so that you don't keep typing "Born in the U>S>A>" by accident. (Don't confuse this kind of alias with what's called an alias by Apple in System 7. You'll find out about *that* kind of alias in Chapter 8. Sorry to interrupt.)

A *Button* is an on-screen button, like OK or Cancel. QuicKeys can click such a button automatically. What's especially nifty is that QuicKeys even knows — in the case of a checkbox-type button — whether the button is on or off. You can tell it to click a checkbox *only* if it's not already selected, for example.

A *Click* is a mouse click or a mouse drag. When you choose this from the Define menu, you'll be asked to *do* the click or drag so that the program gets the idea.

*Date/Time* types out the current date or time, in your choice of several formats.

*Extensions* are pretty neat. They're plug-in special-feature macros. One extension flips your color monitor to black and white (or back again), saving you a tedious trip to the Monitors control panel. Another extension changes printers for you, in case you have more than one connected to your Mac. Once again, QuickKeys has chosen a particularly unfortunate term: an *extension* is actually a special self-loading program in System 7 that you'll read about in Chapter 6. If you last that long.

A *File Launch* macro automatically opens a file, or a program, of your choice. It's peachy because you don't even have to know where the thing's icon is buried on your hard disk. I use Control-W to launch Word. I used Control-D to open the *Macs For Dummies* manuscript while I was writing it.

Don't worry about *FKEYs*. Nobody uses them.

A *Menu Selection* macro pulls down a menu item for you or opens a desk accessory.

*Mousies* are various self-explanatory mouse actions, like scrolling down in a document, closing a window, or opening a window to full size.

A *Sequence* is several of the other types of macros, strung together. Using this kind of macro, you can construct long and complex macros.

*Specials* are miscellaneous handy macros. Shut Down, for example, safely turns off your Mac even if you're not in the Finder. And QuickQuotes automatically pops in a curly quote whenever you type in one of those boring straight ones (see "Top Ten Word Processing Tips" in Chapter 3).

*Text* is how you get QuicKeys to type out some text that's always the same: your end-of-a-letter closing; your return address; boilerplate text of any kind.

Finally, a *Real-Time* macro is one that doesn't zip maniacally through the steps of the macro as fast as its little brain can manage. A Real-Time macro performs the steps you teach it at exactly the same pace, with all the hesitations and mouse movements at which you recorded it. You'd use a Real-Time macro in a painting program to draw a cartoon smile, for example. If you used the Sequence kind of macro instead, QuicKeys would try to save time by drawing a line straight from the beginning point to the end point, which wouldn't look like a smile at all.

Any macro usually needs a little debugging. But once you've mastered the art of putting your Mac on autopilot, you'll save hours of cumulative time which you can use to leave work early and play outside.

# *Apple File Exchange*

Most people will never use this program, so I guess it really doesn't qualify for the top ten. Yet Apple File Exchange comes free with almost every Mac (it comes on those white System disks), and the few people who need a program like this *really* need it.

Apple File Exchange converts IBM PC files to Mac and vice versa. You may have read in the brochures that your floppy-disk drive is a SuperDrive capable of reading both Mac and PC disks — a technical achievement comparable to making a CD player play tapes.

What the brochure *doesn't* say is that it's not quite that easy. You don't slip a PC disk into the drive and watch its icon pop up on your screen. (Especially not the old 5¼-inch *really* floppy disks, which you have to first get transferred to Mac-style 3½-inch hard-shell disks before you can even think about any of this.)

No, what you do is launch Apple File Exchange first. *Now* you can insert a PC disk, and its contents will show up on the right side of the screen:

On the left, you see the contents of your hard drive. To convert a file, you just select it by clicking and then click the Translate button, as shown above.

You get exactly one converter included with Apple File Exchange — from MacWrite to DCA format, whatever that is. Actually, you really don't need to worry about converters if you're performing obvious translations: a Mac *text file* to an IBM *text file;* a Microsoft *Word document* to a *Word for Windows document;* a PC *FileMaker file* to a Mac *FileMaker file;* and so on.

Of course, if you're serious about exchanging files with PCs and PC clones, you might be better off with a program like MacLink. This incredible software gizmo, once installed in your Mac, *does* make PC disks' icons show up on the screen when they're inserted — no Apple File Exchange needed. What's more, MacLink comes with a zillion converters, to and from every kind of Mac and PC program. Apple also sells something called PC Exchange, which is supposed to do the same kind of thing.

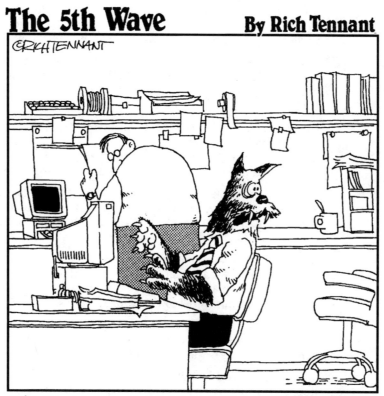

# The 5th Wave
## By Rich Tennant

"I'M GONNA HAVE A LITTLE TROUBLE WITH THIS 'FULL MOON' ICON ON OUR GRAPHICAL USERS INTERFACE."

# *Top Ten Programs That Aren't in the Top Ten*

For your shopping pleasure and entertainment: a double-handful of neat programs that are worth looking into and often discussed at techno-savvy cocktail parties. ("Hi there, baby. Want to come up and see my FreeHand printouts?")

1. *FreeHand* or *Illustrator*. Primo, powerful, professional, pricey PostScript graphics programs. Be prepared to read the manual.

2. *Photoshop*. If FreeHand is MacDraw on steroids, then Photoshop is MacPaint taken to its ultimate conclusion. A stunning, pro-level photo painting program, capable of fantastic transparency effects or undetectably painting your in-laws right out of the family portrait.

3. *Now Up-To-Date*. A sensational calendar program: type your appointments onto the appropriate squares. Up-To-Date can then remind you of them, show your To Do list, and print out gorgeous daily, weekly, or monthly agendas.

4. *Quicken*. The world's greatest and least expensive checkbook/financial program. Perfect for home and very-small-business use. Prints your checks; balances your budget. When stretched, can even do accounts receivable and payable, profit and loss, and that sort of thing.

5. *Persuasion*. It's called *presentation* software. Lets you quickly and easily assemble slide shows — graphs, bullet charts, colorful diagrams — with a choice of many rich, unified color schemes. Print the slides onto slides or transparencies, or use the Mac itself to give a slide show.

6. *Kid Pix*. Mind-blowing, colorful, audio-equipped version of MacPaint. Designed for kids but equally addictive for adults. The drippy paintbrush runs, the eraser makes scritch-scratch sounds, and when you want to start over, the Dynamite Tool blows up your artwork. About $30.

7. *Microsoft Flight Simulator*. A great, almost too-realistic airplane simulator. It's three-dimensional, works in color, and has sounds. You can actually fly across the country — in real time.

8. *Microphone II*. You use this program if you have a modem (a phone hookup for your Mac). Lets you dial friends, bulletin boards, or on-line services like CompuServe. (More about these things in Chapter 7.)

9. *Super QuickDex*. A sizzlingly fast Rolodex program. Can pull up one person's card out of 2,000 in less than half a second. Can even dial the phone if you have a modem. Easier to use than a hairbrush. If you'll want to do much printing, you may prefer the more feature-laden (but much slower) *DynoDex* or *Address Book Plus*. They print out your address books in a billion different formats.

10. *Premiere*. For high-horsepower color Macs. This is the program for making your own digital QuickTime movies right on the screen. And what's QuickTime? Like the man said: digital movies right on the screen. See Chapter 7.

# Chapter 6
# System Folder:
# Trash Barge of the Macintosh

## In This Chapter

▶ What the System Folder is for

▶ Why System 6 isn't System 7

▶ How to get System 7 if you really want it

▶ What junk you can throw out of your System Folder

*T*here it sits. Only one folder on your hard drive looks like it — or acts like it. It's the System Folder, which holds software that the Mac needs for itself. Every Mac has a System Folder. (Correction: every Mac that *works* has one.) Yours probably looks like any other folder, except that it's called System Folder and its icon has a tiny Mac Plus drawn in the middle:

System Folder

There are three important reasons for you, the former novice, to know about this vital folder.

First, someday you, like millions of Mac users before you, will attempt to double-click one of the icons inside the System Folder. With gentle, earnest curiosity, you will shyly move your pointer onto something; with a soft, trusting gesture, you'll click your mouse button twice; and with sarcastic venom, the Mac, your former friend, will reward you with nothing but a meaningless error message.

You get this message because much of the stuff in the System Folder *isn't for you!* It's information *for* the Mac, *by* the Mac. Information — notes it takes — to serve you, its master. I'll give you some specific examples later; for now, suffice it to say that most of the stuff in the System Folder is for the *system* (which explains why Apple hides it away in a folder to begin with).

The second reason you'll be glad you learned about the System Folder is this: you got a brand new computer. It's clean, it's fresh, it's empty. You know for a fact that you haven't put much of anything into it. And yet, one day you open up your System Folder to discover that it's absolutely *crawling* with files! Seething, teeming, overrun with zillions of little icons you've never seen before!

You're perfectly entitled to exclaim, "Jeez, what *is* all this stuff?!" And, before having read Chapter 1½, you might also have exclaimed, like many Mac beginners before you: "For the love o' Mike, all those files are gonna *use up all my memory!*"

Naturally, you now realize the foolishness of this comment. Data resting comfortably on your hard drive doesn't use up *any* memory. It *does,* however, take up *disk space.*

Since disk space, for most of us, is *also* limited, I'm going to show you exactly how much of the System Folder clutter you can safely throw away.

Finally, you should know about the System Folder because it's the nerve center of your whole Mac . . . the heart . . . the brain . . . the headquarters. A Mac without a System Folder is like a car without an engine. A house without a roof. *Groundhog Day* without Bill Murray.

# *Battle of the Systems*

Back in Chapter 1, when you were a rank amateur at this computer thing, I hinted that your Mac may or may not be outfitted with a special feature called System 7. And instead of explaining what that meant, I muttered something along the lines of, "Tell you later." Before we get busy with our System Folder Trash-fest, we need to get this over with.

You know how General Motors comes out with a new model of each of its cars every year? Apple does the same thing: It keeps making minor changes to its computers, trying to make them better (and provide more incentive to buy them).

In 1991, Apple came out with a newer version of the System Folder contents, called System 7. (It replaced the older version, which, with stunning originality, was called System 6.)

System 7 has lots of terrific features, especially for the beginning Mac user. Every Mac sold since early 1991 is equipped with System 7. You'd only have System 6 if you bought your Mac used, or you've had it for a long time.

It's easy to tell which System you have. Remember this handy test from Chapter 1? Look in the upper-right corner of the screen. Do you see this icon ⑦ ? If so, you have System 7. Otherwise: System 6.

# *What's the diff?*

There are about one zillion and fifty-eight differences between Systems 6 and 7. Here are a few of the ones worth mentioning.

- ✔ **System 7 is slower.** It's true. Everything takes longer in System 7: copying files, emptying the Trash, opening windows, and so on. Oh, and if you've already experienced the horror of an "out of memory" message (see Chapter 11), it's worth noting that System 7 hoards a big chunk of your Mac's memory unto itself.

- ✔ **Icons in System 7 are in color and have a neat 3-D look.** All right, it's not a trip to Bermuda, but it's better than nothing.

- ✔ **System 7 has those little list-view triangles.** You may have messed with these in Chapter 1.

- ✔ **System 7 has the ⟨?⟩ menu!** We've been using that little question mark icon as a harbinger of System 7, but that's not really its purpose. Actually, this little guy is called the *Help menu*. If you're at your Mac, try this now: mouse on up to that ⟨?⟩, hold down the button, and choose Show Balloons.

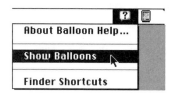

Now roll the cursor around the screen. Don't click — just point to things: icons, windows, disks, the Trash, menus, whatever. As the cursor touches each one, a little cartoon-character balloon pops up. The balloon identifies whatever you're pointing at.

Try this: move the cursor to a menu. Hold down the mouse button and try pointing to different menu commands. When you're tired of seeing what things are and what they do, go back to the question mark menu. This time, choose Hide Balloons.

This Balloon Help feature always works when you're working at the desktop. It *usually* works when you're using your programs (word processor, and so on).

✔ **System 7's Trash never empties by itself.** You have to choose Empty Trash from the Special menu to make it stop bulging. In System 6, on the other hand, the Trash gets emptied by itself whenever you turn off the Mac. (Now, if only they could get the trash can in the *kitchen* to do that. . . .)

✔ **In System 7, you can stick anything into the  menu.** In System 6, as you discovered in Chapter 3, the  menu at the left side of your screen lists miniprograms called desk accessories. But in the newer system, you can make *anything* appear there: a program (such as your word processor itself), a word processing document (like your application to driving school), a folder (your last 14 poetry attempts), and so on.

In fact, *anything that has an icon* can also be listed in your  menu. Some people's  menus are longer than their résumés.

Why would you care about listing some folder or file in the  menu? The primary advantage is efficiency. When you choose an item from the  menu, it opens immediately, just as though you'd double-clicked its icon. The  menu is a much more direct way of choosing something than having to burrow into your folders, three deep, trying to locate the icon you want to open.

If you're still wobbly on your Mac feet, and have already supersaturated your brain with computer info, and just want to know how you're supposed to turn the thing off and go to bed, then you might not care in the least about this nicety. If you *are* interested, here's the trick: double-click your System Folder to open it. Inside the System Folder window is another folder called: Apple Menu Items.

Any icon you drag into this folder appears, *instantly,* in your  menu! And, likewise, you can get rid of anything listed in the Apple menu that you don't use much. Just double-click the Apple Menu Items folder and drag the offending item into the Trash (or into another folder).

Anyway, you'll find out more good dirt on System 7 in Chapter 8 and elsewhere. But you probably get the point that System 7 is a newer, more feature-laden edition of the Mac's *operating system*. ("Operating system," by the way, is a terrific-sounding computer term. In fact, I find that simply walking into a public place and very loudly saying "operating system" works wonders when I'm feeling a little depressed.)

## *Names and numbers*

When people say "System 7," they're not being terribly specific. In typical computer-nerd fashion, Apple keeps making little changes to System 7. Each time, they rename the thing by changing the digits after the decimal point. First it was called System 7.0. Then they made a few touch-ups and called it System 7.0.1. Incredibly, and confusingly, they then made some *more* improvements and dubbed the result System 7.1. (If you can believe this, there's actually even something called System 7 *Pro*. What'd they do, run out of decimal points?)

Now, I don't know about you. But when I was growing up, we were taught: one decimal point per number. Anyway, if you ignore the additional decimals, you can pretty much figure out which system version is more recent. For example, 7.01 is, technically, a smaller number than 7.1, so it's therefore earlier.

Then there's the issue of P. Some system versions have the letter P after them: System 7.1P, for example. That means you have a Performa Mac. More about Performas in Chapter 9.

And then there's x. You'll sometimes hear computer people say that something won't work if you have System 7.x. That's shorthand. It means "System 7.0, System 7.0.1, System 7.1, or System 7-point-anything." As opposed, naturally, to System 6.x.

Want to know what *you've* got? Here's a quick way to find out. Go to the  menu. Choose About This Macintosh. A window appears. In the upper-right corner, it tells you what system version you have.

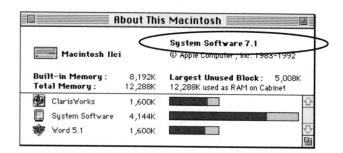

There's no appreciable difference between versions 7.0 and 7.0.1. There's one feature that only System 7.1 has, however: a folder called Fonts. (It's inside the System Folder.) You know all about fonts if you read Chapter 4. Anyway, the Fonts folder makes it much easier for font freaks to add and remove new typefaces to the Mac. In 7.0 and 7.0.1, fonts get installed magically into the System *file,* which is somewhat inconvenient and time-consuming to open when you want to muck around among your font files.

# System-Folder Trash-O-Rama

Who else would be utterly brave enough to utter the following Emperor's-New-Clothes utterance? *Half the stuff in your System Folder is worthless.* It's designed for power-users, or people in big corporate networks, or superweenie NASA scientists and their Mensa-qualifying eight-year-old offspring. Meanwhile, these files are taking up room on *your* hard drive.

Do it right now: double-click your System Folder to open it. (Of course, your System Folder is in your main hard-drive window. Double-click your hard-drive icon first, if need be.) Now click the zoom box, the tiny square in the top right corner of the System Folder window, so you can see as much of the System Folder contents as possible. As a matter of fact, move your mouse up to the View menu and choose "by Name." That should put everything into a neat list.

| System Folder | | |
|---|---|---|
| 32 items | 155.6 MB in disk | 44.1 MB ava |
| **Name** | Size | Kir |
| ▷ 🗀 After Dark Files | 1,701K | |
| ▷ 🗀 Aldus | 1,001K | |
| ▷ 🗀 Aldus folder | 662K | |
| ▷ 🗀 Apple Menu Items | 746K | |
| ▷ 🗀 AppleLink Out Basket | 4K | |
| ▷ 🗀 At Ease Items | 77K | |
| 🗋 ATM Font Database | 1,421K | |
| ▷ 🗀 Claris | 18K | |
| 🗋 Clipboard | 7K | |
| ▷ 🗀 Control Panels | 2,188K | |
| 🖾 DiskDoubler™ App | 158K | |
| ▷ 🗀 Extensions | 3,406K | |
| 🗋 Finder | 371K | |
| ▷ 🗀 Fonts | 2,727K | |
| ▷ 🗀 GlobalFax Files | 5,506K | |
| ▷ 🗀 GlobalFax Personal | 32K | |
| 🗋 Note Pad File | 4K | |
| ▷ 🗀 Preferences | 1,344K | |
| ▷ 🗀 Printer Descriptions | 18K | |
| ▷ 🗀 PrintMonitor Documents | zero K | |

Just *look* at all that junk! *You* sure as heck didn't put it there — what's it *doing* there?

Here's a wonderful, glorious, worth-the-price-of-the-book-right-there list of everything in your typical System 7 System Folder, item by item. I'll tell you which of these things you can safely trash.

Don't have a cow about throwing things away, either. This is *not* like cleaning your attic, where if you toss that box of your drawings from elementary school, you've wounded your inner child forever. No, *this* stuff you can always get *back again* if you need it. It's all on your white System disks that came with your Mac. (If you're a Performa or PowerBook 145 owner, you didn't get System disks; you're supposed to make your own backup of the System Folder. And, as I've mentioned elsewhere, if your Mac has a built-in CD-ROM drive — you'd remember having paid extra for it — you may have received a CD-ROM disc, containing the system software, instead.)

And if you're not the least bit interested in de-junking your System Folder? That's why we chose to make *Macs For Dummies* a book and not a major motion picture: since it's a book, you don't have to sit through the dull parts.

By the way, you may not find *every* one of these files listed in your System Folder. Likewise, you may find files in your System Folder that aren't listed here (especially if your Mac isn't new).

## In your Apple Menu Items folder

Let's start off with the stuff in the Apple Menu Items folder, which is, alphabetically speaking, the first thing in your System Folder. You'll recall, of course, that anything in this folder also appears in the  menu at the left side of your screen.

This is really a two-for-one discussion: each Apple menu item is also a desk accessory like the ones you worked with in Chapter 3. So now you'll get to find out what exactly those things in your  menu are . . . acquire a deep and sensitive appreciation of their importance and value . . . and *then* throw them away.

### Alarm Clock

Try choosing it from your  menu right now. You'll see that it's a tiny clock. You can leave it open on your screen all day, and always know exactly how much time you're wasting. With some difficulty, you can also use it to set an alarm that goes off at a certain time of day. (Some alarm. All it does is beep once and make your  menu icon start flashing at the top left of your screen.)

You can probably trash the Alarm Clock and never miss it. As the song says, does anybody ever really know what time it is?

### Battery

This DA shows you how much juice is left in your battery. Toss it unless you have a PowerBook.

### Calculator, Note Pad

You already know about these desk accessories (see Chapter 3). Leave them for now.

### CD Remote

It lets you play regular music CD discs on your Apple CD-ROM player. If you don't *have* an Apple CD-ROM player, this does you no good whatsoever.

### Chooser

You *definitely* need this, as you found out in Chapter 4.

### Control Panels

This folder is simply a shortcut (an *alias*) to opening your real Control Panels folder. More on aliases and control panels when the informational flood dries up a little.

### Key Caps

Another desk accessory. It helps you find out which combinations of keys you're supposed to press when you want to type wacky symbols like ¢ or ¥ or © (see details in Chapter 5).

### Puzzle

A highly silly desk accessory whose Novelty-Wear-Off Quotient is about five minutes. Upon reaching the sixth minute, trash it.

### Scrapbook

This desk accessory is worth keeping. Using Copy and Paste, you can put pictures, sounds, or blocks of text into it for use later. For example, after you spend three weekends designing an absolutely gorgeous logo for yourself, paste it into the Scrapbook. Thereafter, whenever you need that logo again, open the Scrapbook and copy it, so that it'll be ready to paste into your memo or package design.

## In your Control Panels folder

Control Panels is another folder inside your System Folder. As you read in a previous chapter, a control panel is a tiny miniprogram that changes some aspect of the Mac's behavior.

It's very important — and rarely understood — that Apple's control panels *only* do their work when you actually *change* a setting. In other words, it's perfectly OK to make a setting and then throw away the control panel completely. Your setting will remain in effect forever.

If you ever *do* need to change that setting again, you can always use your System disks. The full complement of control panels is on them, and you don't even have to copy them to the Mac to use them.

### ~ATM™

The first half of Adobe Type Manager (see Chapter 4). It doesn't come with the Mac, but an awful lot of people have it anyway.

### AutoRemounter

Yet another one of these doodads that's only good for connecting Macs to-gether — in this case, a PowerBook and a regular Mac. (It automatically recon-nects the two whenever you wake a sleeping PowerBook.) If you have neither PowerBook nor network, send it Trashward.

### Brightness

This control panel doesn't even *do* anything except on a Mac Classic or Classic II. If you have any other model, march this icon directly to the Trash.

### Cache Switch

This little software switch has two settings: Compatible and Faster. It's useful exclusively on Macs named Quadra and Centris — and even then, only slightly. (Compatible mode makes your Mac run slower, but with fewer problems using really old programs.)

### CD Speed Switch

You need this only if you have an Apple CD-ROM player. It lets you play CD-ROM discs at double speed. Unfortunately, some CD-ROM discs can only be played at the older, slower speed, so you use this control panel to switch.

### Color

If you have a black-and-white Mac, trash this sucker.

It's used on color or grayscale Macs to choose what color you want to use when you highlight some text. (Talk about obscure.) See Chapter 8 for details.

### Date & Time, Numbers

These control panels are for non-Americans. They let you change the way the Mac punctuates numbers and spells dates. For example, when you write down a date in England, you're supposed to put the month *second*. So if Cher's birthday is August 25, you'd say that her 40th birthday was 25/8/83. Along the same lines, the French use *periods* in large numbers instead of commas. You'd say, "Bonjour! You owe moi $1.000.000, Monsieur."

If you're satisfied with the American way of doing things, throw away these control panels. (You only have them if you're using System 7.1 or later anyway.)

### Easy Access

This control panel is designed for people who have difficulty using a mouse or typing with both hands. If you're coordinated and two-handed, throw this thing away.

### File Sharing Monitor

Here's the first of several control panels that have to do with *networking* (connecting Macs together by wire). If you have no plans to plug your Mac into somebody else's, throw this away. (Instructions for setting up a Mac network are beyond the scope of this book. Networking is not, however, beyond the scope of the upcoming *More Macs For Dummies*.)

### General Controls

A useful control panel. (You played with it in Chapter 3.) Set your clock, and so on.

### Keyboard

Use this control panel to change how a key behaves when you keep it pressed. Does a held-down key start repeating like thisssssssssss? And how fast? I find that many first-time Mac users fare better if they turn the repeating-key feature off. That way, if a book happens to lean on the spacebar while you're on the phone for 20 minutes, you won't hang up to find 536 pages of blank space in the letter you were working on.

If you couldn't care less, throw this one away.

### Labels

Look at your menu bar: File, Edit, View, Label, Special.

Labels are a way to categorize your files. You just highlight an icon and choose a label from the Label menu (such as In Progress). It's a wonderful, ingenious, fascinating concept. Almost nobody uses it.

Use this control panel, Labels, to change *what* the Labels menu says (instead of Essential, Hot, In Progress, you can change them to say Late, Past Deadline, Hopeless, or whatever). If you don't use labels, which is probably the case, chuck this.

### Launcher

You only have this if you have a Performa Mac. You *can* throw it away, but only if you want to de-Performatize your Mac. See Chapter 9 for an explanation.

### Map

This control panel is primarily useful for people who do business with different geographical locations. You type in a major city's name and click Find, and the Map shows you where that city is. It also tells you how far away it is, and what the time difference is.

If you pretty much stay in your living room, the Map is a good candidate for trashing.

### Memory

As the French say, *Ne trashez pas!* You'll need this one. Details on memory, and Memory, in Chapter 11.

### Monitors

If you have a black-and-white Mac, throw this out.

If you have a color screen, you use this control panel to switch it between color and black and white.

And why, you may well ask, would you ever want your Mac world in black and white after you've gone to all the trouble and expense of buying a color Mac? Easy — when you set your monitor to black and white, it's *faster*. Much faster. Things like opening windows and scrolling through a document happen about three times quicker in black and white. (They're just not as pretty doing it.)

### Mouse

This control panel adjusts how far the cursor moves on the screen relative to how you move the mouse. It may surprise you that moving the mouse one inch does *not* move the cursor one inch on the screen. In fact, the distance the arrow moves depends on the *speed* of your mouse motion.

Try this: move the mouse very slowly across three inches of desk space. The arrow moves three inches. But now *jerk* the mouse across the same three inches. Now the cursor flies across your entire monitor!

Anyway, the Mouse control panel lets you adjust how much of this speed-exaggeration you'll get when you move the mouse. It also lets you decide how fast two clicks must be to be treated as a double-click.

My advice: set the Mouse Tracking to one of the Fast settings, and the double-click speed in the middle. Then throw this control panel away.

### Network

Yet another control panel used only for networking. In fact, even if you *have* a network, you can toss this; it's used to switch *between* different kinds of networks, such as Ethernet and LocalTalk (whatever *they* are).

### Portable (or PowerBook), PowerBook Display

The first one controls how quickly your laptop Mac goes to "sleep" to conserve battery juice. The second governs what happens when you plug an external monitor into your laptop. Naturally, if you don't have a PowerBook, it's Trash Time for both. (See Chapter 10 for more on PowerBooks.)

### Sharing Setup, Users & Groups

More control panels used only for networking. Throw them away unless you want to connect to other Macs.

### Sound

A keeper. It lets you adjust the volume of your speaker. It also lets you choose from among several, equally uncouth sound effects for use as your error beep (what the Mac does when you make a mistake). And if your Mac came with a microphone, or has one built into the front, then you can record your own embarrassing and gurgly sound effects.

### Speech Setup

Only Macs with AV in their names (such as Quadra 840 AV) come with this control panel. Use this to control how the Mac responds when you talk to it (see Appendix A for details on The Macs Who Listen).

### Startup Disk

You'd use this if you have *more than one* hard drive connected to your Mac. You have one hard drive inside the Mac. Some people purchase another one, or a removable-cartridge thing, that plugs into the back. Startup Disk lets you choose which hard drive's System Folder you want to run the show when you next turn on the computer.

If the hard drive in your Mac is your only hard drive, toss Startup Disk.

### Views

My grandfather's 103 and sharp as a tack. When I showed him my PowerBook last Thanksgiving, he had absolutely no problem using it. But there was one thing that bothered him: the icons' names were too small to read.

Fortunately, I was using System 7. I opened up the Views control panel, typed a new point size, and handed the Mac back to him. He loved it.

He did remind me, however, that when *he* was growing up, they didn't even have *electricity*.

## In your Fonts folder

You only have a Fonts folder if you're using System 7.1 or later. Actually, you probably shouldn't throw away anything in it. See Chapter 4 again for a detailed explanation of what all this junk is.

# In your Extensions folder

An *extension* is a little program that runs automatically when you turn on the Mac. It usually adds some little feature to your Mac that you want available at all times: a screen saver, for example, that automatically blanks your screen after a few minutes of inactivity on your part.

## AppleShare, File Sharing Extension, Network Extension

Still more doodads for networking Macs together.

## ImageWriter, LaserWriter, StyleWriter II, etc.

Recognize these names? They're various *printers* made by Apple. You only need one of them — the one that matches *your* printer. You should definitely throw away all the others. (More on printers in Chapter 4.)

## Apple CD-ROM, CD Remote Init, Foreign File Access

Why does Apple's CD-ROM player need so many little extensions? Heaven knows. All I know is that you should toss these if you don't have a CD-ROM.

## A/ROSE

There's a good joke in here somewhere — something about A/ROSE by any other name — but, alas, this extension is useless. Jettison pronto.

## Basic Color Monitor

This extension lets your Mac work with this one specific low-cost Apple monitor model. If you have any other kind of screen, get rid of this.

## Caps Lock

Only for PowerBooks. Because the Caps Lock key on certain models doesn't light up or stay down when you press it, this little extension puts an up-arrow symbol on your menu bar when Caps Lock is engaged. That way, you know when you're about to inadvertently type 46 pages in all caps.

## DAL

It's ridiculous that Apple even wastes your time with this. It's for hooking up to gigantic humming mainframes in Houston. Nobody uses it. Toss it.

## EtherTalk Phase 2

Sounds suspiciously like something you'd hear uttered on *Star Trek: the Next Generation,* doesn't it? Actually, it comes with Quadras and Centrises, and it's useless unless you're hooked up to a major office network that uses special Ethernet cables.

### Finder Help

Leave this one alone. It's where the Mac stores the information you get when you use Balloon Help.

### QuickTime

You need this little jobber if you plan to use (or are using) digital movies on the Mac. You know, little flicks that play inside a Triscuit-sized window right on your screen, complete with sound (see Chapter 7). This QuickTime extension is what makes those movies possible. If you have a black-and-white Mac, or you're not a Hollywood wannabe, then save yourself the memory and disk space and send this one to the cutting room floor.

### PrintMonitor

Definitely leave this. It's actually a program, not an extension, and it's the genie that grants you the miracle of *background printing,* a concept you probably don't understand unless you've read Chapter 4.

### Tuner

Keep this baby right where it is! This extension repairs some bugs in System 7.0 or 7.0.1, some of which are a wee bit dangerous. If you have any other System version, you can ditch it.

## In your Launcher Items folder

You only *have* a Launcher Items folder if your Mac has *Performa* in its name. And the purpose of this folder is to let you specify what jumbo icons you want to appear in your Launcher window, the Performa's program-launching bay. See Chapter 9 for the gory details.

## In your Preferences folder

The Preferences folder is filled with information, and *none* of it's for you.

Every single file in this folder was put there by *another* piece of software. Let's say you change a setting in your word processor: you always want it to make your typing double-spaced, let's say. Well, where do you suppose the computer stores your new setting? It jots it down in a *preferences file.* And this prefs file lives — wild guess — in the Preferences folder.

Prefs files are famous for frustrating beginners. Because they're for use by your programs, and not by you, virtually every one of them gives you a rude error message if you try to double-click it. *You* simply can't open a Prefs file; only your software can.

### Finder Preferences, Photoshop Prefs, ClarisWorks Prefs, etc.

Like I said. Leave these alone, and don't even think about double-clicking them.

### DAL Preferences

Out it goes. See DAL, above.

### Scrapbook file, Note Pad file

When you paste something into the Scrapbook or Note Pad desk accessories , the Mac actually stores it in these files.

## In the Speakable Items folder

There's no possible way you'll find this folder in your System Folder, except under one circumstance: the letters *AV* are part of your Mac's name (such as Centris 660AV or Quadra 840AV).

If you're using your AV Mac's speech-recognition feature — you know, where you talk to your Mac ("Computer: open MacWrite") — you can "teach" your Mac to recognize the names of certain files or folders by putting them, or aliases of them, into this folder. Don't get greedy, though. You're not supposed to put more than about 50 things in here.

## Loose in the System Folder

### Clipboard

Every time you use the Cut or Copy command in a program, the Mac, according to what you read earlier, socks the selected material away on an invisible clipboard. Well, guess what: it's not actually invisible. Technically speaking, that info you copied has to be put *somewhere*. This is where: in the Clipboard file.

Little-known fact: you can double-click the Clipboard file to open a window that shows the last thing you cut or copied. (Another little-known fact: the last swallow of a can of soda is 69 percent saliva.)

### Finder

This is the most important file on your Mac. Without it, a System Folder is just a folder, and your Mac can't operate. The Finder file is responsible for creating your basic desktop: the Trash, your disk icon, windows, and so on.

### System

This is *also* the most important file on your Mac. It contains all kinds of *other* info necessary for the computer to run: your sounds, for example; your fonts (in systems before 7.1); and reams and reams of instructions for the computer's own use.

### System Enabler

This, too, is the most important file on the Mac. Like the System and the Finder, without this file, your Mac can't even turn on.

However, not every Mac *has* one of these. In fact, only Macs sold in the last couple of years have one: Centris, Quadra, LC III, PowerBook Duos, and a few other recent models. If you have one, don't touch it.

### PrintMonitor Documents

PrintMonitor, as you read in Chapter 4, has to do with *background printing*. After you use the Print command, but before the paper actually starts coming out of the printer, the Mac stores the printout-to-be in this folder. You can trash this folder if you want, but it'll reappear every time you turn on the Mac.

### Startup Items

Fascinating, Captain. Anything you put into this folder (a program, a document, a sound, a folder) gets opened with a mysterious automatic double-click whenever you turn on the Mac. If you don't do anything but word process, for example, drag the icon of your word processor into this folder. Thereafter, every time you power up for the day, your word processing program will be on the screen awaiting your brilliance.

### ~ATM 68020/030

Another component of Adobe Type Manager (see Chapter 4). Leave it here.


# How Come You Can't Double-Click Things

Nobody ever explains this. Not one computer book — including, I'm embarrassed to say, the first edition of *this* book — bothers to mention this extremely annoying syndrome.

You see an icon. You double-click it to see what it does. But all you get is this error message:

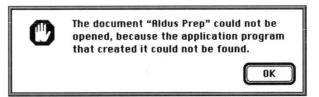

This frustrating occurrence, as you've probably discovered, flies violently in the face of the Macintosh Reputation for User-Friendliness.

Actually, if you've read this chapter from the beginning, you already pretty much know the explanation. Half the icons in the System Folder *aren't for you.* They serve as storage cubbies for the computer itself. The "Application not found" message really means "Sorry, bub, authorized personnel only." And it's really nothing to worry about.

On the other hand, at times in your Macintosh computing life, you'll get a similar error message when the thing you're double-clicking is *not* in the System Folder. That's a very different scenario, particularly when you're double-clicking an icon you *know* is a legitimate, user-openable file.

For an explanation of that irritating event, see Chapter 11.

# Top Ten Other Typical Pieces of System Folder Crud

Unless your Macintosh is brand new, you've probably got a bunch of other System Folder clutter I haven't mentioned. Usually, it's stuff that you (or your guru-friend) purchased and installed.

Remember, the vast majority of this stuff doesn't eat up any of your *memory;* it's only occupying *disk space.* Still, if some piece of unidentified System Folder crud really bugs you, you can always try moving it out of the System Folder for a week or so, long enough to see if your Mac still works without it.

1. **Aldus** — A folder full of stuff for programs made by Aldus (probably PageMaker or FreeHand).

2. **Claris** — A folder full of stuff used by Claris Corporation programs (ClarisWorks, FileMaker, and so on).

3. **CEToolbox** — A component of any program from a company called CE Software (DiskTop, QuicKeys, QuickMail, etc.).

4. **Suitcase** — A font-management program that lets you "turn on" or "turn off" sets of fonts very easily.

5. **GlobalFax** or **Teleport** or **PowerPort** or **Express Modem** or **FaxStf** — The software that controls your modem.

6. **After Dark** and **After Dark Files** — A famous automatic screen dimmer — see Chapter 8 — that features the famous Flying Toasters and Fish.

7. **32-bit Enabler** (or **Mode32**) — These are memory-related add-ons. You need one or the other if your Mac has more than 8MB of memory and it's a Mac II, IIx, IIcx, or SE-30. At this point, you probably don't know or care about memory; if you want to find out more, see Chapter 11.

8. **Hardware System Update (HSU)** — Another one of those little tune-up gadgets Apple sends out from time to time in the hopes of making your Mac run better and faster. It only works if you have System 7.1, and it's only for specific models (LCs, IIsi, IIvx, Classic II, and Quadras). The problems it fixes are unbelievably obscure, so don't work yourself into a frenzy if your Mac doesn't have it.

9. **At Ease Items** — The storage folder for aliases of everything you choose to list on your At Ease screen. See Chapter 9 for more about At Ease.

10. **Launcher Items** — Another folder full of aliases. This one's only for Performa users. It contains aliases of the icons you want listed in your Launcher window.

# Chapter 7
## More Stuff to Buy and Plug In

●●●●●●●●●●●●●●●●●●●●●●●●●●●●●●●●●●●●●●●●●●●●●●●

### In This Chapter

▶ Preserving your favorite belch sound forever

▶ Why a scanner is like an inside-out printer

▶ Hooking your Mac to the telephone line

▶ Making your Mac musical or cinematic

●●●●●●●●●●●●●●●●●●●●●●●●●●●●●●●●●●●●●●●●●●●●●●●

*I*t's probably taken you at least a day to reach this part of the book, and I'll bet you're already chomping at the bit. "FileMaker — fiddlesticks! Printers — piffle!" you're no doubt exclaiming. "Give me something I, the Reader, can sink my teeth into!"

OK, O Reader. In this section you'll find out about several impressive and high-tech gadgets you can spend money on — yes, it's Credit Card Workout #4. These devices give the Mac eyes and ears, turn it into a national network, and turn it into an orchestra. You're not obligated to purchase any of them, of course. But knowing about some of the amazing things your computer can do will help you understand why a Mac is such a big deal.

## Microphones

Almost every Mac model comes equipped with a little microphone. It's the circular thing that looks like a Munchkin smoke detector, about two inches in diameter, with a thin cord trailing out. Or maybe it's built right into the front of your computer, as on the Color Classic and most PowerBooks, among others.

If you bought an older Mac, or for some other reason have a Mac model without a microphone jack in the back, a little money (as always) can remedy the situation. One microphone is called the MacRecorder; another is the Voice Impact (both listed in Appendix B). Both plug into the jack marked by a telephone (in back of your Mac) and do everything the Apple mike can do, and more — they just cost more.

Anyway, you wouldn't be alone if you wondered what the point of a microphone was. Fact is, there isn't a whole heckuva lot you can do with it. Mainly what you do with it is record sounds — sentences, sound effects, belches, whatever you want. You can play back a sound by double-clicking its icon; or, using the Sound control panel, you can designate any sound to replace the beep the Mac makes when you make a mistake. (The offices of Mac freaks are filled with exclamations of *"Not!"* and "Bogus!" — the chosen error beeps of the Mac faithful. For more details on recording your own sounds, see Chapter 8.)

## Casper, the friendly technology

Of course, if your Mac has the letters *AV* in its name, you know pretty darned well why there's a microphone. Can you say *voice control?*

Yup, it's PlainTalk, formerly known as Casper, the speech-recognition ghost. You can actually *speak* to your AV Mac and it will obey your commands. No, no, you can't just go randomly dictating your great American novel and expect the Mac to take it all down; the Mac can only recognize *menu commands,* mainly. And even then it doesn't respond to you for a moment or two. And this feature uses up a *huge* amount of memory (see Chapter 11). And it often doesn't even hear you correctly; if you say "Computer, close window," the Mac may just respond by opening, say, the Puzzle.

Despite all of this, voice control is extremely amazing and cool. If you get the right distance from the mike and speak the right way and don't set your expectations too high, you can get a serious fun-shiver out of this.

## Scanners

You've actually seen scanners before. They're usually known by their technical name: *copying machines.* Yup. When you put a piece of paper on the ol' Xerox machine, the scanner part (glass, bright light, funny hum) takes a picture of your document. Then the printer part prints the copy. Well, if you strip out the printer part, what's left is a scanner.

If the point of a printer is to take something on the *screen* and reproduce it on *paper,* then a scanner is the opposite — its function is to scan an image on *paper* and throw it up on the Mac *screen.* After it's been scanned and converted into bits and bytes that the Mac understands (meaning that it's been *digitized),* you can manipulate it any way you want. Erase unwanted parts, make the background darker, give Uncle Ed a mustache, shorten your brother's neck, whatever. The more dignified use for a scanner is grabbing real-world images that you then paste into your own documents, particularly in the realm of page layout and graphic design. Got a potato-industry newsletter to crank out? Scan in a photo of some fine-lookin' spuds, and you've got yourself a graphic for page one.

# O Say Can U OCR?

Unfortunately, when you scan a page of *text,* the Mac doesn't see English words. It sees lots of itty-bitty dots in funny patterns. When the image pops up on your screen after being scanned, you can't correct a typo — because it's not really text anymore, just a picture of text. (Analogy time: If you take a Polaroid of a handwritten grocery list, you can't then erase Charmin 8-Roll Pack from the *photo* because it's no longer handwriting — just a picture of some writing.)

To convert that picture of text into a true text document, you need a piece of highly brainy software designed for *optical character recognition,* which is so unhelpful a term that people abbreviate it OCR out of sheer disgust. Using OCR, you can save yourself massive amounts of retyping; you can just roll the magazine article, book page, or other text document through your scanner, and wait while your OCR program examines each letter to decide its identity. The result is a text document that's about 98 percent correctly typed.

So how much is all this gonna cost you? A serious black-and-white scanner, one with a big plate of glass like a copier, is around $800. An OCR program costs between $200 and $800, depending on its sophistication.

# Modems

A modem is a phone hookup — a box that sits between the Mac and a phone jack.

## One in the hand

If you doubt you'll be needing to grab images or text every day, consider a *hand* scanner. Instead of being a huge piece of machinery, a hand scanner is a little hand-held doodad about five inches wide. You leave the document on the table and roll this gizmo across it; the scanned image (usually four inches wide, max) appears in a strip on the screen. You can even get a hand scanner with built-in OCR when you need to grab text. Hand scanners have their limitations — the four-inch maximum scan width, for one thing, and the fact that you have to drag the scanner across the page absolutely straight. But they cost less than half what the big guns do.

After your Mac is connected by phone to another computer, all kinds of neat things can happen. You can have a conversation with somebody at the other end where everything each person types appears on both people's screens. You can transfer a file from your hard disk to somebody else's even if they live in Tulsa or Zurich. You can drop written messages into people's electronic mailboxes, which they'll read the next time they check in. (Such messages are called *e-mail,* from the exclamation "*Eeee*-hah! I don't have to send it through the *mail!*") You can make plane reservations, order disks, check your stocks, send cartoon renderings of your face worldwide, and get all kinds of other info by using an *on-line service.*

Depending on how much of a computerphile you intend to become, a modem can be as exciting an addition to your life as, say, taking up aerobics or getting cable TV. If your printer blows up, you could scream for help on an electronic bulletin board, and you'd get it. If you have Macs both at work and at home, you can send documents back and forth over the phone wires. Some people phone *all* their work in to the office; these people are called *telecommuters* (or *lucky slobs,* depending on whom you ask).

In fact, if you have a PowerBook (a laptop Mac) with a modem, you can do something *really* neat. Suppose you're out in the Alaskan tundra and you realize you left those critical third-quarter sales reports on your regular office Mac in Chagrin Falls, Ohio. If the Ohio Mac also has a modem, you can actually dial in to your office, turn on the Ohio Mac automatically, get the documents you need, turn off the Ohio Mac — all by long-distance remote control. To do this, you need a program called AppleTalk Remote Access.

## Coping with bauds

Just like computers, modems come equipped with different amounts of speed and power; just like cars, the more speed you have, the more the thing costs. Instead of miles per hour, which would probably be a more user-friendly measurement, modem speed is measured by its *baud rate.* (Note the spelling. *Bawd* rate is something completely different, having to do with barroom womanizing in 17th-century England.) I wouldn't try to explain what a baud is even if I knew. I *can* tell you, though, that the available modem speeds are 300, 1200, 2400, 9600, and 14400 baud. (All right, you weenies. It's more correct to say 300 *bps,* 1200 *bps,* and so on, but who bothers?)

Almost nobody uses the lowest two speeds anymore. The 2400 and 9600 baud rates are by far the most common; 14400 will certainly be the speed-o'-the-future (but at this point is way-2-expensive).

In addition to the modem, you'll also need some software. If you want to communicate directly to another Mac, you'll need a program like MicroPhone, ZTerm, SmartCom, or White Knight (and so does the person on the other end of

---

## Another stupid etymology

Sorry to do this, but the weenies will claim I didn't do my job if I don't reveal the usual boring explanation for the word *modem*.

The word comes from the first syllables of the words *modulator* and *demodulator*. When a modem modulates, it's sending very rapid on/off pulses, kind of like a Morse code operator on a nicotine fit. That's how it talks to other computers. The computer on the other end translates (demodulates) those on/off signals back into intelligible text (or graphics or music or whatever you're sending).

---

the phone). If, instead, you want to hook up to an *on-line information service* (see below), then you probably won't need to buy any software; the service you're subscribing to usually provides free software that works with their system.

And, of course, you'll need to rig some kind of phone-line connection for your modem, either by adding a Y-splitter jack to your existing phone line or by using a separate line.

## Fax/modems

While we're talking about buying modems, you might also want to consider a *fax/modem*. For only about $50 more than the cost of a plain modem, you can get one that turns your Mac into a big gray fax machine. A fax/modem can receive any kind of fax; the incoming document appears on your Mac screen, where you can read it, print it on your printer, or throw it away.

To *send* a fax, you prepare the document (that you want to send) on your Mac. For most people, that means typing it up in a word processor. This, of course, is the one major disadvantage to owning a fax/modem instead of a real fax machine: you can only send documents that are on the Mac. You can't fax someone, for example, an article from *MAD* magazine because it doesn't exist on your Mac screen. (Unless you go to the trouble of buying a scanner and scanning it in.)

## On-line services

One of the neatest things you can do with a modem is dial into an on-line service. The most popular ones are called America Online and CompuServe. You get a local phone number for each, so calling the service isn't a long-distance call. But you pay by the hour while you're connected to the service: about $3.50 per hour for America Online and about $13 per hour for CompuServe.

# The 5th Wave

"HE MUST BE A MACINTOSH USER. THERE'S A WRISTWATCH ICON ETCHED ON HIS RETINA."

In reality, these services are gigantic rooms full of humming mainframe computers in Virginia (America Online) or Ohio (CompuServe) with gazillions of phone lines coming in so that thousands of computer users can dial in at the same time.

What you see on your screen, however, depends on the service you're using. America Online (and AppleLink, another popular one) looks just like the Mac screen you're used to: there are friendly icons and folders and buttons to click. If you want to send an e-mail message to somebody, you just click a button that says Send Mail. CompuServe, on the other hand, has no graphics at all; it's basically some small text that scrolls endlessly up your screen. Most people would agree that CompuServe (and GEnie, Delphi, and other text-based services) is much harder to navigate and learn, *even* if they buy a program called CompuServe Information Manager that adds an icon-based front end to that Mother of All Networks.

On both kinds of services, though, there are some wicked-cool things to do. You can find up-to-the-minute news, sports, and weather reports, for starters. There's an electronic ("on-line") encyclopedia, for those middle-of-the-night bursts of curiosity about dead German philosophers. You can hook into the same airline reservation systems that travel agents use so that you can literally book your own flights. You can send faxes to anybody in the world for about a dollar a page (even though you don't have a fax machine or even a fax/modem). You can get help, overnight, for just about any computer problem.

What's especially fun about America Online is that you can have face-to-face meetings, live encounters, with up to 22 other people at once in an electronic "room." It's a real social encounter — wisecracks, social gaffes, falling in love, the whole bit — except you don't even have to comb your hair. Nobody knows your age, gender, weight, skin color, or whether or not there's spinach caught between your front teeth. There are also *private* rooms, where, legend has it, people from different parts of the world participate in the ultimate safe sex.

## *Bulletin boards*

Much less exotic, but especially practical, are local electronic bulletin board services, known commonly (according to the Universal Rule that Computer Terms Must Be Cryptically Abbreviated) as *BBSs*. A BBS is local and run by some computer guru. Since they're local and usually free, they're less polished than the expensive commercial services, but they make up for the glitz by being hotbeds of local information. You wouldn't have much luck selling your used printer on a national service, for example, but you could put an ad on a BBS for nearby computer users to find.

Like the commercial services, BBSs usually stock a huge amount of trial software free of charge, which you can transfer to your own Mac (in a process called downloading). This kind of software is called *shareware* (a computer term I actually *like*) because the programmer who wrote it wants to share it with fellow Mac owners everywhere. Instead of paying $400 for a beautifully packaged, heavily advertised program, you can download a piece of shareware from a local BBS and pay only $15 for it. And your payment is on the honor system, at that: you only mail the guy his money if you really like the software. (Try *that* with a Microsoft program.) It's the ultimate try-before-you-buy, win-win, everybody's-happy system.

So how do you find out the number of a local BBS since that's probably the best way to try out your new modem? Well, you can ask around, of course. But a surefire (albeit roundabout) method is to call Apple at 800-538-9696 and ask them which Macintosh User Group is nearest to you. Once you know, call up the user group and ask *them* what some phone numbers of local BBSs are. Then dial away and have fun! I can almost guarantee it — you won't remember having tied up the phone for so long since you were a teenager.

# CD-ROM

Nothing spices up a good discussion like a baffling computer equipment acronym, y'know?

Fortunately, you already know half of this one: CD stands for Compact Disc, just like the ones that let you play Ella Fitzgerald on your stereo. Instead of holding music, though, a CD-ROM disc holds computer information — *tons* of it. (Don't even worry about what ROM stands for. It'd leave you more confused than you may be already.)

If you have a CD-ROM player — a $400 gizmo that plugs into the back of your Mac — you can play CD-ROM discs. They contain pictures, sound, movies, graphics, and text . . . enough to keep you busy for days. Typical examples: One CD-ROM contains an encyclopedia, complete with color pictures, some of which are movies that show the motion of, say, the Venezuelan Sun Gekko. Another is a dictionary where you actually hear a guy read the pronunciation of each word. Another CD-ROM is a video game — an *interactive* one, like a TV show where *you* control where the main character goes next.

Apple Computer vows that CD-ROM is going to be the next big thing. In fact, you can get a built-in CD-ROM player as an option on Centris and Quadra Mac models, and on some Performa and LC models. We'll see if CD-ROM catches on. At the moment, there aren't all that many CD-ROM discs to choose from, and $400 is still too much for most people to pay for the privilege.

# Music and MIDI

Oh, groan . . . it's another abbreviated computer term! All right, let's get it over with.

*MIDI,* pronounced like the short skirt, stands for Musical Instrument Digital Interface. What it *means* is "hookup to a synthesizer." What it *does* is let your Mac record and play back your musical performances using a synthesizer attached to it. When you record, the Mac makes a metronome sound — a steady click track — and you play to the beat. Then, when you play back the music, your keyboard plays *exactly* what you recorded, complete with feeling, expression, and fudged notes; you'd think that Elvis's ghost was playing the instrument, except that the keys don't move up and down.

The advantage of recording music in this way (yup, there's a term for this, too — it's *sequencing*) is that once you've captured your brilliant performance by recording it into the Mac, you can edit it. You can take *out* those fudged notes. You can transpose the piece into a different key. You can speed it up or slow it down *without* affecting the pitch. Why? Because this isn't a tape recording; it's a *digital* recording. Your musical MIDI information is a stream of computer numbers that describe each note you play; the Mac might instruct the keyboard, for example, to "Play middle C with this much volume. And hold the note for one-tenth of a second."

## A one-person orchestra

In the real world, the most useful application of MIDI information, though, is that a single musician (or even semimusician) can make a recording that sounds like an entire band. How? you ask, eyebrows raised.

Simple: You record one musical line at a time. You play the bass line, for example; the Mac records it, nuance for nuance. Now, while the bass line plays back, you record the piano part. Then while those *two* tracks play back, you record the violins, and so on. Hate to break it to you, but virtually *all* popular music (and advertising jingles) are now recorded this way — by one Mac musician alone in a studio with a big pile of realistic-sounding synthesizers. (And I still haven't recovered from finding out, at age eight, that the whole band isn't actually at the radio station every time a song comes on.)

## What you need

What you *don't* need to make MIDI music on the Mac is much musical ability. Remember, you can record something as slowly as you want, at a tempo that would slow a turtle's pulse. Then you can just change the tempo when the music plays back, and instantly you sound like you've got 18 fingers and six hands.

You do, however, need a little box that connects your Mac to the synthesizer. It's called a MIDI *interface,* and it shouldn't cost more than about $50. You also need a program that can record and play back the music, called a *sequencing program.* Some easy-to-use and inexpensive ones are EZ Vision, MusicShop, and Trax. And, of course, you need to get your hands on a synthesizer. Check out a music store and get jammin'.

## Other things MIDI can do

Another popular use of the Mac is to make it write out your music for you in standard sheet music notation. Several *notation* programs (Finale, Finale Allegro, Encore) actually write down every note you play, let you edit it, add lyrics or chord symbols, and then print it out as gorgeous sheet music. These programs can even play back your music; you can listen to your masterpiece, correcting any wayward notes before committing them to paper. Presto, you're Mozart.

## A Camcorder

"Say *what?*" you're saying. "This crazy author is suggesting I plug my camcorder into my computer? What's next, plugging my microwave into the vacuum?"

**Hot:** *(1) Expensive.* He bought a hot new computer. *(2) Trendy.* What do you use your new computer for? Well, nothing, but it's hot, isn't it?

It's true. The hottest new use of a Macintosh is as a movie-making machine. You can actually plug your VCR or camcorder into the computer and watch in awe as your home movies pop up on the Mac screen. After you've captured your videos onto the Mac (or, more correctly, *digitized* them), with full color and sound, you can edit them, play them backward, edit out the embarrassing parts, or whatever. The technology and the movies are called QuickTime, and no other computer can do it.

## The caveats of the proletariat

That's the end of the good news. QuickTime video editing takes some serious Mac horsepower: you need a fast color Mac. And unless you have a Mac model with *AV* in its name, you also need to buy a video *digitizing card* (the thing you actually plug your VCR into) and some movie-editing software. And you need a *lot* of hard-disk space: every minute of digitized movie on your Mac consumes about *15MB* of disk space (for those whose calculators don't work in megabytes, that's a hefty chunk of a typical hard disk). Even with all that, the movies play back pretty jerkily, in a tiny window about the size of a Triscuit.

At this writing, the most cost-effective way to get started making your own digital movies is to buy either a Video Spigot or a Movie Movie. Each is a digitizing card (a circuit board you install into your Mac IIsi, IIci, or whatever) that costs around $400.

If you've got the bucks (more like $5000), you can get one of the new generation of pro digitizing cards; instead of watching jumpy, Max Headroom-ish movies in a window on your screen so small you need a magnifying glass, you can watch very smooth, full-screen movies with stereo sound!

They still take up tons of hard-disk space, though. Of course, people just have to go buy additional hard disks to hold their movies. And when *they* fill up, then — hold on a second. Maybe it's time to talk about less expensive storage gadgets.

# SyQuests, Bernoullis, and Tapes, Oh My!

In Chapter 1½ you learned all about hard disks. You learned that the hard disk (usually built inside your computer) is a terrific place to store your data when the computer is turned off. You found out that it's sort of expensive, but it delivers data very quickly into the Mac's little head.

There's only one thing wrong with hard disks: like closets, garages, and land-fills, they fill up. No matter how much of a neatness nerd you are, even if you promptly throw away anything you're finished working on, you'll gradually watch your "MB available" count go down, down, down over the months, until your hard disk is completely full. (Thousands of experienced Mac users all over the world are sagely nodding their heads in sorrowful acknowledgment.)

So what are you supposed to do? Go back to writing on Post-It notes?

Well, you could buy another hard disk, of course. The one *inside* your computer is called an *internal* hard drive. If you buy another, you could plug it into the back of your Mac and have access to its contents as well. (This, as you may have guessed, would be called an *external* hard drive.) But that's an expensive proposition, and the darndest thing of all is that *that* hard drive will fill up, too.

## Remove it

For thousands of storage-starved people, the solution is to get a *removable-cartridge* system. This device looks just like an external hard drive, except when the spinning platters get full, you can just pull them out of the machine (they're sealed into a  plastic cartridge) and put in a new, blank, virgin cartridge. Since an 88-megabyte cartridge only costs about $75, and a new hard disk costs $400, you can see why a removable cartridge is an attractive idea.

A removable-cartridge system solves another chronic problem, too: how to *back up* your data. To back up is to make a spare copy of your important files, so if something should happen to your main hard disk (or *you* do something to it) and all your files get erased, you haven't lost your life's work.

But placing a second copy of everything on the *same* hard disk doesn't make much sense; if the hard disk croaks, then you lose both copies. Many people copy their data onto floppy disks. That's certainly cheap, but it's inconvenient, especially if you work with large files that take forever to copy. With a removable-cartridge system, you can back up your entire hard drive in five minutes.

There are two primary makers of removable-cartridge systems: SyQuest and Bernoulli. A SyQuest drive costs about $400. The newer SyQuest drives accept 105MB cartridges, which are slightly more expensive than the 88MB or 44MB ones. The huge advantage of SyQuest drives: they're extremely common. Thousands and thousands of people own them, and cartridges can be swapped freely back and forth.

A Bernoulli removable-cartridge drive is, technologically speaking, a slightly superior solution. Each cartridge holds 90MB of data, and the cartridges are incredibly tough and long-lasting. (You hear occasional stories about a SyQuest cartridge going bad, but you never hear about a Bernoulli going bad.) The possible drawback: there aren't as many Bernoullis in the world, so finding a fellow cartridge-swapper isn't easy (if, indeed, you care).

Another possibility for making backup copies is a *tape drive.* Instead of storing your information on metal platters, a tape drive stores it on a plain old cassette-like tape. The advantage: the special tapes are dirt cheap. The disadvantage: they're slow as frozen ketchup. Also, you can't easily retrieve just one file from a tape-backup cartridge because the computer can't easily jump from one place on the tape to another. So don't bother with tape backup; I'm telling you about tape backup only so that you'll know to whom you're entitled to feel superior.

# *Networks*

You already know what a *network* is. It's the television company that broadcasts stuff like *Love Connection* so you'll have something to watch when you're burned out from computer work.

In the computer world, though, a network is defined as *more than one Mac hooked together.* In some offices, hundreds of Macs are all interconnected. Some advantages of being networked: You can send e-mail to other people, which pops up on their screens; you can have access to each others' files and programs; and you can save money by buying just one printer (or scanner or modem) for use with a whole bunch of Macs.

The goal of this book is to get you going with your *own* Mac. If you really, truly, honestly want to read about connecting Macs together (normally the domain of gurus, computer whizzes, and paid consultants), read *More Macs For Dummies.*

# Plugging the Stuff In

Suppose you win the lottery. You buy every Mac peripheral there is. Only two things left to do: give half your winnings to the IRS and figure out where to plug the stuff in. In Appendix A, you'll find a pretty good diagram of the jacks in the back of your Mac. Here's where everything goes:

**Peripheral:** *An expensive add-on gadget for your Mac, like a scanner, printer, or hard disk. From peripheral vision, which is how you'll see all this stuff cluttering up the edges of your desk.*

✔ *Scanners, CD-ROM players, external hard drives, removable-cartridge drives, tape-backup devices:* the SCSI port. It's the wide one with screws on each side. So how are you supposed to plug in so many different things if there's only one port? Simple — by *daisy-chaining* them, one to another. Daisy-chaining is an act of utter bravery, however, and should not be undertaken until after you've read the "Scuzzy SCSI" section in Chapter 11. Until then, plug *one* machine only into the SCSI jack of your Mac.

✔ *Apple microphone:* There's a special jack, a miniplug, just for this.

✔ *Modems, MIDI interfaces (music), label printers, MacRecorder, or other non-Apple microphones:* These all go into the modem port. It's the little round jobber marked by a telephone icon. So how are you supposed to plug more than one of these into your Mac? (No, there's no such thing as daisy-chaining modem-port devices.) You have two choices, both of which involve using only one device at a time. First, you can just unplug one device before using the next. Or second, you can get an A/B switch box that acts like a Y-splitter; you plug both modem port pluggables into this box and then turn a knob to select which one you want the Mac to pay attention to. (You can even buy an A/B/C/D box that accommodates *four* devices if you've really gone crazy with this kind of peripheral.)

✔ *Camcorder, VCR:* There's no built-in jack for this, except on AV Macs. But after you buy a digitizing card and install it into one of your Mac's *expansion slots,* there will be a new little jack protruding from the back of the Mac (extending from the card inside).

**Expansion slot:** *A receptacle for a plug-in circuit board inside certain Mac models. Only the Classic, the Plus, the Classic II, and the PowerBooks lack expansion slots. The majority of people never use their expansion slots. You can fill your slots with things like accelerators (to make your Mac faster), digitizing cards (so you can make QuickTime movies), or internal fax/modems.*

✔ *Printer, network:* You've probably figured out, all by yourself, that the printer gets connected to the printer port (another small, round jack, next to the modem port, and marked by a printer icon). But it's good to know that this is where you plug in the cabling for a *network,* too, if you have one. (So then where does the printer go if your printer port is used up by a network connection? Easy — it gets hooked into the network so that anyone can use it. See your resident guru for details.)

---

### SCSI trivia not worth the paper it's printed on

Daisy-chaining is the act of connecting more than one peripheral gizmo to a single jack on your computer by plugging each into the back of another one. So called because, when you discover how frustrating it can be to connect multiple devices like hard drives, you'll be reduced to sitting in a field by yourself tying flowers together.

SCSI is the annoying acronym for Small Computer System Interface, pronounced even more annoyingly: "scuzzy." Actually, it refers to the wide jack with two rows of little holes located on the back of the Mac.

---

# *Top Ten Non-Costly Mac Add-Ons*

Like people, Macs that go unaccessorized are likely to be shut out of the most important social functions. But not every add-on has to cost a million bucks, as the following list demonstrates.

1. *A mouse pad.* It's a foam rubber mat that protects the desk and the mouse from each other, gives your mouse better traction, and keeps cookie crumbs out of the mouse mechanism. It often carries the same kinds of promotional graphics as T-shirts and bumper stickers.

2. *A dust cover.* Basically, it's a specially shaped bag you drape over your Mac at night to keep the dust storms out. You might get one for your keyboard, too.

3. *A glare filter.* I think they make the screen too dim, but lots of people use them and think they make the screen easier to look at.

4. *Disk boxes.* They hold your floppy disks. A nylon disk *wallet* holds about ten disks in a fold-up thing you can put in your breast pocket. Disk boxes hold between ten and 100 disks, and come in every possible material from plastic to polished teak. (Actually, I've found that one of those colorful plastic Thermos-brand *lunch boxes* from Woolworth's makes the very best disk box. It holds 100 floppies perfectly, has a handle, and snaps securely shut. Just remember not to get it mixed up with your *kid's* colorful plastic Thermos-brand lunch box — peanut butter and jelly can impair the performance of your disk drives.)

5. *A carrying case.* For the Classic, Plus, SE, or PowerBook, these rugged, padded protective bags are extremely helpful in transporting your machine. Even if it's in one of these cases, don't ever check your computer as baggage on a plane (unless it's in the original cardboard box with its Styrofoam protectors).

6. *A trackball.* People who don't like mice (computer mice, of course) often take great delight in replacing their Mac mouse with a trackball. A trackball looks like an eight ball set into a six-inch square base; you move the pointer on the screen by rolling the ball in place with your fingers. (The PowerBook has a built-in trackball, right in the center below the keyboard.)

7. *A surge suppresser.* This thing looks like an ordinary multiple-outlet extension cord from the hardware store, but it's supposed to have an additional benefit — circuitry that can absorb an electrical voltage surge, and thus protect your Mac from a wayward bolt of lightning. Not many people realize that the Mac already has a *built-in* surge suppresser, however; furthermore, a surge suppresser's value has long been debated. (They're not designed to protect you from acts of God, though. I've known people with surge suppressers whose Macs got fried by lightning, as well as people *without* surge suppressers whose houses were struck by lightning without affecting the Mac.) Let your paranoia be your guide.

8. *A one-switch multiple-outlet box.* In other words, an extension-cord thing that lets you plug in your Mac, hard drive, printer, and so on, so that they all turn on when you flip a single switch. Such devices usually have a surge suppresser built-in, by the way. My favorite is the PowerKey, which is designed especially for the Mac, has four surge-protected outlets, and lets you turn the Mac on by pressing the big triangle key on your keyboard (even if you have a Classic, Plus, SE, or LC, whose big triangle keys usually do nothing).

9. *A paper clip.* Man, talk about low cost. Nonetheless, the true Mac cognoscenti keep a straightened paper clip next to their machines — it's the only way to remove a floppy disk that's stuck in the disk drive. (See the sidebar in Chapter 2 entitled "Dweebs' Corner: Alternative disk tips" for instructions.)

10. *Spare printer cartridges.* Have an extra ribbon, cartridge, or drum for your printer (depending on what it is) at all times. Murphy's Law, or whatever law governs computers, states that the printer cartridge you're using now will not wear out until you're halfway through a large printing project that's due shortly and all the stores are closed.

# Chapter 8
# Putting the Mouse to the Metal

· · · · · · · · · · · · · · · · · · · · · · · · · · · · · · · · · · · · · · · · · · · · · · · · · · · · · · · · ·

## In This Chapter

▶ Uncovering the forbidden secrets of the Option key

▶ Duplicating, finding, and splitting the personality of icons

▶ Vandalizing your own Mac, without spraypaint or a sledge hammer

▶ Utilities with no monthly bill

· · · · · · · · · · · · · · · · · · · · · · · · · · · · · · · · · · · · · · · · · · · · · · · · · · · · · · · · ·

*T*his chapter is about honing the basic skills you already have. It's about becoming more efficient in the way you work — shortcuts, hidden secrets, and slick tricks to astonish your friends. And it's about turning the basic Mac that *millions* of people have into one that's unmistakably yours.

Maybe it'd be better if I avoided the term that's about to apply to you . . . *power-user.* Maybe those words will strike fear once again into your soul. But even if you started *out* as a Mac virgin, either leery or outright petrified about the alien technology before you, by now you've almost completely mastered the Mac. The only tidbits left to explore are the ones normally classified as — yes — *power-user secrets!*

## The Efficiency Nut's Guide to the Option Key

Yeah, yeah, everybody knows that you can close a window by clicking its close box. But you didn't fork over good money for this book to learn something that's on page 1 of the Mac manual.

No, these tips are much choicer. They show you how to unlock the power of that most overlooked of keys, the Option key. It's been placed closer to you than any letter key on the keyboard — and that's no accident.

## *Closing all windows at once*

Suppose that you've opened a gaggle of folders and their windows are lying open all over the screen. And suppose that the niggling neatness ethic instilled in you by your mother compels you to clean up a bit. Here's the "before" picture:

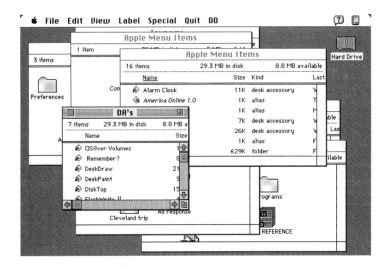

You could, of course, click the close box of each window, one at a time. But it's far faster to click only *one* window's close box while pressing the Option key. Bam, bam, bam — they all close automatically, one after another. Here's the "after" picture:

# *Windows and folders: Developing tunnel vision*

When you're trying to find a document icon that's inside a folder inside a folder inside a folder, it's hard to avoid having COWS (Cluttered, Overlapping Windows Syndrome). By the time you finally arrive at the darned icon, your screen is filled with windows.

If you press Option while double-clicking each nested folder, though, the Mac will neatly close the *previous* window before opening the next one. Criminy — this computer even *cleans up* after you!

In the figure below, you could press Option while double-clicking the Oregon folder (left); the USA folder that contains it would automatically close as the new window opened (right):

OK. So here we are in the Oregon folder. What if we want to backtrack and go back to the USA folder (or the World folder)? There's a little-known trick that lets you jump to the folder that *contains* it: press the ⌘ key and click the window's title!

In the figure to the left, you ⌘-click the word Oregon at the top of the window. Now you slide down the pop-up menu that lists the nested folders from innermost to outermost. Let go when you reach the folder you want (following left); the Mac opens the folder you selected (following right).

And, logically enough, if you press ⌘ *and* Option as you choose the new folder name, you'll simultaneously close the original nested window.

## The silence of the Trash

Let's review: You drag an icon on top of the Trash can and the icon disappears. The Trash can bulges. You smile gently at the zaniness of it all. Then you choose Empty Trash from the Special menu, and a little message appears on the screen, saying something like:

That's all very well and good, but busy Americans concerned with increasing their productivity may not always have time for such trivial information. Therefore, if you want to dump the trash, but you *don't* want that message to appear, press our friend Mr. Option Key while you choose Empty Trash. (Option is also the key for emptying the trash when the Mac tells you there's something "locked" in the Trash can.)

'Smatterafact, you can shut up the Trash's warning permanently, if your little heart is so inclined. It's easy and fun!

Click the Trash can. Choose Get Info from the File menu. Turn off "Warn before emptying." There — what an improvement!

## *Multitasking methods*

As you discovered early on, the Mac lets you run more than one program simultaneously. (Remember when you tried some tricks with both the Note Pad and the Calculator open on the screen at once?) You can switch from one program to another by choosing the program's name from the Application menu at the top right of your screen, marked by the ▣ icon (or the icon of whichever program is currently in front).

We haven't yet examined the other commands in this menu, such as Hide Others and Show All. These are anti-COWS commands that help keep your screen neat and clean. For example, suppose that you're trying to use the Calculator, but so many other programs are running that your eyes cross:

By choosing Hide Others from the Application menu, all windows that belong to other programs disappear, leaving the frontmost window all by itself:

The other programs *are* still running, and they *do* still exist, but their windows, plain and simple, are now hidden. You can verify this by checking the Application menu, where you'll see that their icons appear dimmed.

So how does the Option key play into all this? When you switch from one program to another, you can make the program you're *leaving* hide itself automatically if you press Option while choosing the new program's name (or clicking in its window). That way you always keep nonessential programs hidden.

## *Making an instant document copy*

In most Mac graphics programs, the Option key has a profound effect on a selected graphic item: it peels off a copy of the selected graphic as you drag the mouse. For example, the left eye (right) is selected and then Option-dragged to the right:

You can accomplish essentially the same thing in the Finder, making duplicates of your files instead of eyeballs. Normally, when you drag an icon from one folder to another *on the same disk,* of course, you simply move that icon. But if you press Option while dragging an icon to a new folder (or to the Desktop — the gray background), the Mac places a *copy* of the file in the new folder and leaves the original where it was.

## Alphabetize them icons!

For the neat freak, there's nothing worse than a mass of messy icons cluttering a window (below, top). If you choose Clean Up Window from the Special menu, the Mac will align each icon to an invisible grid so that at least they're neatly arranged (below, lower left). But (1) that won't alphabetize them, and (2) that won't maximize space in the window by eliminating gaps.

Folder before cleaning up

Normal Clean Up          Clean Up using the Option key

If you press (guess which key?) Option while choosing Clean Up Window, though, it changes to say Clean Up by Name. And the effect is totally different — the Mac (1) alphabetizes your icons, and (2) moves them so that they take up as little window space as possible (above, right!).

## *Funny little hidden Option key stunts*

**Control panels:** *Little programs that govern the way your Mac works: the color of the background, how fast your mouse pointer moves, stuff like that. To see your list of control panels — and to play around with them — choose Control Panels from the ★ menu.*

Those wily Apple guys! The sneaky programmers! The funsters in Apple Land have buried all kinds of amusing little surprises in the control panels and other places (of System 7). Try these:

✔ The weird little Map control panel lets you find any major city by latitude and longitude, and tells you what the time zone difference is. If you Option-double-click the Map control panel, the map will appear at double size.

✔ You use the Monitors control panel to switch from color to black and white (if you have a color monitor, of course). If you hold the mouse down on the little "7.0" in the upper-right corner, you'll see a list of the programmers. Press Option while you do so, and watch the smiley face — you'll find out what they really think of you.

✔ When you're in the Finder, the first item under the ★ menu normally says About This Macintosh. Choose it to view some critical specifications about your machine — how much memory it has, for example. But if you press Option while choosing it, the command changes to say About the Finder and shows you a pleasant Silicon Valley scene. Wait long enough, and you'll eventually see some scrolling credits.

✔ Open the Memory control panel. See the part called Virtual Memory? (Some older Macs don't have this section.) Click the On button. Then, while pressing (what else?) the Option key, click the pop-up menu on the right side and keep the button pressed. And move the pointer to the right so that the submenus pop out. Wow — it's more fun than reading the phone book!

## *Buried Treasures*

Did you enjoy those obscure, mostly useless Option key tricks? Then you'll really love these equally scintillating techniques, not one of which requires the Option key.

### *How to find a lost file*

You haven't really poked around much with the Find command, but it's a doozie. Just choose Find from the File menu (or use the keyboard equivalent ⌘-F), and this box appears:

In the highlighted text box, type a few identifying letters of the name of the file you're looking for. For example, if (by some improbable cosmic accident) you can't find your System Folder, you could just type *SYS* and then click Find (or press the Return key). It doesn't matter whether you type capitals or lowercase letters. The Finder will look for the nearest file that *contains* (not necessarily *begins with*) the letters you've specified.

You can buy any of a zillion programs and desk accessories that are designed to find lost files. But the Finder's Find command is the only one that actually produces the lost file's *icon*, opening its folder for you and highlighting the icon:

But what if there are several files on your disk that contain the same letters? Easy. Each time the Find command displays the wrong icon, choose Find Again from the File menu. Or just press ⌘-G, as in, "Guess again, diskbrain." The Mac will hunt through your files and highlight the next one it finds that contains those same letters.

If you click the More Choices button, the dialog box expands to show you some other search criteria, such as date, file size, and so on. You could, if you really wanted to, find a certain document whose name you couldn't remember, but that you're certain you created at 3 p.m. during a NoDoz-crazed fit on August 4th.

## Make an alias of a file

In the File menu, there's a command called Make Alias. Although you might expect this command to generate names like One-Eyed Jake or Bubba Wilcox, the term *alias* in the Macintosh world represents something slightly different —

a duplicate of a file's icon (but not a duplicate of the file itself). You can identify the alias icon easily because its name is in italics, as shown in the following figure. (The original file is on the left.)

Word 5

*Word 5 alias*

What's neat about aliases is that, when you double-click an alias icon, the Mac opens the *original* file. If you're a true '90s kinda person, you might think of the alias as a beeper — when you call the *alias,* the *actual* file responds.

So who on earth would need a feature like this? Well, there's a little bit more to the story. An alias, for one thing, only requires a tiny amount of disk space (a couple of K) — so it's not the same as making an *actual copy* of the original file. (And you can make as many aliases of a file as you want.) Therefore, making an alias of something you use frequently is an excellent time-saver — it keeps the alias icon (and thus the real file) readily accessible, even if the real file is buried four folders deep somewhere.

Another very common trick: Place an alias of a program, or a document, into your  menu, where you don't have to open *any* folders to get at it.

Here's the drill:

1. Click the real icon.

2. Choose Make Alias from the File menu.

3. Open your System Folder.

4. Drag the alias into the folder called Apple Menu Items (within the System Folder).

5. Now look in your  menu.

Sure enough — there's your file! Choose it from the menu to open the original file.

## Trash, aliases, and a word of caution

When you trash an alias, you're only deleting the alias. The original file is still on your disk. If you delete the *original* file, however, the alias icons will remain uselessly on your disk, rebels without a cause, babies without a mother, days without sunshine. When you dcuble-click an alias whose original file is gone, you'll just get an error message.

Likewise, if you copy your inauguration-speech file's *alias* to a floppy disk, thinking that you'll just print it out when you get to Washington, think again: you've just copied the alias, but you *don't* actually have any text. That's all in the original file, still at home on your hard disk.

And yet, because you used an alias, the *real* file can be anywhere on your hard disk or on a different disk. You can move the real file from folder to folder or even rename it, and the alias still opens it properly.

## Creating the L.L. Mac catalog

Every now and then, you might find it useful to create a list of files or folders on your disk. But it's hardly worth your time to go to the Finder, look at the first file's name, switch to your word processor and type it, and then repeat with the second file. Here's a much faster way:

1. Select the files whose names you want to copy. (You might want to use the Select All command in the Edit menu, at which point you can press the Shift key and click "off" the items you don't want.)

2. Choose Copy from the Edit menu.

3. Launch your word processor (or even the Note Pad desk accessory under the  menu) and choose Paste from the Edit menu. Presto: a neatly typed list of file names!

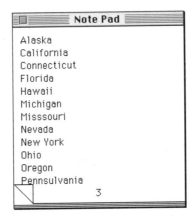

(P.S. — The list can't be a terrifically long one; the Mac copies only 256 characters of text at a time, but you can always repeat the process.)

## *Have it your way — at Icon King*

You don't have to accept those boring old icons for files, programs, and folders. If you want anything done around the Mac, heaven knows, you've got to do it yourself.

1. Go into HyperCard or ClarisWorks or some other program that lets you paint stuff. Make a funny little picture. And I mean *little* — remember, you're drawing a replacement icon for some hapless file. Like this guy here, for example:

2. Copy it to the Clipboard.

3. Go to the Finder, and click the file whose icon you want to replace.

4. Choose Get Info from the File menu so that this box appears:

5. See the folder icon in the upper left? Click that sucker —

and then paste away!

From now on, that little picture will be the new icon for the file (or folder or disk). To restore the original icon, do the Get Info business, but click the icon and press the Clear key.

## *Taking a picture of the screen*

In this book, you've probably noticed a number of pictures that illustrate objects on the Mac screen. Now I'll show you how to take your own snapshots of the screen.

It involves pressing three keys simultaneously: Command (⌘), Shift, and 3. You hear a satisfying *kachunk!* camera shutter sound. After a moment, a new file appears in your hard disk window, called Picture 1. (If you take another shot, it'll be called Picture 2, and so on.) If you open this Picture file (with the TeachText program that came with your Mac, for example, or a graphics program like ClarisWorks), you'll see that you've successfully captured the entire screen image.

Unfortunately, you don't have much control over this photo session business. You can't take any pictures while a menu is pulled down, and you can't take a picture of only *part* of the screen. (You can buy programs for those tasks: Screenshot and Capture, for example.)

So why did I wait until this chapter to clue you in on this? Easy — I didn't want you to write and illustrate your *own* Mac book before you'd finished reading this one!

## *Just saying no*

There's a wonderful keyboard shortcut that means *no* in Mac language. It could mean *No, I changed my mind about printing* (or copying or launching a program); *stop right now.* It could mean *No, I didn't mean to bring up this dialog box; make it go away.* Or: *No, I don't want to broadcast my personal diary over worldwide e-mail!* Best of all, it can mean *Stop asking for that disk! I've already taken it out of your slot! Be gone!*

And that magic keystroke is ⌘-period (.).

When you begin to print your Transcripts of Congress, 1952–1992, and you discover — after only two pages have printed — that you accidentally spelled it "Transcripts of Congrotesque" on every page, ⌘-period will prevent the remaining 14 million pages from printing. Because the Mac has probably already sent the next couple of pages to the printer, the response won't be immediate (but will be light-years quicker than waiting for Congress).

Or let's say you double-click an icon by mistake. If you press ⌘-period *right away,* you can halt the launching and return to the Finder. And if the Mac keeps saying, "Please insert the disk: Purple Puppychow" (or whatever your floppy disk was called), you can tell it to shut up by doing that ⌘-period thing over and over again until the Mac settles down with a whimper. Show it who's boss.

# Colorizing, Editing the Menus, and Other Cool Acts of Vandalism

The great thing about the Mac is that it's not some stamped-out clone made in Korea. It's one of a kind — or it will be after we get through with it. These tips illustrate some of the ways you can make the Mac match your personality, sensibility, or décor.

## Changing the background pattern

When you first turn on a new Mac (Performas not included), the desktop area (the background) presents a lovely shade of uninteresting gray. You can easily change this to any other pattern of black-and-white dots — or, if you have a color Mac, to any elaborate arrangement of colored dots. Here's how.

From the  menu, choose Control Panels. Double-click the General Controls icon, and you'll see this:

Click here or here to see some patterns to choose from.

This is a magnified view of the pattern. Click a black dot to make it white, or vice versa.

As you edit the dots in the magnified view, you see an actual-size view here. When you get the pattern the way you want it, click here to fill in your whole desktop background.

As shown in the diagram, the upper-left quadrant of the General Controls panel contains the tools you need to change the backdrop pattern. At left, there's a magnified view, which lets you easily edit each dot that constitutes the overall pattern. At right, you see the overall pattern — in other words, you see what's in the "magnified view" repeated over and over again.

If you have a color (or grayscale) monitor, you can use the row of eight colored squares beneath the magnified view. Double-click one of these squares to change the color it displays. Once that's done, treat these color swatches as a palette — click a swatch and then start clicking dots in the magnified view to change their colors.

Anyway, the point is that when you're finished editing the magnified view at left (to show, for example, your initial), you have to click in the normal-size view (to its right) to make the pattern "take" and fill in your desktop backdrop. Furthermore, you have to *double-click* the normal-size view if you want your new pattern saved for future use.

Here are a few pattern ideas to get you started.

## *Color-coding your icons*

There's another pretty neat colorization feature that hardly anyone uses, but it's still worth knowing about: color-coding. All you do is select an icon or a whole passel of them, and choose a color from the Label menu.

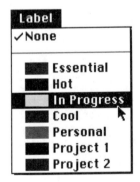

If you don't have a color monitor, you can still attach descriptive labels to your icons (Essential, Hot, In Progress, and so on), even though you won't see the colors.

Two questions, then: (1) How do you change the colors and labels into something more useful, and (2) what's the point?

Well, it seems like most people never bother with labeling their icons. You could argue, though, that it makes life more convenient since you can sort by label (you could see all your In Progress files grouped together in a window). You can also use the Find command to search for a file that has a certain label. You might give one label to everything related to, say, a certain book project —

"Sadam Hussein: The Sensitive Side" — and then when it's time to back up your work, use the Find command to round up all files with the Hussein label, so you can copy them all at once. (Or, when the project is over, you could happily *delete* them all at once.)

Anyway, if you *do* want to use this feature, you'll probably want to change the labels Apple suggests (Essential, Hot, In Progress, and so on) to something more useful. To do that, choose Control Panels from the  menu. When the Control Panels window appears, double-click Labels.

To change the wording of a label (remember, you're actually changing the wording of the Label *menu*), just double-click a label and type in something new. To change the color — if your monitor is thus equipped — click the color swatch; a dialog box appears where you can select a new color by clicking.

## Blue language

Here's one more treat for color monitor owners: you can make highlighted text turn some color other than drab black. In other words, when you select some text in your word processor, it usually looks like this:

To change the highlighting so that it looks more like, well, a *highlighter,* choose Control Panels from the  menu. When the Control Panels window appears, double-click Color. This control panel appears:

By choosing a new color from the upper pop-up menu, you can make your highlighted text any color you want, like this:

a vile mixture of Jack Daniels, sparkling water, and Pond's skin cream.

Let your innate fashion sense be your guide.

## Views

Open the Views control panel. This baby is the control freak's best friend — it can change almost every aspect of the way the Finder displays icons.

Using the font and size controls at the top of the window, you get to choose what text style you want the Mac to use for all icons in the Finder. If your vision is going — or you're trying to demonstrate the Mac to a crowd — make the font huge. If you want to make your icons as high as possible per square inch, pick a tiny, compact type style. A couple of unorthodox possibilities are shown here:

The Icon Views controls let you specify how icons should arrange themselves when you drag them around. If you select "Always snap to grid," icons will smartly jump into position whenever you drag them and let go, according to your Icon Views setting: "Straight grid" places them into neat rows, and "Staggered grid" offsets every other icon so that their names won't overlap when they're placed side by side.

The List Views control governs how icons appear when you're viewing them in a list format.

All those checkboxes on the right side ("Show size," "Show kind," and so on) control which pieces of information show up when you're in a list view. "Calculate folder sizes" is neat because it lets you see how much disk space each folder takes up. (If this checkbox isn't selected, then all you get is an unhelpful "—" in the Size column of a list view. On the other hand, some people think that turning on this option tends to make window contents appear more slowly.)

Finally, "Show disk info in header" puts a separate information strip at the top of each window, which shows you how full your disk is.

## Using that microphone

With most new Macs, you get a free microphone. It's not exactly the same one Madonna licks in her videos, but it's good enough for what we're about to do. And that is to change the little beep/ding sound the Mac makes (when you make a mistake) into some other sound, like "Oops!" or a game show "wrong answer" buzzer or a burp or something (depends on your mental age, I guess).

---

## An almost unnecessary list view refresher

There are two ways to view your files in the Finder: as icons or in a vertical list. You choose how you want them arranged using the View menu.

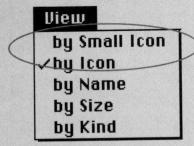

These two commands let you arrange your icons freely.
The remaining commands create list views and determine how your files are sorted: alphabetically, by file size, by type, and so on.

You control which items appear ("by Size," and so on) in the View menu by your checkbox selections in the Views control panel. That is, if you've elected to show only the Size and Date of each file, then you won't see "by Kind" or "by Comments" in the View menu.

---

Here's how it works:

1. From the  menu, choose Control Panels.

2. Double-click the Sound icon.

3. When you see the Sound control panel, click the Add button (if your Mac didn't come with a microphone, the Add button will be dimmed). Now you see this:

4. To record, just click Record and speak into the microphone.

   Be ready to click Stop when you're done or else you'll accidentally include a bunch of silence and fumbling at the end of your sound.

There's a plethora of ways to play back your new sound. You could, mnemonically enough, click the Play button. Then again, you could click Save and give the sound a title so that you'll be able to preserve it for your grandchildren. When you return to the list of sounds in the Sound control panel, click your new sound's name to play it. If you leave it selected in the list, though, you've just selected it to be your new error beep.

## A sound-playing fact for the detail-obsessed

Here's a way to play a sound that doesn't even involve opening a control panel. If you're a double-clicking kinda person, open your System Folder and then double-click the System file. It opens into a window where you'll see a list of all your fonts and all your sounds. Just double-click any sound's icon to hear it played.

# Utilities with No Monthly Bill

Even as you've been taking your first tremulous steps on this most wondrous of computers, thousands of hackers, in a grand effort to make this insanely great computer even greater, have been slaving away late at night, for weeks at a time, subsisting primarily on three-cheese pizza and Jolt cola ("Twice the caffeine! And all the sugar!").

You'd be amazed at the things they come up with. Today you can buy programs that make your hard disk hold more, automatically type out your return address on cue, or — most important of all — put an animated sarcastic moose in a corner of your screen. These are called *utility* programs; here's an overview.

## Compression programs

Run a large file through a *compression* program, and it emerges from the other end at about half its original size. (Too bad you can't run the government through one.) Multiply that size-reduction process by all your files, and all of a sudden your hard disk can hold twice as much. It's almost like getting a second hard drive free.

Some of the best-known file-compression programs are StuffIt, Now Compress, and the shareware program Compact Pro. The simplest and most useful, however (if you ask me), is DiskDoubler. This ultra-clever program adds a new menu to your menu bar in the Finder, containing Compress and Expand commands. To shrink a file, just click it and then choose Compress.

## Geek's nook

If you own a modem (a phone hookup for your Mac), you'll discover another great benefit to owning a file-shrinker—if a file is smaller on your disk, it'll take less time to send over the phone lines. And when you're paying by the minute, that means cold, hard cash.

Best of all, DiskDoubled files decompress themselves automatically — a double-click does the trick. Why is that a big deal? Because in most other compression programs, you have to launch a special program each time you want to compress or decompress a file.

Oh, and P.S.: Do *not* fall for the programs called things like Times Two and Stacker. They're advertised to make your disk hold twice as much information, but they use a scary method of doing so — you'll definitely slow your Mac down, and you'll also run the risk of losing all your files. "Other than that, Mrs. Lincoln, how did you like the play?"

## Screen savers

If you've ever seen the ghost of a cash machine's welcoming screen permanently etched in the display, you'll understand the reason for *screen savers.* By automatically blanking the screen after a few minutes of disuse, these programs ensure that your Mac monitor won't suffer the same burn-in syndrome if you accidentally leave the computer on for the whole week you're in Acapulco. To signal you that the computer is still on, however, a screen saver must bounce some moving image around the screen. That's where the fun comes in.

The programmers of these utilities figure: if you've got to display some "I'm still on!" signal on the monitor, it might as well be entertaining. That's why today's screen savers let you choose from dozens of different patterns or animations to fill your screen while you're ignoring the Mac: wild, psychedelic lava-lampish images, sharks swimming back and forth, fireworks, swirling lines, slithering worms, and so on. The most popular commercial screen saver is After Dark, which displays the now-famous Flying Toasters in Space or a Lawnmower Man whose riding mower gradually eats up whatever document you were working on. You get your regular screen back by touching the mouse or keyboard.

Do you really need one of these? Nah. You'd have to leave your Mac sitting idle for weeks to get screen burn-in. On the one-piece Macs, you can just turn down the screen brightness; on a Color Classic or LC520, you can use the built-in Screen Power Saver. But frankly, screen savers are really, really neat, and sort of *de rigeur* among the computing elite. And they help you justify having bought a color monitor.

## The bright person's guide to dim screens

Here's how you dim your screen. On a Macintosh Classic or Performa 200, choose Control Panels from the  menu, double-click Brightness, and move the slider. On a Mac Plus, SE, or SE/30, there's a dial built into the underside of the front of the screen. (Two-piece Macs have a brightness dial on the side of the monitor, but it doesn't go all the way down to black.)

## Anti-virus software

A computer virus, as you may have read, is a program written by some jerk from a dysfunctional family who seeks to bolster his own self-worth by gumming up other people's Macs. There have been a dozen or so Macintosh viruses — little self-duplicating programs that attach themselves to innocent software, whereupon they duplicate some more, until every disk that passes through your floppy-disk drive is infected. You can't get a computer virus unless you (1) swap disks with friends or (2) use a modem to connect to other Macs over the phone.

Once infected, your Mac usually just acts weird: beeps occasionally, slows down, that kind of thing. No widespread Mac virus has ever destroyed files. Nonetheless, that potential exists. Playing on the resulting paranoia, many companies have offered anti-virus programs for sale, cleverly charging you money for an update every time a new virus is discovered. Virex, S.A.M., and Gatekeeper are a few.

My advice is not to spend any money at all on this — instead, get Disinfectant, which is free. It watches over your Mac, tells you if you've contracted a virus, and wipes it out for you. (Disinfectant comes from the usual sources of noncommercial software: your local user group has it, and you can get it from a dial-up on-line service or bulletin board. Or just send a disk to the author; I've provided his address in Appendix B.)

## The Talking Moose and other just goofy stuff

There's no good reason for you to spend any time or money in acquiring these things. It's worth knowing, however, that this computer of yours actually has a decent sense of humor.

The Talking Moose is a hilarious, nearly indescribable little software doodad. It makes a cartoon moose pop up in the corner of the screen every few minutes, utter a sarcastic or silly morsel, and then disappear again. "Let's get a move on," he'll say after a few minutes of boredom. Or "We never go out anymore."

If such silliness piques your interest, you may also want to consider SoundMaster. This one is *shareware* — not sold in any store — and it finally gives you a good use for that microphone of yours. It lets you designate a sound for the Mac to play when it ejects a disk, starts up, shuts down, or does any other conceivable computer action. This means you can jazz up your holiday season with fa-la-las or make the Mac shut down with a parting shot like "Now get some exercise, lardball." The most famous example is making the Mac say *Bleeccchh!* when spitting out a disk, although playing the Looney Tunes theme upon startup isn't too shabby either.

# Top Ten Free or Almost-Free Utility Programs

A moose may be charming, as the producers of *Northern Exposure* will tell you, but it's expensive. Your other Mac utilities don't have to be. Here are ten good ones, all of them shareware. (In case you missed it, you get shareware from a user group, electronic bulletin board, or on-line service like America Online.)

1. *Before Dark.* Hey, look, I'm not ungrateful that the Mac lets you change your background desktop pattern. But jeez, they only give you a few tiny screen dots from which to create your new pattern. Before Dark lets you plaster your desktop with a choice of 30 stunning, 3-D, brilliantly colored background textures and patterns that blow the standard set of Mac patterns out of the proverbial water.

2. *Disinfectant.* As described earlier.

3. *Compact Pro* or *StuffIt Classic.* File-compression programs. Not as convenient — and not nearly as fast — as DiskDoubler, but then again much cheaper.

4. *SoundMaster.* As described earlier — at last your Mac can make yawning sounds and grouchy mumbling when you wake it up in the morning.

5. *System 7 Pack.* When Apple upgraded its system software (i.e., all that junk in the System Folder) to System 7, many Mac owners rejoiced. But a few sighed because System 7 makes things in the Finder slower — things like opening windows and copying files. But System 7 Pack, written by a teenager in New Jersey, takes care of both problems. It makes windows open faster and makes your Mac copy files three times faster.

6. *SCSI Probe.* You power up the Mac, but your hard-drive icon doesn't appear. If you have SCSI Probe (or the nearly identical SCSI Info), you can find out the make, model, capacity, and SCSI address of every SCSI device attached to your Mac, and more. It has a Mount button that can often bring a SCSI device on-line if it's acting flaky. (SCSI is like that.) More about SCSI in Chapter 11.

7. *Save-O-Matic.* The software for the chronic Mac procrastinator: a safety net for people who forget to save their documents regularly. This thing'll do it *for* you, every five minutes or ten minutes or whatever you specify.

8. *Remember?.* It's a desk accessory calendar thingie. You type your appointments into its clean, colorful calendar, and it actually reminds you of each upcoming event. If you want, it presents you with a list of the day's schedule when you turn the computer on in the morning. If anybody cares, I think it's better than most of the high-priced calendar/reminder programs.

9. *Moire.* It's a screen saver, as described above. No, it doesn't have flying toasters or lawnmower guys. But what the heck — it's free, and the patterns it bounces around on the screen are plenty pretty.

10. *Pixel-Flipper.* Do you know how to switch your color monitor to black and white (and back again)? It's a long, boring process: choose Control Panels from the  menu, double-click Monitors, and click Color or Black and White. The whole thing is much easier if you get Pixel-Flipper, which pops a menu up anywhere you click, from which you choose any setting: black and white, color, whatever.

# Part III

## Special Macs for Special People

The 5th Wave     By Rich Tennant

# In this part...

*I*n 1984, you could have any Mac you wanted, as long as it was the beige, hard disk-free, 128K original Mac.

Fifty Mac models later, the line has begun to differentiate itself into peculiar breeds of Mac. A Performa is exactly like a regular Mac, only different. A PowerBook is exactly like a regular Mac, only smaller. The Newton is *nothing* like a regular Mac, but, as a product of Apple, is of acute interest to many a Mac fan.

# Chapter 9
# Yo: It's Da Performa

Apple Computer has never seemed totally content simply to manufacture the greatest computer the world has ever known. No, they feel lonely over there in those rarefied computer stores. They wanna make it big. They want Apple products cropping up in department stores, mail-order catalogs, discount marts . . . it wouldn't surprise me one iota if, a year from now or so, we started seeing a chain of Apple casual-wear shops in America's finer malls.

Anyway, Performas (this chapter) represent one direction the company's plan for world domination is taking. PowerBooks and Newtons are another (next chapter). In any case, I'll be concise in these chapters for two reasons. First, I don't want to bore everybody who *doesn't* own one of these specialty Macs. And second, as my cousin Anne always says, no computer book should weigh more than the machine it purports to describe.

## Principles of Performa

Your Mac is a Performa if: (a) it says Performa on the front; (b) you bought it from an office or appliance store like Sears, The Wiz, Price Club, and so on; and (c) when you say your Mac's name, you sound like Sylvester Stallone trying to say "performer."

Most of this book applies equally well to Performas and non-Performas. This section, however, covers a few items exclusive to this, the Family Mac.

# The Deal

A Performa is actually a great deal. It saves you hassle because you get the complete setup — a Mac, a monitor, a keyboard, and (usually) even a modem — for one fixed price. It saves you money because you get a bunch of ready-to-use software programs already installed. And it saves you headaches because you get a year of *on-site* service. Know what that means? Some guy will actually come to your house to fix the computer for free if something goes wrong! (When, oh when, will electricians and plumbers adopt that policy!?)

Despite all of these yummy freebies, you also get, for the same price, just a little bit ripped off. First of all, you don't get a set of those all-important white System disks to which I've referred about 1,000 times in this book. (More on this topic later.) Second, you don't get the *manuals* for the free software! You're supposed to send in some money (fortunately, not much) if you want the users' guides.

Just wanted to make sure you knew what you were getting into.

# The Launcher

A Mac is, to be sure, a user-friendly computer. It's no longer the *most* user-friendly, though: a Performa is. Its System software (see Chapter 6) has been specially tinkered with to make it even simpler to operate. Case in point: the Launcher.

What the Launcher *is:* a control panel, just like the ones described in Chapter 6. What it *does* is display a winderful wondow — I mean a wonderful window — containing jumbo icons for your programs.

As you know, you normally *double-click* an icon to launch a program. But anything in *this* window opens when you click it *once*. (This is progress, folks.)

You can move, resize, or close the Launcher window just as you would any window (Chapter 1). Once closed, it will reappear if you double-click the little Launcher icon on the desktop (see the next figure).

So who decides which icons appear in the Launcher? You do. Inside your System Folder is a folder called Launcher Items. Any file or folder icon you put in Launcher Items shows up in the Launcher window. (Actually, more typically, you wouldn't put the icon itself into this folder; you'd put an *alias* of that item. See Chapter 8 for info on aliases.)

And who decides whether or not the Launcher window appears when you first turn on the Mac? You again. Open the System Folder; open the Startup Items folder; and drag the Launcher alias outta there. From now on, the Launcher window won't appear until you double-click the Launcher icon on your desktop.

## The Documents folder

For many people, the purchase of a Mac is a primal attempt to get their lives, so full of traffic and turbulent relationships and scraps of paper, into some kind of order.

Little do they know what awaits them on the typical Mac: their important documents get every bit as lost as their paper-based counterparts once did. Even the great Mac gurus of our time have, at one time or another, saved some document created on the Mac — and then found themselves unable to find it again because it got arbitrarily stashed in some hidden folder somewhere.

Enter the Documents folder. See its icon in the following figure? As you work with your Mac and create different documents, the Performa housekeeps for you by storing them *all* in this folder automatically. Every time you use a program's Open or Save command, you're automatically shown the Documents folder's contents.

In theory, you'll never lose anything again; everything you do will always be in one place. (That feature makes backing up your work simple, too; you just copy that one folder, and you know you're covered.)

If this document magnet bothers you, however, just rename the Documents folder. Then you'll have to file your documents in your own folders, just like everybody else.

## Turning it all off

The Launcher is responsible for more Performa characteristics than just the Launcher window. It also creates the Documents folder. It's even responsible for *hiding* one program when you launch another (unlike other Macs, where all windows remain simultaneously on the screen).

To kill off these behaviors, thus de-Performatizing your Mac, choose Control Panels from your  menu. Drag the Launcher control panel clear out of the System Folder — onto the desktop, for example.

Now restart the Mac. From now on: no Documents folder, no program hiding. You *can* still use the Launcher window; double-click that Launcher control panel, wherever it is now (not in the System Folder), and the Launcher window will appear like always.

## Apple Backup

Apple saved itself a precious $7 by failing to give you System disks with your Performa. Instead, the System comes preinstalled on your hard drive, and you're supposed to back it up onto your *own* floppy disks using the Apple Backup program.

Two extremely important points: (1) Do it! Call up Mac Connection (see Appendix B) and order a box of high-density disks. Use them to back up your System Folder as soon as possible.

(2) If your System Folder gets trashed *before* you've made a backup, call the toll-free Apple help line number that came with your Performa. Give them the bad news. Apple will Fed Ex you a free set of System disks. (Methinks they should just include these disks to begin with.)

# All About At Ease

In addition to some cool work software like ClarisWorks, America Online, and so on, your Performa also comes with a fascinating piece of system software: At Ease. (You can also buy it for use on *any* Mac for $60.)

Remember all that talk of folders, windows, and disks that you slogged through in the beginning chapters of this book? It must've made your head spin at first. Now imagine that you're a ten-year-old, and you'll understand why Apple invented At Ease. It's a sweet little program that *covers up* all that stuff you've spent so much time and effort learning: folders, the Trash can, dragging icons around, and list views. In fact, the entire Finder (the desktop) gets hidden when At Ease is running.

In its place, you see something like this:

Click here to see the screenful of document icons.

If there are more than 20 icons, click here
to see the next screenful of them.

What's neat is that, exactly as with the Launcher, you can launch any program
or document with a *single* mouse click, not a double-click. You hear a cool
clicky sound when you click one of these icons.

When you launch a program, the At Ease window itself disappears, only to
reappear when you quit that program. (What's also neat, for those who care, is
that At Ease takes up 200K less memory than the regular Finder desktop, and
that means 200K more memory for your programs to use.)

At Ease is designed for teachers, parents, or trainers who want to hide the
confusing world of folders and icons from beginning Mac fans. It's also good for
*protecting* your regular Mac universe from unwitting (or witting) disrupters.
Because At Ease denies a user access to control panels, the Trash, or moving or
renaming files, your hard drive is safe.

You can switch back and forth from At Ease to the regular Finder by choosing the appropriate command from the File menu (Go to Finder, for example). If you want even *that* escape hatch closed, you can create a password so that only you, The Parent, can escape to the Finder.

# *Make Yourself At Ease*

At Ease is a nice idea if you have kids, students, or visitors of any kind; it provides a lot of simplicity and reassurance if you don't want your normal Mac environment messed with.

Unfortunately, At Ease won't help *you* avoid learning the Mac; you still have to know the Mac just to install and set up At Ease. Here, then, for the sake of Ye Who Must Administer, is a step-by-step guide. (I'm assuming you've already installed At Ease by double-clicking the Installer icon on the At Ease disk, and then restarting the Mac.)

1. From the  menu, choose Control Panels. When the Control Panels window opens, double-click At Ease Setup. This box appears:

2. Click On. Then click Select Items. Now you see this:

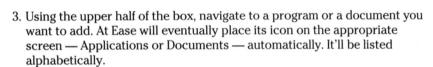

3. Using the upper half of the box, navigate to a program or a document you want to add. At Ease will eventually place its icon on the appropriate screen — Applications or Documents — automatically. It'll be listed alphabetically.

4. Double-click the name of a program or document. You'll see that its *alias* (an italicized reference to the original file) appears in the lower half of the box. These are the icons that will appear when you use At Ease. If you ever feel like going mucking around in your System Folder, you'll find these alias's icons in the At Ease Items folder.

5. When you're finished adding items, click Done. Now restart the Mac . . . you're in business! Remember that to get back to your old world, choose Go to Finder from the File menu.

To turn off At Ease, repeat step 1; but when you get to Step 2, obviously, you should click Off and not On.

To remove At Ease for good, you *must* run the Installer that comes on its original disk. Click Customize, hold down the Option key, and click Remove. Don't just drag the At Ease files to the Trash, or you'll trash your computer and have to write *I will not meddle irresponsibly with my system software* 500 times. (See the At Ease manual for details.)

# Chapter 10
# PowerBooks, Newtons, and You

*A*s the years go by, the size and weight of Mac models bloat and atrophy more wildly than your average lifetime dieter. First, they were small and light (the Mac Plus). Then they got big (the Mac II). Then they got really small (the PowerBook). And then they got really big (the Quadra).

Lately, Apple has made their computers so small that a keyboard won't even fit; you have to write on it with a pen (the Newton). Now, the Newton isn't a Mac. You can't even stick a floppy disk into it. But Mac fans will recognize quite a bit of Mac in this little handheld fellow.

Anyway, this chapter looks at the lighter side of Apple: the PowerBooks and Newtons.

## The PowerBook Survival Guide

It's a little bit mind-blowing when you find out that a tiny PowerBook Duo 230 has more computer horsepower than a Mac IIci. Apple made almost no compromises: the speed, storage capacity, memory, and back-panel jacks on a PowerBook are almost exactly the same as regular Macs — but they're crammed into a book-sized case that weighs four or six pounds and conceals dirt. You can get them with black-and-white, grayscale, or color screens, and usually for less money than you'd pay for a regular Mac (henceforth called a *desktop Mac*).

In fact, working on a PowerBook is so much like working on a desktop Mac that you may forget to make certain allowances. Use these tips to help you get extra mileage out of your machine and its battery.

## Get a case

The PowerBook comes with neither handles nor a carrying case. There are a million cases for sale, designed to carry and protect the PowerBook and accessories; call up one of the mail-order companies like Mac Connection. Almost all of them are tough, attractive, and beautifully designed (the cases, I mean, not the mail-order companies). A company called Magenta Seven makes a really neat one; they also sell a lightly padded slipcover with handles, for people who don't need a full-fledged case because they carry the PowerBook in a briefcase.

## Power options

There are all kinds of ways to milk more juice out of your PowerBook battery; they're outlined in the Top Ten list at the end of this chapter.

In the meantime, consider buying a power accessory or two. Car (or boat) cigarette lighter adapters for the PowerBook are available from Lind or Empire Engineering. If you look in the pages of *Macworld* magazine, you'll also find an absurd number of carry-along, external superbatteries for sale that keep your PowerBook kicking for eight hours or more (compared with the regular battery's two). Keep that in mind the next time you have to fly to Europe.

My favorite alternative-power product, though, is a second regular PowerBook bat tery. Not very innovative, I know, but you really get your $60 worth from the thing.

## When trouble strikes

One of the best things you bought with your PowerBook was Apple's emergency-repair program. For the first year, you can call Apple at 800-SOS-APPL, wherever you are. They'll send a messenger to pick up your sick PowerBook, repair it in one day, and overnight it back to you — all at *no charge*. Ladies and gentlemen — an American bureaucratic program that really works.

Before you dial, though, you may as well know ahead of time that burned-out *pixels* (the tiny square dots of your screen) may not qualify as broken. Apple says that up to five burned-out pixels (on a PowerBook 170 or 180 or Duo 250) are within its definition of "not really broken."

Yeah, well, I bet *their* PowerBooks don't have burned-out pixels.

## Keeping an eye on juice

Mac insiders have known for years about SuperClock!, an ingenious control panel that puts a digital time readout in the upper-right corner of your screen, like this:

When you install it on a PowerBook, though, a funny thing happens: you also get a battery "fuel gauge" so that you can keep an eye on your battery life:

A solid black battery indicates a full charge; as the battery juice runs out, the blackness empties out of the little battery icon. (You get SuperClock! wherever fine shareware is sold: on electronic bulletin boards or from a local user group.)

Alternatively, of course, you can just leave the Battery desk accessory open on the screen in a convenient place.

## Those darned X-ray machines

Some people claim that airport security X-ray machines are bad for your Power-Book. Others claim that X-rays can't hurt electronics. The first group replies that, "It's not the X-rays, it's the magnetic fields in the conveyer-belt mechanism." So the second group, getting annoyed, replies that they *always* put their PowerBooks through the machine and have never had a problem. The first group, claiming it's better to be safe than sorry, rebuts that it's no big deal to turn the machine on for inspection (which is the alternative to running it through the machine) and throws a spitball at the second group.

Finally, both groups agree to disagree and start swapping tips on maximizing battery life.

## Walking during sleep

Then a few minutes later, they start arguing again. Some people will tell you that you should never transport the PowerBook when it's in Sleep mode. They point to the Apple manual, which does indeed tell you to fully Shut Down your PowerBook before moving it. The other group scoffs and tells you that they carry their machines around all the time while asleep (the machines, not the owners) with no problems.

**Sleep Mode:** *A low-power condition for a Macintosh laptop. Very similar to Off, actually, except that the contents of memory are preserved. When you wake up the computer (by touching a key), you're right where you left off, complete with programs and documents open.*

The first group insists that you'd better let sleeping-laptops lie, elaborating on Apple's concern — that you might really bump the heck out of the PowerBook, enough that a key gets pressed, which will wake up the computer, which will start the hard disk spinning, which puts your data at risk of another bump. The living-dangerously group kicks sand in the faces of the conservative group, jeering that such a sequence of events is incredibly unlikely and insisting that it's OK to carry the thing around, as long as you don't dribble it like a basketball. And they finally whip out a memo from Apple conceding that, well, OK, they (Apple) were being a little overcautious, and that it's fine to carry the thing asleep after all.

## Insta-Printer

You can get a fax/modem as an optional accessory for any PowerBook. (Global Village and PSI make superior fax/modems for the PowerBook.)

*That's* not the tip, though. The tip is that if you have a built-in fax/modem, you really don't need to lug along a printer (even if you did have the money to spend on a portable Diconix printer). Instead, just fax the document you want to print *to yourself,* using a fax machine at the airport or hotel to receive the fax you're sending from the laptop. Ingenious, eh?

## Preventing your battery from bursting into flame

If you carry an extra PowerBook battery with you, keep it in a baggie. (Or, if a plastic battery case didn't come with your PowerBook, call Apple and get your free one.) Otherwise, it's theoretically possible for a paper clip or a coin to create a short circuit between the battery terminals, starting a fire.

And, as we all know, it's impolite to smoke in public.

## Sittin' on the dock

If you bought a PowerBook Duo, you must've turned this four-pound beauty over and over in your hands, mystified as to where you're supposed to plug stuff in. There's no place to hook up a monitor; no SCSI connector for plugging in another hard drive; there isn't even a floppy-disk drive!

Then again, you don't *need* any of those items when you're sitting on the airplane typing, and that's exactly what Apple discovered. That's why there's the Duo Dock — a housing that sits on your desk at home, which has expansion slots, a floppy drive, and every connector you can think of. The MiniDock is a more portable, less full-fledged piece of gear that only adds the jacks and a monitor connector.

Into the big Dock or the MiniDock you can plug in a big-screen monitor, a regular keyboard, and a mouse. So when you come home from your trip with the PowerBook Duo, you slide the laptop into its dock. It gets slurped into the Duo Dock like a videocassette, or it clips firmly onto the MiniDock, and presto: you've just handed all your data — and the Duo's brain — to the machine on your desk, so you can now work merrily away as though it wasn't a laptop at all. Pretty cool.

Oh, and by the way, there *is* one jack on the Duo itself. (You have to flip down one of the Duo's little legs to see it.) You can plug *either* a printer *or* a modem into it — precisely the two items you'd need most on the road.

## *When you get desperate*

Now look, I don't want to get angry letters from spouses and significant others, blaming me for converting their beloveds into hermitic power nerds. What I'm about to tell you should be socked away in the back of your mind, only for emergencies.

It's about airplanes and airports. We all know that PowerBooks and airplanes were made for each other. But what you may not know is what to do when the dreaded "Your screen has been dimmed" message pops up, warning you that you only have a few minutes of battery power remaining, and you're in the middle of a brilliant brainstorm.

First of all, I happen to know that there are publicly available power outlets at every gate of every airport (and bus and train station, too). They're there, actually, for the benefit of the cleaning staff's vacuums, and as such they're sometimes concealed on the side of a pillar. And I happen to know that they're *never* convenient to a seat, so if your Mac habit is stronger than your pride, you're going to have to sit on the floor.

I also know what to do when you run out of juice *on the plane.* Yes, that's right: I'm going to call to your attention the electric razor outlet in the bathroom of almost every plane in America. You feel like an absolute idiot, of course, wedged in there on that toilet with your adapter cord snaking up to the plug above the doll-sized sink, while your laptop recharges.

That's what I've been *told,* anyway. Naturally, *I* would never do anything that pathetic.

# Newton: Not Just Figs Anymore

Now, I'm only 30 years old, but I'm old enough to remember when *PDA* stood for public display of affection.

Not anymore. PDA, according to Apple, stands for personal digital assistant — a new class of yuppie appliances, of which the Newton is the first. The Newton, Apple's newest computer line, is a handheld thing, about the size of a 4 x 6 index card. You use it for taking notes, dialing the phone, and scheduling your day. It can print, send faxes (if you buy the plug-in fax/modem), and beam information via infrared to other Newtons. And it's *really* good for meeting people. "Hey, baby. Wanna write on my PDA?"

## How to make the Newton understand

The Newton is much too small to have a keyboard. So you're supposed to use the inkless pen to *write* on its screen (which covers practically the entire thing). The Newton translates your handwriting into neat, typed text.

Well, more or less. Everybody's got their favorite Newton stories. How it interprets your handwritten "testing, testing, one two three" into "nestling, termites, one twin choo." How it won't put the hyphen into phone numbers. Well, this isn't *Newtons For Dummies,* but here are a few tips from a war-torn Newtonian.

TIP

## A Newton guide for people who like surprises

Not everything the Newton does is spelled out in its video, its Getting Started tour, and its little manual. Here are three undocumented goodies for you to play with during your next helpless eight-hour layover in a boring airport.

Surprise #1: First, hold the pen tip steadily on the clock icon at the bottom-left of the Note Pad screen. You'll see the internal temperature of the Netwon! (No, they *didn't* put a thermometer into the Newton just for the sake of this little gag. The thermometer is there for the purpose of adjusting the screen contrast automatically depending on the heat.)

Surprise #2: On the Note Pad screen, write *About Newton.* Then tap the Assist button at the bottom of the screen. Hey—who are all these crazy people!? And why do they have such funny handwriting!?

But #3 is the best: Tap the Find button at the bottom of the screen. Write *Elvis.* (Then you'll have to correct the Newton's guess because *Elvis* isn't in its dictionary!) Now tap All. The Newton will tell you — and show you on the Map — where the King was last seen!

As in any intimate relationship, your partner, the Newton, requires some time to get to know your quirks — and vice versa. I tell people not even to bother assessing how they like the thing until they've spent at least three days with it. During that time, the Newt (as the insiders call it) will get better and better at translating your handwriting.

There are two mechanisms by which it learns. First, there's the handwriting game that comes on the Getting Started card. Play that game a *lot*. Don't worry if the boss catches you playing it on company time; this time, you can explain honestly that this is an important part of getting to be productive on the Newt.

The second way the Newton improves is by studying the ways in which you correct it. Watch it, though: There are *three* ways to correct a word, and only *one* of them actually teaches the Newt to improve for next time. (1) You can tap the Undo button and rewrite the word. (2) You can correct individual *letters* of the word by writing over them. (3) You can double-tap the word and correct it using the little on-screen keyboard. This last method is the *only* one that will help the Newton's recognizing capabilities improve.

## *Get extra mileage from Extras*

The Newton, as you'll rapidly discover, has a lot in common with a Mac, but it's quite a bit different, too. For example, you know those little "dialog boxes" that appear on the screen when you tap the Extras button? Interestingly, unlike Mac dialog boxes, you don't have to put these screens away before proceeding with your work! You can leave them floating right there on the screen.

I mention this not to impose my natural affinity for clutter upon the rest of the world, but to suggest a tip. If you tap Extras and then tap Styles, you get a floating palette of text styles: Bold, Underline, Simple, Fancy, and various sizes. My suggestion: If you have to do much text formatting, *leave* this miniwindow open on the screen. Go ahead and close the larger Extras screen, if you want, and reposition the Styles box by dragging its edge; but now you can go ahead and highlight pieces of text, immediately change the style, and highlight the next piece of text, all without closing the Styles box on the screen. Shoot, this is better than menus!

Another Extras tip: Don't overlook those fabulous Formulas screens. (Tap Extras, and then tap Formulas.) One of the most useful is Currency Exchange. It works a little strangely: you tap the little hollow dot next to the line you want the *Newton* to compute. Then you fill in the other two. For example, darken the Currency 2 dot; then fill in the dollar amount as Currency 1, and the rate of exchange to francs as the Exchange Rate. Instantly, Newton does the math.

Quit yawning. This is leading up to something truly practical. Here's Pogue's Ultimate Restaurant Trick: Write in 1.15 as the Exchange Rate. Now, when you write into Currency 1 the food total from your restaurant check, you instantly get the total including a 15% tip! All done with minimum effort and (with the possible exception of pulling a $700 appliance out of your pocket) with maximum subtlety and discretion.

## All kinds of things to plug in

Just so you know, Apple will be delighted to help you achieve any of the following, if you're prepared to spend a few more bucks.

- **Send faxes:** Just buy the fax/modem card.

- **Transfer your Newton information to a Mac:** Just buy the Newton Connection Kit. It comes with Mac programs that precisely duplicate the "programs" on the Newton so that you can keep your Rolodex list up to date using either the Mac or the Newton, for example.

- **Receive pages:** If you can't stand to be out of touch, you can buy a paging card that makes your Newton act like a pocket pager. You dial up a special number to receive the messages of people who've tried to call you (or you can get the Newton to display their phone numbers). Do me a favor, though, *please* don't get one of these and then sit behind me in the movie theatre, OK?

- **Play games:** All kinds of new programs, including games, are available for the Newton. Like all add-on Newton software, they come on cards that go into the little Newton slot at the top of the machine.

- **Add memory:** If you've added so many names and numbers that your Newton's memory is almost stuffed full, you can buy a card that expands its memory.

Trouble with these add-on cards, of course, is that the Newton MessagePad only has *one* card slot. So you can't have a pager card *and* more memory. You can't have a game card *and* the fax/modem. And so on. That, I guess, is why Apple's working on a two-card Newton.

# Top Ten Tips for Maximizing PowerBook Battery Power

Many new PowerBook owners are devastated to find that, instead of getting "two to three" hours of life out of each freshly charged battery, they only get 90 minutes or so. These excellent tricks will solve that problem in a hurry.

1. The backlighting for the screen uses up *half* of the power. The more you turn it down, the longer your battery will last.

2. I've actually overheard PowerBook owners asking the airline gate agent for a seat not merely next to a window but on a particular *side* of the plane, and now I know why. They want to be where the sun will be shining. Bright sunlight is enough to illuminate a PowerBook screen, so you can turn the backlighting all the way off.

3. As you go through life with your PowerBook (model 140 through 180), repeated partial chargings of your nickel-cadmium battery gradually decrease its potential life. The problem is called the *memory effect* (camcorder batteries do this, too), and it results from not allowing the battery to fully discharge before recharging begins.

   To restore the battery to its good-as-new, virginal, strong-as-ever condition, deliberately let it run down to the ground. That's right, just keep your PowerBook on, not letting it sleep, and click OK every time a message appears telling you that the battery is running down. At the very end, the Mac will literally tell you "Good night," and it will put itself to sleep. You've now drained the battery — and undone the memory effect — and it's now OK to plug the adapter in to charge it.

   When the battery is finally restored, it should last much longer. Do this routine once a month.

4. If you want to get serious about tip #3, you can actually buy a device that performs that whole sequence automatically. It's called a Battery Reconditioner/Charger, and it's made by Lind. It plugs into the wall; you put your battery into it, and it deep-empties the battery and then safely refills it to full. The whole cycle takes over seven hours, but the company claims that it rejuvenates the battery even more than the process described in tip #3 does. (Lind also makes a charger for the PowerBook 100 battery, which is a lead-acid battery, and thus doesn't suffer from the memory effect.)

5. When you want to make sure your battery is as full as it can be, allow all day for it to recharge — and don't trust the Battery desk accessory fuel gauge. You see, the PowerBook battery gets charged 80 percent full in only two hours or so. At that point, the Battery gauge will tell you that it's full. But to charge the battery fully — to charge that extra 20 percent — it takes another *five or six hours* of what they call "trickle charging." (This isn't true of Duo, whose battery charges fully in two hours.)

6. Turn off AppleTalk! This incredible power drain will sap a half hour of life from your battery. To do so, choose Chooser from your Apple menu. In the lower-right corner, make sure that AppleTalk Inactive is selected.

7. If you're not going to use the machine, even for a couple of minutes, put it to sleep by choosing Sleep from the Special menu.

8. If you have any PowerBook numbered 160 or higher, open the PowerBook control panel and click the Options button. You'll be presented with two battery-saving options: Processor Cycling and Processor Speed. These options slow down the Mac's brain, but they do eke out a few more precious minutes of battery juice per charge.

9. If your PowerBook has a built-in modem, quit your modem software promptly when you're finished telecommunicating. Otherwise, as long as that modem program is open, the Mac is sending precious juice to that modem.

10. The other major drain to your battery is hard disk usage. Whenever you hear that darned disk spinning, it's like voltage down the drain.

    The only way to completely avoid using the hard disk is to transfer *everything* you'll be working on into memory. If everything's in memory, the Mac never needs to wake up the hard disk, and your PowerBook can run happily for hours and hours. (I've heard people say they get five hours from a charge this way.)

    If you have 6MB of RAM or more in your little gray marvel, read on.

    In order to fit everything into memory, you need to create a *RAM disk* — a portion of memory that the Mac believes to be a big floppy disk. A RAM disk even shows up on the screen as a floppy disk icon. But anything you drag onto its icon is copied into memory, and stays there.

    To create a RAM disk on your PowerBook, choose Control Panels from the Apple menu, and double-click Memory. This window opens:

Click On...    ...and then use this slider to
change the size of the RAM disk.

Click On, as shown, and then drag the slider until the "RAM Disk Size" number is large enough to contain (1) your System Folder, (2) your program, and (3) your document. This can become a game of mental Twister if you're not careful — even though you're going to be putting these items into *memory,* the size you're worried about is *not* how much memory they need to run. You're worried about how much *disk space* they take up at the moment.

You're not going to be able to pull this off at all, unless you strip down your System Folder. If I were you, I'd start with the absolutely minuscule System Folder on the Disk Tools disk that came with your PowerBook — with only a single font and no desk accessories, it only takes up 1.2MB of disk space. Be sure it includes the Enabler File (see Chapter 6) your PowerBook needs to run. (I doubt you'll survive for very long with only Geneva 9-point type, though, so feel free to add another font or two.)

After you've prepared this mini System Folder, carry it on a floppy disk with your PowerBook. Now here's how it all works.

Set up the RAM disk, as described above. Restart the computer by choosing Restart from the Special menu. When the Mac comes alive again, you'll see the RAM disk on the screen:

Onto this imaginary disk, copy your stripped-down System Folder, the program you'll be using, and the document you'll be using. After that's done, choose Control Panels from the Apple menu and double-click Startup Disk; in the window that appears, select RAM Disk. Restart the PowerBook.

If all has gone well, the Mac will now use the RAM Disk as the startup disk and heed the instructions in *its* System Folder instead of the one on the hard disk. If you now double-click the program on the RAM Disk and use its Open command to open your *document* on the RAM Disk, you've successfully created a completely memory-based workstation. The Mac will *never* need the hard disk, and will thus never waste any battery power making it spin.

When you save your work, you'll be saving changes to the document on the RAM Disk — which isn't, of course, a disk at all. In other words, you'll be making changes in memory and *saving* them into another part of memory!

If this were happening on any normal Mac, you'd be scolded for attempting anything so foolish. After all, what if your system crashes? Then every-thing in memory — including the document you've been working on — vanishes forever, right? Aren't you out of your mind to save a document into RAM?

On a PowerBook, no, because the contents of its memory are preserved, even if you put the machine to sleep, and even if you restart the machine. (*Restart,* friends, *not* Shut Down. If you Shut Down, you *will* lose the contents of the RAM disk.) So if you do have a system crash, don't do anything rash, and *don't shut off the computer by pushing the On/Off button.* Instead, take a pencil or a straightened paper clip, and carefully push it into the tiny hole on the back of the machine — the Restart switch, which is marked by a little left-pointing triangle. The machine will restart, once again using the System Folder on the RAM Disk, and there you'll find your document, safe and sound.

# Part IV
# Becoming Your Own Guru

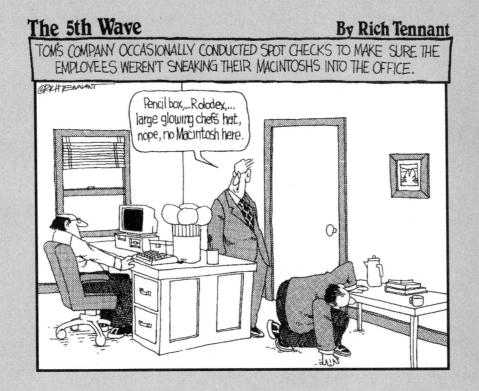

## In this part...

Now it's time to take the bull by the horns, the sword by the hilt, the fish by the gills, and really take off. First, I bestow unto you Chapter 11, the Mother of All Troubleshooting Sections. And then you'll find out where to go from there, with your trusty Mac ever by your side.

# Chapter 11
# When Bad Things Happen to Good Machines

## Introduction to Computer Hell

As a new computer owner, it probably doesn't cheer you up very much that this troubleshooting guide is the fattest part of the book.

But let's face it: Computers are appliances — and, as such, they have minds of their own. And, like other expensive appliances (cars, homes, pacemakers), they tend to get cranky at the worst possible times.

Fortunately, several million Mac users have been this way before, and they've uncovered the most common glitches already; you'll find them, and their solutions, explained here. Again fortunately, most computer problems cost you nothing but time.

Some computer glitches also cost you some data (that is, your work). Well, you've been told to floss if you want to keep your teeth; I'm telling you to back up your work if you want to keep your data, job, and sanity. Saving your work frequently and making backup copies minimizes the number of midnight sobbing sessions you'll have when your important projects vanish into what's left of the ozone.

# The three most common causes of computer problems

A guy once called a software company in a panic. "Help!" he told the help-line woman. "Your program made my monitor go out!"

The woman tried to soothe him. "Don't worry," she said. "A cable probably came loose. Why don't you look in back of the computer to see if everything's connected?"

The guy replied, "How can I look back there? It's too dark — the power in my building is out!"

That story is a tactful, nonthreatening way of introducing one very common cause of computer glitches: operator error. Nothing's actually *broken,* but there's something simple that you, the operator, may have overlooked. Be sure to read the "Top Ten Beginner Troubles," later in this chapter.

Another common cause of computer troubles arises when you attach other equipment (or peripherals, as the Mac intelligentsia call them) to the back of the Mac. Be sure to read "Scuzzy SCSI" for some chilling truths on this topic.

By far the most common and frustrating computer problem, though, is caused by software bugs. Writing a software program that works with every Mac model, under every circumstance, and is compatible with all *other* programs, is spectacularly difficult. It's like trying to work out the seating for a 100-guest dinner party, where no two people of different political, dietary, or hygiene habits can be seated together — and everyone, incidentally, happens to be schizophrenic. There are just too many variables; and in the computer world, everything changes all the time.

**System crash:** *The Mac suddenly stops working, usually displaying a picture of a short-fused bomb accompanied by the not-very-comforting words "Sorry, a system error has occurred."*

**System freeze:** *The cursor freezes in place on the screen and neither the mouse nor the keyboard works, but no error message appears.*

Therefore, even when Silicon Proboscis Software thinks it's ironed out every single bug in its nose-imaging plastic surgery program, *you* may have trouble with it because there's something on *your* hard disk that's incompatible with that program. The result may be a system crash, a freeze, or something equally horrifying.

# *Shooting your own troubles*

**Extension:** *In this context, a System extension is a little miniprogram that you drop into the System Folder. It adds some feature to the Mac — one that automatically dims your screen after a few minutes of idleness, adds a little clock to your menu bar, and so on. Called inits by the old-timers.*

Therefore, what I'd *really* like to teach you is how to be your *own* Mac guru: how to ferret out the cause of a problem yourself.

There are only a certain number of ways a person can set up a Mac. The elements are what model it is; how much memory it has; what printer it's connected to; what *extensions* and control panels are in its System Folder; what order you take steps in; what program you're using; and how everything's wired together.

When something doesn't work, then the object is to try changing *one* of those variables and repeating whatever-it-is-that-didn't-work.

Here are a couple of typical examples.

Walter, a New Jersey tollbooth operator, tries to print out a picture he made of a Maserati flying off the highway at high speed — but nothing comes out of the printer. Flicking his earlobe, he wonders whether it's the *printer* that's not working or the *program*. To find out, he goes to his word processor, types TESTING TESTING and prints *that*. It works. Now he knows that the printer works fine — the problem is related to the drawing program. Next, he successfully prints a different document from the same drawing program, and thus learns that the problem is with his Maserati *document*, not the drawing program in general.

Or Nina, the political figurehead for an emerging third-world nation, is given an expensive fax/modem as a bribe by a company that wants to strip-mine for sulfur. She hooks it up, drops the necessary software (an extension) into her System Folder, and tries to send a fax — but the mouse freezes, unmovable, on the screen. Calmly, she wonders what's unusual about her particular Macintosh that would cause a popular gizmo to malfunction. She opens the Extensions folder and removes all the extensions that didn't originally come with her Mac: a screen saver, a spelling checker, and Adobe Type Manager. She restarts the Mac, and this time the fax/modem works beautifully. She correctly assumes that the fax/modem's extension has a *conflict* with one of her other extensions; with a little experimentation, she is able to figure out which one, and the desecration of her country's natural resources proceeds unhindered.

**Extensions folder:** *A special folder inside the System Folder that houses System extensions. In fact, if you drop an extension's icon on top of the System Folder icon, the Mac will replace it in the Extensions folder automatically.*

Do you see the connection between Walter and Nina? Each became a Mac sleuth, changing one variable at a time, until the problem was cornered. Neither one knew *what,* technologically speaking, the problem was. But both figured out *where* the problem was, and that's the first step to working around it and getting on with your life.

Here, then, is a chapter full of typical snafus encountered by typical Mac users. If you never need to refer to this section, the gods smile on you; read it anyway, to find out how lucky you really are.

# *The Top Ten Beginner Troubles (That Don't Actually Need Shooting)*

If you've read this book to this point, a couple of these troubles will seem obvious. But believe me, I've seen these typical troubles zap the confidence of many a first-timer.

1. *The screen is all gray, there's no window open, you can't find any files or folders, but the Trash can is in the corner.*

   If you want a window to appear, you have to open a disk icon. In the upper-right corner of your screen, there's an icon representing a disk. Point to it and double-click the mouse button to make it open into a window.

2. *You try to work, but nothing happens except beeping. Every time you click the mouse button, there's another beep.*

   When the Mac requests some information from you, it displays a *dialog box* — a box with some questions for you to answer. This one, for example, appears when you try to print:

   ```
   ┌────────────────────────────────────────────────────────────┐
   │ LaserWriter  "Silentwriter 95"            7.1.1   │ Print  │
   │ Copies: 1          Pages: ◉ All  ○ From:     To:    │ Cancel │
   │ Cover Page:    ◉ No ○ First Page  ○ Last Page              │
   │ Paper Source: ◉ Paper Cassette  ○ Manual Feed             │
   │ Print:        ○ Black & White   ◉ Color/Grayscale         │
   │ Destination:  ◉ Printer         ○ PostScript® File        │
   └────────────────────────────────────────────────────────────┘
   ```

   What's not very nice about dialog boxes, though, is that they commandeer your Mac. You're not allowed to do *anything* until you answer the questions and get rid of the box. If you try to keep working, the Mac will keep beeping at you, and the box will sit on your screen until doomsday.

Every dialog box, therefore, has a button you can click to make the box go away. Usually you can choose a button that says OK or one that says Cancel. (In the figure, the buttons say Print and Cancel.) Anyway, you have to click one of those buttons before the Mac will return control to you.

3. *You double-click an icon, but you get an irritating message that says "Application not found" (or something equally unhelpful).*

This is a confounding one for beginning users. As it happens, it's also a confounding one for *experienced* users. So I'll refer you, at this point, to the same item in the section called "Error Messages."

4. *A whole document window just disappears.*

Every now and then — and this happens even to the greats — you'll be trying to do something with the mouse, when suddenly your entire spreadsheet (or manuscript or artwork) vanishes, and you find yourself in the Finder. No message appears — no "Save changes?" no "System error," nada.

What's probably happened is that, in the process of clicking the mouse, you accidentally clicked *outside* your document window. Of course, clicking a window (or outside a window) is the universal Mac signal that you want to bring some *other* open program to the front.

If your arrow's aim misses the document window (usually when you're trying to use a scroll bar, as shown below), you're most likely to click the gray background — the Finder.

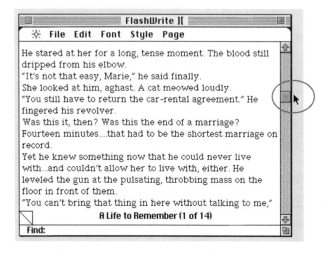

The Finder promptly jumps to the front, showing your folders and files, and the document you were working on gets shoved into the background. (All together now: "It's a feature, not a bug.")

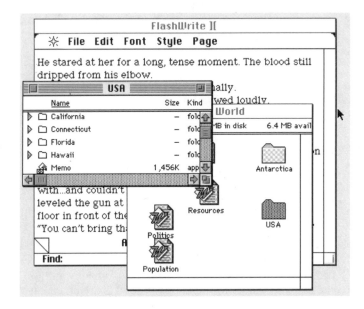

Now you know why, in the Performa Macs, Apple decided to make the Finder get hidden automatically whenever you launch a program.

To bring it back, choose the name of the program you were in from the Application menu.

5. *There's a pile of stuff next to the Trash can.*

All the Mac books and manuals tell you how you chuck a file you no longer want: drag its icon "to the Trash," meaning the Trash can icon in the lower-right corner of your screen.

What's usually *not* made absolutely clear is that, as you drag the icon to the Trash can, you have to place the *tip* of the arrow cursor directly *on* the Trash can icon. You have to see the Trash can itself turn black.

That may seem awkward, especially if you're dragging a whole group of icons at once. For example, in the illustration below at left, one of the icons being dragged is already bumping up against the edge of the screen.

You have to ignore that, though, and keep on moving the mouse until the arrow is directly on the Trash can (above right).

6. *You're word processing, and suddenly all your text disappears.*

There are two possibilities, neither of which means you've really lost your text.

First of all, not everyone is aware that, when you fill up a screenful of text, a word processor automatically shoves that screenful upward off the top of your screen, in effect advancing you to the next clean sheet of paper. This diagram shows how the first page of text has scrolled off the top of the window:

As she slipped out of the silky almost-nothing she'd been

wearing, her shiny chestnut hair cascaded down across her

creamy shoulders.

"What you *don't* know about me, Arthur," she cooed, "is

that I'm not a woman at all."

An odor of electrical smoke touched his nostrils, and he

looked in horror as her graceful, womanly fingers—the very

fingers he'd kissed only moments before—grappled with a

seam near her collarbone. His breath quickened. A clock

ticked. Somewhere, in the distance, a wolf howled.

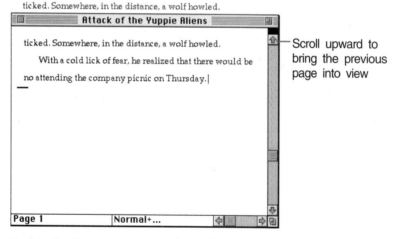

Scroll upward to bring the previous page into view

But suppose you *do* know all about scroll bars and scrolling. And you scroll, and you decide that your text really *has* disappeared.

You may well be the victim of another not-immediately-obvious Mac "feature": that any highlighted text, from a single letter to a 4,000-page encyclopedia, is *instantly replaced* by the next keystroke you type. Usually this is handy. For example, if you want to replace the word "kickback" with the words "incentive payment," you don't have to *delete* the word "kickback" first. You just select it (below, top) and then type (below, bottom):

to accept the occasional kickback of
to accept the occasional incentive payment of

The danger is that, if you've inadvertently (or advertently) selected a bunch of text, and you touch any key — the spacebar, Return key, or any letter — you'll replace everything you've selected with a space, a Return, or a letter.

If this happens, the solution is easy: choose Undo from the Edit menu.

If it's too late for Undo — in other words, if you've done something else *since* deleting the text (because Undo only undoes the *most* recent thing you do) — you may be able to recover some of your text. Close your document *without* saving changes. Reopen it. At least you'll see as much text as was there the last time you saved your work.

7. *There's a thin horizontal line all the way across your color monitor.*

Believe it or not, *all* Apple 13-inch and 16-inch color monitors show this faint line (it's about a third of the way up the screen). It's a shadow cast by a wire inside. Just grit your teeth and remember: "It's a Sony." (Sony makes these monitors.)

8. *You drag a file into a window, and it disappears.*

Once again, you have to watch your tip, if you'll excuse the expression. When you drag an icon, it's the cursor arrow's *tip* that actually marks where the icon is going, *not* the icon itself. What probably happened is that you accidentally released the icon when the arrow tip was on top of a *folder* within the window, as shown here:

---

## A word to writers

If you're a writer, or anybody who plans to do a lot of typing, there's a way to protect yourself against *any* of the text-loss problems described above. Even if you (1) experience a system crash before you've had a chance to save your work, or (2) accidentally replace all your text, or (3) *deliberately* delete some text, but then later wish you hadn't, there's a little piece of software that can save you. It's called Last Resort, and it lurks in the background of your Mac, silently logging everything you type into a text file. You never see it, never notice it — *but,* if the unmentionable happens, you can open the Last Resort text file and recover everything you've typed (ever since you installed Last Resort, in fact). See the Resource Resource for info. (Thunder 7 and Now Utilities have similar features.)

As a result, the Mac dropped the file *into* the folder, making it disappear from the screen.

9. *You can't print.*

   There's a delightfully thorough discussion of printing problems later in this chapter.

10. *You become addicted to working with your Macintosh. The image of the Trash can gets burned into your corneas. Friends, family, and job seem to recede and eventually go away.*

    Congratulations! You've graduated from this book.

# Error Messages

Let's start the Troubleshooting session in earnest with a few good old American Error messages. Yes, kids, these are the '90s equivalent of "DOES NOT COMPUTE." These are messages, appearing in an *alert box* like the fictional one shown below, that indicate something's wrong.

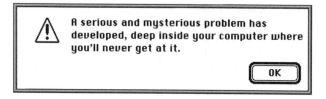

Note that these aren't the same as *System errors,* which are described later; a System error box shows a bomb with a short fuse and indicates a much graver problem.

## *"Application is busy or missing." or "Application not found."*

I promised to return to this one: here we go.

***First resort:*** Not everything in the Mac world is meant to be a plaything for you. The Mac reserves a few files for its own use. If it came with your Mac — like the Scrapbook file, the Clipboard file, and so on — then you at least get *someplace* when you double-click an icon: the Clipboard file opens up into a window where you can see the most recent stuff you copied; the Note Pad file automatically launches the Note Pad desk accessory; and extensions or control panels at least identify themselves (with a message on the screen, like "System Extension: This file adds functionality to your Macintosh").

**Preferences folder:** *One of the special folders inside your System Folder. It contains private data files that are used exclusively by other programs, and are not meant for you to mess with.*

But if you double-click a file belonging to non-Apple software — like any file in the Preferences folder, for example, or various other support files for non-Apple stuff — you'll just get a beep and an unhelpful error message.

That's what's going on *most* of the time.

***Second resort:*** Every now and then, though, you'll double-click a file that you yourself created, and *still* you get the "Application not found" message. Refer back to Chapter 3, where you learned about programs and the documents they produce (like parents and children). In this case, you're trying to open a document (child), but the Mac can't find its parent (the program used to create it). So if you double-click a Word document, but the Word program itself isn't on your hard disk, then the Mac will shrug its shoulders and tell you, in effect, "Yo — how am I s'posed to open this?" To remedy the situation, copy the application program back onto the hard disk.

***Third resort:*** Sometimes you may get the "Application not found" message *even* if (1) you're positive it's not a System file that you can't open, and (2) you're sure that the document's parent program is on the disk. (You double-click a Word document, and you're told that the application — Word — can't be found, even though it's *sitting right there* on the disk in plain sight!)

In a situation like this, the Mac's genealogical gnomes have become confused: the computer has lost track of which program is associated with which kinds of documents. Don't ask me how such confusions happen: just rejoice that it's an easy problem to fix. In the words of Mac gurus everywhere, "You gotta rebuild the Desktop."

Now then. Before you grope for your woodworking tools, let's analyze this concept of rebuilding the Desktop. The Desktop referred to is a very important file on your disk. So how come you've never seen it? Because the Desktop file is *invisible.* (Yes, Mac icons can be invisible. Remember that if you ever get involved in antiterrorist espionage activity.) It's something the Mac maintains for its own use.

In the Desktop file, the Mac stores two kinds of information: First, it stores the actual pictures used as icons for all your files; second, it stores information about the parent-child (program-document) relationships you're having trouble with.

If the Desktop file becomes confused (which results in the "not found" message), you have to reset it. You have to brainwash it, forcing it to unlearn the misconceptions that are giving you trouble, and relearn the correct relationships between documents and the programs that gave birth to them. See the "Rebuilding the Desktop file" sidebar for instructions.

---

## Rebuilding the Desktop file

Restart the computer (choose Restart from the Special menu). As it starts gearing up to turn on again, press and *hold* the Option and ⌘ keys. Don't let go. Keep them down until the Mac explicitly asks you if you want to "rebuild the Desktop." (Obviously, you should click OK.)

After that's done, your document double-clicking will work if, in fact, the parent program is on the disk. And your Mac, having been cleansed of all obsolete icon pictures, will also run faster and more smoothly.

---

**Last resort:** There's one more circumstance when you'll get this message: if you try to open a generic text or graphics file that's not associated with *any* particular program.

(Sigh.) Yes, I know, this contradicts everything you've learned about programs and documents being like parents and children. But suppose that somebody wants to give you a memo she has written, yet she is not sure which brand of word processor you own. The smart thing would be to give you the memo in *text-only* format: a generic, no-frills, raw-typing format. A text file. Or, as the weenies say, an *ASCII* (pronounced ASKie) text file. No matter which program was used to create this file, *any* word processor (even on non-Mac computers, for that matter) can open it.

However, a text file isn't double-clickable. (Actually, in System 7, the Mac will offer to open it with TeachText, but let's just pretend I have a point here.) To read it, you launch your word processor *first*. Then use the Open command in the File menu. The usual list box appears, and you'll see the text file listed there. Double-click to open it.

The same applies to generic picture documents, too; the weenie-word here is *PICT* files. If you try to double-click a generic PICT file, you'll be told (yawn), "Application not found." Once again, the solution is to launch your graphics program (like MacDraw) *first* and then open the PICT file via the Open command.

## *"There is not enough memory to open Word."*

This is a biggie. It gets a section all by itself; see "Out of Memory."

## *"The application has unexpectedly quit."*

You're probably out of memory. Once more, see "Out of Memory."

However, even if your Mac has plenty of memory, the individual *program* that just "unexpectedly quit" may not have enough memory allotted to it. See the sidebar called "Memory tactics" on page 272 to find out how to give your program a more generous helping of memory.

## *"The disk is full."*

This means the disk is full. It happens to the best of us: Over time, your hard disk gets fuller and fuller. Then, with only a megabyte of storage space to go, you try to do something (like saving an important file), and you're told there's no more elbow room.

**Application menu:** *The menu in the upper-right corner of all System 7-equipped Macs, which you use to move from one open program to another.*

You'll have to make some more room. From the Application menu, choose Finder. Root through your files and find some things to throw away. Drag them to the Trash can, and don't forget to *empty* the trash (using the Empty Trash command in the Special menu).

## *"PrintMonitor has reported an error." or "Can't open printer."*

Look these up in the Printing troubleshooting section.

## *"Can't empty trash."*

There's probably a locked file in the Trash can. Press Option while choosing Empty Trash from the Special menu. Or restart the Mac and try again.

## *"An error occurred while writing to the disk."*

Something went wrong while you were trying to save a document — probably your disk was full, or it's a flaky floppy disk. (See "Floppy-Disk Flukes" for more information on flaky floppies.)

## *"The file could not be copied because a disk error occurred."*

Here again, see the section on disks later in this chapter.

## "Microsoft Word prefers 2048K of memory. 2000K is available."

Once again, you're out of memory. The Mac will give you the chance to launch the program anyway — but it'll run slowly and may crash if you get too ambitious with your work. See the "Memory tactics" sidebar for a more lucid explanation.

# Out of Memory

As a service to you, the Tremulous Novice, I haven't even whispered a word about Memory Management, which is a whole new ball of wax. I hoped that you'd never need to think about it. Memory only really becomes an issue when you get the message "There is not enough memory to open Word" (or whatever program you're trying to open) — and that's why you're reading about memory in a troubleshooting chapter.

Your Mac has a fixed amount of memory. Think of it as a station wagon. You can pack it with camping gear, or you can pack it with your kid's birthday party friends, but probably not both. Even if you manage to cram in the kids and the gear, if you *then* try to cram in the dog, somebody in the family is going to say, "There is not enough room to take Bowser."

That's what the Mac is trying to tell you.

Each program you open consumes a chunk of the Mac's limited memory. You're entitled to run as many programs as you wish simultaneously: the Note Pad, the Calculator, your word processor, and so on, *provided* they all fit into the amount of memory your Mac has. If you try to open one too many programs, you'll get that message about the dog. *(You* know what I mean.)

## First resort: Quit programs

If you're told you're out of memory, then the easiest way out of the situation is to quit one of the programs you're already running. (You quit a program by choosing Quit from the File menu.) So if you're running Word, and you try to open the Calculator, and you're told there's not enough unused (free) memory, you'll just have to quit Word first.

# Memory tactics

Here's how you can get a clue.

- ✔ Go to the Finder. From the  menu, choose About This Macintosh. This helpful dialog box appears, showing several important numbers about your use of memory:

This is how much memory your Mac has. (If you want to convert this number to megs, mentally replace the comma with a decimal point.)

This is the largest chunk of memory you have left, into which you can open more programs. (There may be smaller chunks available, too.)

In the bottom part of the box, you can see what's already taking up memory and how *much* each program is taking up (see those bar graphs?).

You may find it useful, however, to *change* the amount of memory each of your programs uses. For example, if you're experiencing a lot of system crashes, the program may need a bigger memory allotment. And if memory is at a premium, you may be able to give a program *less* memory, freeing some up for other purposes.

Here's how:

- ✔ Quit the program whose memory appetite you want to change. Click its icon.
- ✔ From the File menu, choose Get Info. This box appears:

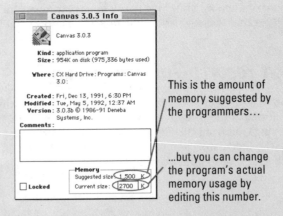

This is the amount of memory suggested by the programmers...

...but you can change the program's actual memory usage by editing this number.

- ✔ Change the number in the Current size (or, in System 7.1, the Preferred size) box. It's the amount of memory the program will actually consume when you run it. Unless the system crashes make life seem more interesting, don't set the Current size much below the Suggested size, though.

Actually, if you use System 7.0 or System 7.0.1 (find out by choosing About This Macintosh from the  menu), there's a *pre*-first resort here: make sure that there's an icon called System 7 Tune-Up in your Extensions folder, within the System Folder. And make sure it's version 1.1.1 or later. If you don't find it, and you've even checked your white Apple floppy disks looking for it, get System 7 Tune-Up right away from a user group or an Apple dealer (it's free). It makes the Mac much kinder and gentler when it comes to dealing with you and your Mac's memory, thus eliminating some of these out-of-memory messages.

## *Second resort:*
## *Make the Mac give back some memory*

Quitting programs, of course, isn't a very convenient solution — especially if having multiple programs open is part of what you're *trying* to do, like copying numbers *from* the Calculator *to* Word.

Therefore, your next attempt to solve the problem should be to make the Mac itself use up less memory. Oh yes indeed, the Mac's own behind-the-scenes operations use memory like a silicon hog — at a minimum, System 7 grabs 1.5MB of your memory. If your Mac only has 2MB to begin with (or even 4), you can see already why it's easy to run out of memory.

Here are some tricks to make the Mac use less memory.

✔ Use fewer *extensions,* the little auto-loading programs whose icons appear across the bottom of the screen when you start up the Mac. Each one that didn't originally come with your Mac (screen savers, menu clocks, virus-checkers, and so on) eats up another nibble of your memory.

✔ Turn off File Sharing. Those of you advanced enough to be using this complicated feature know who you are. March right up to that Control Panels command in the  menu, young man/woman, choose Sharing Setup, and click the Stop button. You'll immediately get back one-fifth of a megabyte of memory.

And while you're shutting things off, open the Chooser (by selecting its name from the  menu), and select AppleTalk Inactive, if it's not already. If you have a laser printer, you've just killed your ability to print — but you've reclaimed another one-fifth of a meg of memory. Turn AppleTalk back on when you have to print.

✔ Turn off Adobe Type Manager (ATM) if you have it. And how do you know? Choose Find from the Finder's File menu and look for it. (Actually, if you have ATM, you'll probably remember buying it for $7.50.) This amazing piece of type enhancement software is nifty (see "Font format #2½: Adobe Type Manager" in Chapter 4), but it gulps up memory like there's no tomorrow. Either turn it off or turn it down (use its control panel to decrease its memory allotment).

✔ Another potentially huge memory stealer is the Disk Cache. This little gimmick is something you can blissfully ignore for most of your computing days . . . until you start running out of memory.

Suppose that you're innocently word processing, and you make some text boldface. Because the word processing program resides on your hard disk, the Mac consults the disk to find out how it's supposed to create bold type. This disk-reading business takes, let's say, one second. If you use boldface a lot, those one-second disk searches are going to cumulatively slow down you and your Mac.

Therefore, the Mac reserves a piece of memory (called the Disk Cache) just for such frequent pieces of information. *Now* when you make text boldface, the Mac consults the disk (taking one second), but stores the "how-to-make-bold" information in the Disk Cache. The *second* time you need to create bold text, the Mac *already knows* how to do it; your text becomes bold in $\frac{1}{100}$ of a second (because memory delivers information to the Mac's brain 100 times faster than the disk). Cumulatively, all those little tidbits of information the Mac stores in the Disk Cache give you quite a speed boost.

The larger this piece of memory, the faster your Mac will go. But there's the rub — if you make this Disk Cache memory *too* big, you'll use up memory that you could be using to run programs.

Even if I've totally lost you, here's what to do when you're strapped for memory: From the  menu, choose Control Panels and double-click Memory. Clicking the arrow as shown below, make the Disk Cache smaller (you can go all the way down to 32K).

This has been a long explanation for a small reclamation of memory, I know, but it do feel good to know what's going on behind the scenes, don't it?

## Third resort: Defragment your RAM

Sometimes the Mac will appall you: here it is, the equivalent of a whole *room* full of 1950s-style computers, yet it can't even add.

Here's the scenario. Your Mac has 5MB (megabytes) of memory, let's say. You know your System uses up 1.5MB. And you're running Excel, which, let's suppose, takes 2MB.

Then you try to launch ClarisWorks, which we'll suppose needs 1.5MB of memory. And you get the out-of-memory message! How can this be — after all, the System (1.5) and Excel (2) together only use up 3.5 of your 5MB. There ought to be 1.5MB left over, right? What's going on?

*Memory fragmentation,* if you must know. It works like this: at noon, you start the Mac. Your memory usage looks like this:

Then at 12:05, you open the Calculator. For this example, let's say its memory requirement is half of a megabyte. When you then launch Excel, your Mac's memory map looks like this:

At 12:15, you close the Calculator. Your memory map looks like this:

If you look at this last drawing, you'll see you can't launch ClarisWorks (which needs 1.5MB) now because there aren't 1.5MB of *contiguous* memory left! Because of the sequence, you've inadvertently chopped your remaining memory into two smaller chunks, neither of which alone can fit ClarisWorks.

The solution to the I-*know*-I-have-enough-memory-to-launch-this syndrome is to *quit* all your programs so that only the Finder is running. *Then* launch all the ones that are supposed to fit in your Mac's memory; and this time, it will work.

## Fourth resort: Starve your software

So far we've assumed that each program has a certain memory requirement — 1MB, 2MB, 3-potato, 4. What you may not realize is that *you* can determine how much memory a program eats up. See the "Memory tactics" sidebar on page 272 for instructions.

Why is this useful? Because sometimes when you first install a program, the Current size (the amount of memory it consumes) is set to a much higher number than it needs to be, which can only make your memory-shortage problems worse. Word, for example, comes set to 2048K (which equals 2MB), when it *really* only needs 1MB, or less, to run. Its programmers assumed that you'd be using all its fancy features: the grammar checker, the thesaurus, the automatic hyphenator, and so on. Besides, those programmers tend to do *their* work on Macs the size of a Buick.

If you *don't* plan to use these features, drag them out of the Word Commands folder, and by all means reset Word's memory allotment to something more reasonable.

## Fifth resort: Virtual memory

There's another rather technical but interesting possibility for avoiding out-of-memory problems. Fortunately, it lets you run programs whose combined memory requirements add up to much more than your Mac's memory should be able to handle. Unfortunately, it requires you to learn a new term. Ponder this tradeoff for a moment; then read on if you dare.

**Virtual:** A '90s computer word meaning fake. Virtual memory isn't really memory, and virtual reality isn't really real. I don't know why they don't just say "fake," or faux if they're after prestige. Maybe it's because virtual has more syllables. I guess it gives computer-weenies virtual status.

The term is *virtual memory.* Under this scheme (unique to System 7, and not available on older models), the Mac attempts to use the *hard disk* as emergency memory.

Suppose that your Mac has 4MB of memory, but you want to run both LimerickWriter (which requires 2MB) and BrailleMeister (which also requires 2MB). Since your System requires 1.5MB by itself, you can already see that 2 + 2 + 1.5 is going to equal more than your 4MB.

But if you were using virtual memory, the Mac would allow you to run both programs simultaneously. Where would it get the extra 1.5MB of memory it needs to fit everything? It would use an empty hunk of hard-disk space.

Read this slowly: When you're in LimerickWriter, the Mac stashes the excess 1.5MB worth of BrailleMeister information on the hard disk. Then when you bring the BrailleMeister window to the front, the Mac quickly feeds that 1.5MB worth of information back into actual memory, displacing that amount of LimerickWriter instructions (which, needless to say, it writes back onto the hard disk). Each time you switch programs, the Mac juggles the overflow.

This doesn't take place instantaneously. That's a lot of information for the Mac to shuttle back and forth between memory and the hard disk. (Maybe it's time to reread Chapter 1½, where memory and hard disks are described in pulse-quickening detail.) In fact, there may be quite a lag when you switch from one program to another. But a little waiting sure beats not being *able* to run those two important programs at the same time.

For some mysterious technical reasons, the amount of hard-disk space the Mac needs to perform this stunt isn't just the amount of pretend memory you want to *add* to your real memory. That is, if your Mac has 5MB of memory, and you'd like your Mac to think it has 8MB, you can't just set aside the difference (3MB) in hard-disk space; golly, no. You have to allow a chunk of disk space that's the size of *all* the memory — real and imagined; in this case, 8MB.

OK. All that having been said and read, let's get to the actual process of using virtual memory.

1. From the  menu, choose Control Panels. Double-click Memory.

   The control panel appears, like this:

See the Virtual Memory area? If not, then your Mac isn't equipped for this feature. (Some of the older ones aren't, and neither is the original Classic or the original LC.)

2. From the pop-up menu, specify the hard disk you want the Mac to use as its temporary fake-memory dumping ground.

If you only have one drive — the one inside your Mac — skip this step.

3. Using the little up-and-down arrow keys, specify how big you want that virtual memory file (on your hard disk) to be.

Remember, there has to be a chunk of empty hard-disk space that's big enough to hold the *total* of your real memory and the extra, phony memory you'd like to have.

Don't create total memory more than double your *real* memory. If you have 4MB of RAM, your total memory (including virtual) shouldn't exceed 8MB; things will get so slow as to be unworkable.

Oh, yeah: if you're going to set the virtual memory *higher* than 8MB, you also need to turn the "32-bit addressing" switch, if your Mac displays one, to On.

The Mac may tell you that there's not enough room on your disk. Maybe it's time to go on a cleaning binge.

When you're done setting up your virtual memory setup, restart the Mac.

## *Last resort: Buy more*

After a certain point, knocking yourself out to solve out-of-memory problems (like those listed in this chapter) reaches a point of diminishing returns. You get so worn out from workarounds that they're not worth doing.

At that point (or much sooner), just spring the $45 per megabyte and *buy more memory*. You can get it from any mail-order company (like MacConnection). You can install it yourself fairly easily on many Mac II-something models. Installing it into a one-piece Mac like a Classic, or into a Quadra, is trickier and requires some funky tools. Anyway, when you call a mail-order company to buy memory, tell them what Mac you have and find out what you'll need. Sometimes they send you a how-to video, which is very handy, and when you're done with it, you can use it to record *Seinfeld*.

Fair warning: Installing memory yourself is not that difficult, but if you cause any other part of the computer to malfunction as a result of your installation, you risk voiding the one-year Apple warranty.

Having lots of memory to kick around in is a joy. Your Mac runs faster, has fewer crashes and glitches, and acts like a new machine. It's a situation I heartily recommend.

# Starting Up

Problems you encounter when you turn on the Mac are especially disheartening when you're a new Mac user. Does wonders for your self-esteem to think that you can't even turn the thing *on* without problems.

## No ding, no picture

***First resort:*** Chances are very, very, very good that your Mac simply isn't getting electricity. It's probably not plugged in. Or it's plugged into a power strip that has an On/Off switch that's currently in Off. Or, if it's a PowerBook, the battery is completely dead. (Plug in the adapter for 15 minutes before trying again.)

***Second resort:*** If you have a two-piece Mac, you normally turn the machine on by pressing the triangle key on the keyboard — maybe the keyboard isn't plugged in. Check that.

***Last resort:*** If that's not the problem, then your Mac is as dead as Elvis. Get it in for repair. But that's virtually never the actual problem.

## Ding, no picture

If you hear the startup chime (or ding) but the monitor doesn't light up, then something's wrong with the monitor.

**Screen saver:** *A little program that runs behind the scenes; after it notices that you haven't touched the Mac for several minutes, it blanks out the monitor to prevent an image from getting permanently etched into the screen.*

***First resort:*** Is the screen brightness turned up? On most Macs, there's a brightness dial on the edge of the monitor. On a Classic, you have to use the Brightness control panel.

***Second resort:*** I don't mean to insult your intelligence — but is it possible you have a screen saver program installed? To find out if that's the cause of the current blackness, click the mouse button. If the screen picture doesn't appear, read on.

***Third resort:*** If you have a two-piece Mac, the monitor has to be (1) plugged into the Mac, (2) plugged into a power source, *and* (3) turned on. (Not everybody realizes that your monitor has an On/Off switch.) Often the monitor is plugged into the AC outlet on the Mac itself; that's OK.

*Last resort:* Does your monitor require a graphics card? Some old models do. Of course, if your Mac needs a graphics card, you would have discovered this problem the very first day you got your system.

## Picture, no ding

Every Mac makes a sound when it's turned on. In fact, even if you've set the volume level of your Mac's speaker to zero (using the Sound control panel), you still get a sound when you start up the Mac.

*First resort:* Look at the little speaker jack in the back of the Mac. If there's some kind of plug in it — usually some kid's Walkman headphones, a cord connected to a stereo, or occasionally a pretzel stick — then no sound can come out of the Mac speaker.

*Last resort:* There's a remote possibility that somebody, mucking around inside your two-piece Mac, unplugged the speaker-wire cable. Find that person, yell firmly into his or her nearest ear, and insist that the cable (inside the Mac) be reconnected.

## Four separate musical notes

If you hear an arpeggio, then something's seriously wrong inside the Mac. (Why is the music prettier the worse the problem? I guess life's just like that.)

Fortunately, 80 percent of the time you hear this just after installing new memory. It means that one of the memory chips is loose or defective — something you (or whoever installed the memory for you) can fix relatively easily.

*First resort:* If you've just installed or otherwise messed around with the memory chips in your computer, that's certainly the problem. Reopen the Mac. Carefully remove each memory chip and reinstall it, checking the little centipede legs to make sure none are bent. Come to think of it, get someone who knows what he or she's doing to do this.

*Second resort:* The other common source of funny startup notes is a SCSI problem of some kind. Yes, I know we haven't defined this in awhile; see "Scuzzy SCSI," on an upcoming page, for instructions — or, for a quick fix, just unplug any external hard drives or scanners from the SCSI jack (the very wide one) in the back of the Mac, and try starting up again.

*Last resort:* If it's truly not a memory chip or a SCSI problem, call your Apple dealer. This baby's sick.

## The Restart switch

*Almost* every Mac has this switch. There are always two buttons side by side somewhere on the Mac's casing — and the one with a left-pointing triangle is the Restart switch.

Pressing this plastic button is the same as turning your Mac off and then on again — except that it doesn't send a wall of sudden electricity thudding into the machine's delicate electronics, and thus is better for your Mac. It's good to keep the Restart switch in mind when you have a System freeze or crash, too.

Old Macs, like the Plus and SE, come with the Restart switch loose in the box; you have to install it yourself. And many recent models — the LC series, PowerBook Duos, IIsi, Color Classic, Performa 400 series, some Quadras — have no Restart switch; instead, you press Control-⌘-Power button to make the Mac restart.

# A question mark blinks on the screen

The blinking question mark is the Mac's international symbol for "I've looked everywhere inside me, and I can't find a System Folder anywhere."

Usually the System Folder is on your hard disk. If it's an *external* hard disk (one that's plugged into the back), check to make sure it's plugged in and turned on and securely connected to the Mac. If you have other pieces of equipment attached to your external hard drive, like a scanner, you might have a SCSI problem. See "Scuzzy SCSI" later in this chapter.

If your hard disk, like most people's, is inside the Mac, the blinking question mark means that it's not working right — or that it's working fine, but somehow your System Folder got screwed up. In either case, here's what to do.

*First resort:* Panic. (Who are we kidding? I know you're going to do this anyway.)

*Second resort:* After ten seconds of that, turn the Mac off and try starting again. Or just press the Restart switch (see the sidebar above).

*Third resort:* Find a floppy disk with a System Folder on it. The best bet is the white System disks that came with your Mac; the one called Disk Tools usually does the trick. Put it into the disk drive.

If it pops out again, then it doesn't have a System Folder. If you arrive at some kind of Installer screen, then you must have used a System Software Installer disk, and (alas) it's not going to help you get going. And if it says something about needing a newer version of the System software than 7.1, the disk doesn't have the little *enabler file* your Mac needs to run. (See Chapter 6 for a discussion of these important little rascals.)

But if the Mac happily accepts the disk, gives you the smiling Mac picture, and goes on to the familiar desktop, look for your hard disk's icon to appear. If it's there, in its customary upper-right-corner-of-the-screen position, reinstall the System software (using those same white floppies, starting with the Install disk) and start over — after first making sure you have a copy of everything useful on the disk, of course.

**Fourth resort:** If the hard drive icon still doesn't appear, read "Scuzzy SCSI," later in this chapter.

**Fifth resort:** This one is really, *really* technical. I've never even seen it work. But repair people say it could theoretically work. It's called (do *not* learn this term) *zapping the PRAM.* (They pronounce it PEA-ram.)

First, turn off (or restart) your Mac. Then turn it on again, but hold down four keys at once: ⌘, Option, P, and R; don't let go until the "Welcome" screen flashes a second time. Supposedly, this can help.

**Last resort:** If nothing has worked, and you still can't make your hard-drive icon appear on the screen, then your hard drive is sick. Call up your local dealer or Mac guru, and do *not* freak out — chances are very good that all of your files are still intact. (Just because the platters aren't spinning doesn't mean they've been wiped out, just as your Walkman tapes don't get erased when the Walkman runs out of batteries.)

In fact, you can probably rescue the data from your disk yourself if you buy a disk recovery program like Norton Utilities or MacTools Deluxe. That won't fix the drive, but it'll let you grab anything useful off the disk in case the drive's ailment is terminal.

## *"Sorry, a System error has occurred."*

This grammatically ungraceful message pops up under various circumstances; see "System Crashes and Freezes," later in this chapter. When it appears while the Mac is starting up, though, it's almost certainly what the nerds call an *extension conflict,* or an *INIT* conflict.

Trouble is, each extension was written by a programmer who had no clue what *other* extensions you'd be using. The result: Two extensions may fight over the same piece of memory, resulting in that polite disclaimer, "Sorry, a System error."

These things are super easy to fix, once you know the secret. Shut off your Mac and then turn it on again (or just press the Restart switch). But this time, as it's starting up, hold down the Shift key. Keep it down until (1) you see the message "Extensions off," or (2) you arrive at the desktop, whichever you notice first.

Now you're running without *any* of your cute little extension programs. No screen saver, no macro program, and so on. Burrow into your System Folder to find the Extensions folder, where these little guys live. Drag a few of their icons out of that folder (and out of the System Folder) onto the gray desktop — that's how you prevent *selected* extensions from loading. You don't have to throw them away; just take them out of the System Folder and restart the computer. (Use the Restart command in the Special menu.)

If the Mac doesn't crash this time, then you can pretty much bet that one of the extensions you removed was the guilty party. If it *does* crash again, repeat the whole process, but take some more extension icons out of the System Folder.

Through trial and error, eventually you should be able to figure out which pair of extensions doesn't get along. Sometimes just renaming one so that it alphabetically precedes its enemy is enough to solve the problem.

## Some crazy program launches itself every time you start up

In the words of Mac programmers everywhere: "It's a feature, not a bug."

Inside the System Folder, there's a folder called Startup Items. Look inside it. Somebody put a program or document in there.

Anything in the Startup Items folder automatically opens up when you turn on the Mac. It's supposed to be a time-saver for people who work on the same documents every day.

# System Crashes and Freezes

There are two scary conditions that are enough to make even semi-pro Mac jockeys swallow hard and feel a little helpless. A system *crash* is when this message appears on the screen:

Your current work session is over, amigo. You have to restart the computer. Anything you've typed or drawn since the last time you saved your work is gone. (Safest way: Press the Restart switch, as described in "The Restart switch" sidebar a couple pages ago.)

A system *freeze* is different — and, as horrific computer nightmares go, it's preferable. You get no message on the screen. Instead, the mouse cursor freezes into place. You can't move the cursor, and nothing you type on the keyboard changes anything. The Mac, as far as you can tell, has silicon lockjaw.

## Escaping a System crash

You can't. Restart the computer (don't even bother trying to click the Restart button on the *screen,* which doesn't do anything).

What you *can* do is understand why system crashes occur. Ninety percent of the time, they're related to memory: either you're out of it, your program is out of it, or two programs are fighting over the same piece of it.

*First resort:* Increase the amount of memory allotted to the program you were using, as described in the "Memory tactics" sidebar on page 272. Give it 150K more, for example.

*Second resort:* There may be a bug in the program that's crashing; call up the company that makes it and ask. More likely (and this is what the company will probably tell you), the program's incompatible with something in your System Folder. Go through the taking-extensions-out-of-the-System-Folder routine described under "Sorry, a System error has occurred" (a few pages back).

*Third resort:* If that step didn't stop the crashes, there may be some other weird memory-related thing going on under the hood. Some programs are allergic to virtual memory, for example; so your second step should be to turn off Virtual Memory (open your Memory control panel and hit the Off button). And if you're advanced enough to know what "32-bit addressing" is, go to the Memory control panel and turn *it* off, if your Mac lets you. A lot of programs break out in puffy hives when *that* is on, too.

*Fourth resort:* You may have a SCSI conflict on your hands, especially if more than one external gizmo is plugged into your Mac. See "Scuzzy SCSI," later in this chapter.

*Fifth resort:* It's possible that something in your System Folder got gummed up. Reinstall the System software. (1) Turn off the Mac. (2) Insert the white Install 1 (or Install Me First) disk into your disk drive. (3) Turn on the Mac. (4) Double-click the icon called Installer; follow the directions on the screen.

*Sixth resort:* You don't, by any chance, have *two* System Folders on your hard disk, do you? That's like throwing two baseballs at once to a Little League shortstop — chances are he'll panic and won't catch either one. Usually people have added another System Folder accidentally, in the process of copying new software onto the hard disk from a floppy. If you don't want your Mac to (forgive me) drop the ball, use the Finder's Find command and search for "system" to make sure you have only one.

***Last resort:*** If you're *still* having system crashes, particularly if they don't seem to be related to any one program, then the fault may lie in the way your hard disk was prepared. Once again we're wading in waters too technologically deep for my comfort. But particularly if you're using a Mac purchased in 1991 or before (in other words, before System 7), frequent system crashes are a telltale sign that you need to *reformat* the hard disk.

That tiresome task involves copying *everything* off the disk (onto a million floppies, for example, or just onto another hard disk), and using a hard-disk formatting program to erase it completely. One such reformatting program is on your white Disk Tools disk that came with your Mac; it's called Apple HD SC Setup. Other popular programs are Drive 7 and FWB Hard Disk Utility. Or if you bought an external hard drive, you may have a drive-formatting program on a floppy disk that came with it.

In any case, the main thing is to ensure that your formatting program is *System 7-compatible.* (The programs I specifically named above all are compatible.)

When you've completely erased and reformatted your hard drive, copy all your intellectual belongings back onto it. You'll probably be amazed at how many fewer crashes you experience.

## System freezes

If your system freezes, and your cursor locks in place, you can't save the work in the program you were working on. You don't, however, have to sell your Mac or even restart it. Instead, try this amazing keystroke: ⌘-Option–Esc. (It's about the only time you'll ever use the Esc key.)

If it works, you'll get a dialog box that says "Force [this program] to quit?" Click Force Quit, and you exit the program you were working in.

So what's the big whoop? Well, if you had several programs running, this technique only dumps the one you were working in — the one that crashed. You now have a chance to enter each of the *other* programs that are still running and save your work (if you haven't done so). Then, to be on the safe side, restart the Mac.

And what causes a system freeze? Pretty much the same kinds of things that cause system crashes (see above).

## A note about the ID numbers or error messages in the bomb box

In the "Sorry, a system error has occurred" box, there's usually an ID number or a cryptic little error message (like "bad F-line instruction" or "Unimplemented trap").

It always cracks me up to read, in other books, the tables that explain what these codes mean. Here are a few actual examples:

| Error message | Error Code | Helpful translation |
|---|---|---|
| bus error | 01 | Software error |
| address error | 02 | Software error |
| unimplemented trap | 12 | Software error |
| bad F-line instruction | 11 | Software error |

Big help, huh?

The point is that these error codes are pretty much meaningless. They'll never help you figure out what *led* to the problem — only *that* there was a problem. But you probably could have figured that out all by yourself.

# Scuzzy SCSI

I've tried to shield you as much as possible from the term *SCSI* and all it entails. But since it's (alas) one of the most common sources of trouble, it's time to put on the overalls and get dirty.

If there's nothing attached to your SCSI jack in the back of the Mac (like a scanner or a removable cartridge drive), then you *have* no SCSI problems, and you should skip this entire section. You don't know how lucky you are.

## What's SCSI?

They pronounce it "scuzzy" for some reason. Here on the East Coast, we used to pronounce it "sexy," which I prefer, but the Valley girls and boys held sway.

Anyway, it stands for Small Computer System Interface (or *Serial* Interface, or *Standard* Interface, depending on where you look it up — it's such a messed-up technology they can't even get the *name* right). It describes the widest connector on the back of your Mac: the *SCSI port*. It also describes the fattest cable of any Mac appliance: the *SCSI cable.* And it describes the kind of hard drives, scanners, SyQuest drives, computer CD players, and other gadgets that you attach to this jack: *SCSI devices.* It also describes the type of information that flows from those devices through those cables to that jack along the *SCSI chain.*

But frankly, the term you hear most often is: *SCSI problems.*

What's especially frustrating to people who write computer books is that you can't pin SCSI down. Even if you obey the "rules," which I'll give you anyway, things still go wrong.

The only good thing to say about SCSI problems is that once you've figured out the problem with your setup, that problem is gone for good.

# System crashes, slow-as-molasses performance, no external drive icon, CD-ROM won't work

These are only a few of the delicious symptoms you have to look forward to in the world of SCSI problems. Now here are some of the equally delicious solutions.

*First resort:* Unhook the SCSI devices from your Mac. That's right, put the Mac back the way it was when you bought it: bald and buck naked, with nothing attached. This way, at least, you can figure out if SCSI *is* the problem. If the problem went away, then you have a SCSI problem indeed.

*Second resort:* Somewhere in this book I've mentioned that you can string more than one SCSI device together, or *daisy-chain* them, which is how you can use both an external drive and a scanner (for example) even though the Mac only has one SCSI jack. When the Mac attempts to talk to various devices along this SCSI train, it must be careful not to say "start scanning!" to the hard drive or "start spinning!" to the scanner. In other words, it has to address its messages carefully.

For that reason, every SCSI device in the world has a *SCSI address* between 0 and 7. Usually there's a little number wheel that looks like a one-digit odometer on the back or the bottom of your SCSI device. Each SCSI device connected to your Mac must have a *different* SCSI number (address) so that the Mac can speak to each appliance individually.

The Mac, since it's part of the chain, has a SCSI number, which is always 7. If you have an internal hard drive, it has a SCSI number, too — and it's always 0. (If your Mac has a built-in CD-ROM player, its address is always 3.) So for your external drives, scanners, and so on, you can choose numbers from 1 to 6; just make sure that no two have the *same* number, or you're cruisin' for a bruisin'.

***Third resort:*** I wish I didn't have to mention SCSI Rule #2: The last device on the chain has to be *terminated.*

When I say terminated, I mean taken out and shot.

But if you've paid good money for these things, I suppose you'd prefer to keep them. The second meaning for terminated is a little bit more complicated.

As the Mac sends its little instructions to the various SCSI devices attached to it, it shoves them out the door with such force that they sometimes go all the way to the end of the cable and *bounce back* toward the Mac. Sometimes they make it all the way back, in which case you get nutty problems like a hard drive icon showing up *twice* on the screen.

To soak up any messages that were pushed with too much oomph, you're supposed to put an electronic shock absorber at the beginning and the end of the line of devices. This absorber is called a *terminator*, Arnold Schwarzenegger notwithstanding.

If your Mac has an internal hard drive, like most Macs, then you don't have to worry about the beginning terminator: your SCSI chain is already terminated inside. And if you only have one SCSI device outside your Mac in addition, you also don't need a terminator on the outside end. (I'm perfectly aware that this contradicts Rule #2. But it doesn't contradict Rule #3, which is that these rules don't always apply. Including Rule #3.)

After you have two or more SCSI things attached to the back of your Mac, though, it's time to start thinking about termination. You add termination by attaching a three-inch stopper plug (called, obviously, a terminator) to the empty SCSI jack of the last device on the chain. Some devices, however, have a terminator *switch* on the back or bottom, which you can just flip between terminated or unterminated positions.

Worst of all, some devices may or may not be *internally* terminated, meaning you can't *tell* whether or not they're already terminated. Rule #4 is that you don't want a device in the *middle* of the chain to be terminated! And the only way to find out whether or not a device is internally terminated (if it's not in the manual) is to call up the cheap, lazy company that made it. And if it *is* internally terminated, that device *must* go at the end of the SCSI chain.

Is this the most pathetic technology ever, or what?

So if you have *two* devices that are both internally terminated — well, you're basically up the creek. You can't use them both at once. You may be able to call up the company and have them explain to you over the phone how you open up the case and, with a pair of pliers, rip out the little circuits that terminate the device . . . but it's an ugly, unenviable operation.

I guess the point is that, when you shop for hard drives, scanners, or other SCSI devices, don't buy one that's terminated internally. It only means trouble.

## For Mac IIfx owners only

You people have an additional SCSI Rule to worry about. When it comes time for you to add a SCSI terminator plug at the outer end of your SCSI chain, you're supposed to use a special, black, IIfx terminator plug.

Truth to tell, though, my ex-girlfriend has a IIfx, and she uses a regular, gray, non-IIfx plug, and it works fine. Yet another SCSI Rule that doesn't seem to work.

**Fourth resort:** Try rearranging the physical order of the devices in your SCSI chain. It makes no sense, and there's no Rule of SCSI about it, but sometimes that makes things work when nothing else does. And at this point, you're entitled to be a little irrational.

**Fifth resort:** If everything else seems hunky-dory, then it's conceivable that the trouble is the *combined lengths* of your SCSI cables. They're not supposed to add up to more than 20 feet or so, and, like speeches and Willie Nelson songs, the shorter the better. Oh, and while we're talking about SCSI cables: they go bad. It's true. One rich guy I know threw out an 800MB hard drive because he thought it had died permanently. Upon rescuing it from the dumpster, an enterprising Mac buddy discovered that the drive was fine — but the *cable* had been crimped by a piece of furniture. After spending $30 on a new SCSI cable, the drive was good as new. It's probably worth replacing or at least switching around the cables if you're still having SCSI problems.

Oh, yeah, one guy I know solved his SCSI woes by switching his cable from one SCSI jack on his CD-ROM player to the other (of the two identical SCSI jacks). It makes *absolutely* no sense, but that's what happened.

**Last resort:** OK. You've made sure every device has its own address. If you have more than one external SCSI device, you've terminated the last one. But things *still* aren't working right.

In this case, try taking *off* the terminator. I'm perfectly serious: Rule #5 of SCSI is: If a rule isn't working, try breaking it. Here at home, for example, I have a hard drive and a SyQuest removable-cartridge drive both plugged into the back of my Mac. And *no* external terminators. What sense does that make? I don't know — but I do know that if I follow Rule #2 and add a terminator, then nothing works, and my hard-drive icon doesn't appear on the screen.

Someday we'll laugh and tell our grandchildren, "Why, when I was your age, we used to have to *add terminator plugs to our external devices!*" Until that golden day, though, we have to put up with this cranky and unpredictable technology. Good luck to you.

# *Printing Problems*

After the brutal experience of solving SCSI snafus, these'll seem like child's play.

## *"Printer could not be opened."* *or "Printer could not be found."*

***First resort:*** These messages appear when you try to print something without turning on the printer first (or letting it warm up fully). Turn it on, wait a whole minute, and then try again.

***Second resort:*** Of course, it may be that you haven't performed the critical step of selecting the printer's icon in the Chooser desk accessory. (Or even if you did, the Mac sometimes gets a little feebleminded and forgets what you selected in the Chooser. Just repeat the procedure.) See Chapter 4 for step-by-step instructions.

***Last resort:*** Maybe a cable came loose. Track the cable from your Mac's printer port all the way to the printer. (Important: Make sure it's really the printer port since the modem port looks exactly like it.) If it all seems to be firmly connected, try replacing (1) the cable or (2) the little connectors.

## *A million copies keep pouring out*

This big-time hazard for novices has to do with Background Printing (see Chapter 4). When you print something, *nothing happens* for a minute or two. (The Mac is storing the printout behind the scenes so that it can return control of the Mac to you.)

Trouble is, your first time at bat, you probably don't *know* what the delay is. All you know is that the printer isn't printing. So you figure you'll just try again — you pick Print from the File menu again. Still nothing: so you print *again*.

The thing is, the Mac is duly *storing* all your printing requests; at some moment when you least expect it, all of those copies will start to print!

To stop them, choose Print Monitor from the Application menu (the tiny icon at the far right of your menu bar); select each document and click Cancel Printing.

## *You get jagged text in your printouts*

If this is your problem, I'll have to punish you by making you reread Chapter 4, where there's an entire section devoted to this topic. There you'll discover that getting jagged type when you print on a laser or inkjet printer is a matter of which fonts you've used in your document.

There's only one other oddity I want to mention. If you're printing a graphic, it may be text you made in a program that has *Paint* in the title (SuperPaint, MacPaint, and so on). The trouble here is that the Mac no longer thinks of your text as *text;* it knows only about a bunch of dots in a certain pattern, and they'll never print out smoothly. See Chapter 5 for details on painting programs.

## *"Font not found, using Courier"*

Your document contains a PostScript laser font (see Chapter 4 for excruciatingly detailed definitions), but the Mac can't find the printer font file for the font you're using. Find the printer font (the file with the abbreviated name, like FrankGothBol) and install it into your System folder.

## *Nothing comes out of the printer*

Sometimes the Mac fakes you out: it goes through the motions of printing, but nothing ever comes out of the printer.

***First resort:*** Go to the  menu. Select Chooser. Click the icon for the printer you're using, and make sure your actual printer's name shows up in the list on the right. (This process is explained more patiently in Chapter 4.)

***Second resort:*** Is there paper in the paper tray, and is the tray pushed all the way in?

Or if it's an ImageWriter: Is the little Select light on? If not, push the Select button.

***Third resort:*** Alas, your document is probably overwhelming the printer's feeble memory, and the printer is giving up. You can try using fewer different fonts in the document. Try printing only a page at a time. Or try using fewer *downloadable* fonts in the document — that is, fonts that aren't built into the printer (see #3 of "Top Ten Free Fun Font Factoids" in Chapter 4).

***Fourth resort:*** If you're printing something complicated, there may be a messed-up graphic. Programs like SuperPaint, FreeHand, and Illustrator are known for generating very complex, sometimes unprintable graphics. For example, here's a graphic from SuperPaint that won't print out:

If you're printing something that includes both text and graphics, try removing your graphics and printing the same document. If it prints without the graphics, you know where the problem is. Call up the graphics program company and complain abrasively.

***Last resort:*** If your printer truly has run out of memory, you can usually pay to have it upgraded with more memory. In the computer world, as always, a little cash can surmount almost any problem.

## *PrintMonitor won't go away*

If you're using the generally wonderful Background Printing option, as described in Chapter 4, sometimes you may encounter the bizarro PrintMonitor program.

What's so baffling is that you never remember launching this program by double-clicking. But there it is, listed in your Application menu. And sometimes it beeps at you, demanding some intervention on your part (such as when the printer runs out of paper).

Anyway, you can't make PrintMonitor quit on cue. To make it really go away, you have to cancel any printing jobs it's still working on (by clicking the Cancel button). Then go to another program. Eventually, PrintMonitor should disappear from your Application menu.

## *Streaks on Laser printouts*

If they're *dark* streaks, then there's some crud on some element of the paper path inside the laser printer. Open the lid. Examine the rollers (but be careful if the printer has just been on — those rollers get incredibly hot). You're looking for a single blob of grit or toner dust. Clean it off with a Q-tip, preferably damp with alcohol (the Q-tip, not you).

Also look for a series of thin, one-inch diagonal wires. Make sure those are sparkling clean.

Then again, if this streaking business just started after you've returned from a three-month trip, the cartridge probably went bad from sheer loneliness. Replace it.

If there are *light* streaks on the printouts, open the printer lid. Remove the toner drum (usually a big black plastic thing) and gently rock it from side to side. Basically, you're running out of toner dust; this procedure may give you a couple days' worth of extra time, but you'll be needing a new cartridge soon.

## Every time you turn on the laser printer, it cranks out a stupid startup page

This is an annoying one, but easily fixed. See #8 in "Top Ten Free Fun Font Factoids" in Chapter 4.

# Finder Foulups

The Finder, you'll recall, is your home base. It's the Desktop. It's the Trash can and icons and all that stuff. It's where you manage your files, rename them, copy them — and sometimes have problems with them.

## The Find command doesn't find a file that you know is there somewhere

The Find command is pretty literal. Suppose you're looking for a letter called "Mr. Ted Smith." You use the Find command, and where it says "Find what," you type "Mr. Smith," or "Mr.Ted Smith" (see the missing space?), or "Mr Ted Smith" (no period), or "Mr. WilliamSmith." In any of these circumstances, the Find command will draw a blank. Try searching for "smi," or "Mr.", or any portion of the letters you're certain of.

Capitalization, however, *doesn't* matter.

Of course, the problem may not be what you type into the "Find what" box. You may have misspelled the name of the file itself — say, "1993 Salries" — and no matter how many times you search for the word "salaries," the Finder will always come up empty-handed.

## You try to rename an icon, but the Mac highlights some other icon

To rename an icon, click once on it and then press Return (or click its name and wait a second) so that the little rectangle appears around its name.

Now you can edit the name.

If you start to type *before* the little rectangle appears, though, the Mac will think you're trying to select an icon by typing its name, and it will highlight the icon whose name most closely matches what you're typing. It's a feature, not a bug.

## You can't rename a file

The file is probably locked. Click on it, choose Get Info from the File menu, and deselect the Locked checkbox.

```
╔════════════ Review Info ════════════╗
║                                      ║
║      📄  Review                       ║
║                                      ║
║    Kind: Word 5 document             ║
║    Size: 18K on disk (16,896 bytes used) ║
║                                      ║
║   Where: Tsunami:                    ║
║                                      ║
║ Created: Wed, Jun 17, 1992, 4:41 PM  ║
║ Modified: Wed, Jun 17, 1992, 6:51 PM ║
║ Version: n/a                         ║
║                                      ║
║ Comments:                            ║
║  ┌────────────────────────────────┐  ║
║  │                                │  ║
║  │                                │  ║
║  └────────────────────────────────┘  ║
║ ☒ Locked          ☐ Stationery pad   ║
╚══════════════════════════════════════╝
```

# *Floppy-Disk Flukes*

Floppy disks are cheap and handy and make excellent coasters. But when they start giving you attitude, read on.

## *"File could not be copied and will be skipped."*

This one's a pain, isn't it?

***First resort:*** If you were copying a whole group of files, try dragging the troublesome file by itself.

***Second resort:*** Make a duplicate of the file (click it and choose Duplicate from the File menu). Now try copying the duplicate.

***Third resort:*** If the unruly file is a document, launch the program that created it. For example, if it's a Word file, launch Word.

Now go to the Open command in the File menu and try to open the file. If it opens, use the Save As command to save it onto a different disk.

***Fourth resort:*** Eject the disk. Open and close the sliding shutter a couple times. Manually rotate the round hub. Try again.

***Fifth resort:*** Try inserting the obnoxious floppy into somebody else's Mac.

***Last resort:*** With a little expenditure, you can almost certainly retrieve the file. The rescue programs are called things like 911 Utilities (the best for floppies) or Norton Utilities (best for hard disks). They're listed in Appendix B, the Resource Resource.

## *The Mac keeps asking for a disk that you've ejected*

***First resort:*** You probably ejected the disk by using the Eject Disk command in the Special menu. In general, that's a no-no, precisely because the Mac will continually ask for it.

You can get out of this scrape by pressing ⌘-period several times. And next time, eject a disk using the Put Away command in the File menu (or by dragging the disk icon to the Trash can).

**Last resort:** Sometimes, even if you use Put Away, a ghost of the disk's icon remains on the screen, and the Mac keeps asking for it, and ⌘-period doesn't solve anything. In this case, you probably opened a file on that disk — and it's still open. As long as something on that disk is open, the Mac won't forget about the disk; it would be like canceling the space program while some astronauts were in the middle of a mission.

Choose the program in question from the Application menu, and make sure you close all documents. Now you should be able to drag the disk icon to the Trash can.

## You can't rename a disk

In System 7, you can't rename those really old, "single-sided," 400K disks. Period. You also can't rename any disk you're sharing on a network (you power-users know who you are).

## You can't get a floppy disk out

**First resort:** Press ⌘-Shift-1. That should pop out the disk, even if you can't see its icon.

**Last resort:** Use the paper clip trick described in the sidebar "Dweebs' Corner: Alternative disk tips" in Chapter 2.

## "This disk is unreadable. Do you want to initialize it?"

If it's a brand new disk fresh out of the box, there is *no* problem. *All* brand new floppies are initially unreadable, unless they have already been initialized. Go ahead and click Erase, and follow the disk-naming process that the Mac takes you through. But if it's a disk you've used before, you certainly don't want to destroy it.

**First resort:** Click Eject. *No*, you do not want to initialize (that is, erase) the disk.

**Second resort:** Remember that there are three different kinds of floppy disks: single-sided (400K), double-sided (800K), and high-density (1400K). If you have an older Mac (say, one made before 1990), it may not have a high-density disk drive, and you may be trying to insert a high-density disk that it can't read.

Actually, it's even more complicated than *that*. Another typical problem: you insert a new 800K disk into a high-density disk drive. You go through the usual "Initialize?" routine. But then you discover that the disk won't work in somebody else's old 800K disk drive! Strange but true.

In any of these cases, again, the main thing is that you do *not* give the Mac permission to erase the disk; just take it to a more modern Mac, rescue the files, and bring them home on a kind of disk that *your* Mac can read.

**Third resort:** If it's a disk that you know has data on it, and you have a disk drive of the right type, then there may be something actually wrong with the disk. Eject it, shake it around a little. Try it a couple more times.

**Fourth resort:** There may be something wrong with your disk *drive* — and not the disk itself. That's easy enough to find out: insert the disk in another Mac's drive.

If it does turn out to be a problem with your drive, the culprit is often dust and crud. Some of my technoid friends say it's dangerous (static-wise) to use a vacuum or blower in the disk drive slot, but I've actually rescued a disk drive or two this way (and have never damaged one).

**Fifth resort:** Buy a recovery program like 911 Utilities. If anything can get your files off that disk, 911 can.

**Sixth resort:** You're not trying to insert an IBM PC disk into your Mac, are you? If you are (having read in the ads that any Mac can read a PC disk), give it up — it's not that simple. You're going to need some special software, described at the end of Chapter 5, if you want your Mac to read PC disks.

**Last resort:** If the problem is not your disk drive, and even 911 can't get your data off the disk, then the disk is really broken. Don't even erase it and reuse it: throw it away!

One occasional source of zapped floppies, by the way, is magnetic damage. Just like audio tapes, a disk stores information by magnetizing tiny particles of metal stuff. So if the disk gets magnetized by accident, the metal particles get rearranged into some random pattern that the Mac correctly deems "unreadable."

I know this sounds crazy, but *somebody* has to put this into print: Don't put refrigerator magnets on your Mac. That hard disk inside the machine is, after all, a disk, and magnets do to disks what gravity does to a watermelon dropped at 39,000 feet.

# Your floppy disks don't hold the amount they're supposed to

It's true. You can't fit 800K of information on an 800K disk, nor 1.4MB on a 1.4MB disk.

The missing storage capacity is filled by an invisible file, on every disk, called the *Desktop file*. This file is the Mac's accounting department and is described in more detail under "Error Messages" earlier in this chapter. The point is that it takes up 7K or more on every disk. If it's taking up a lot more than that, you may have a *bloated* Desktop file; see the "Rebuilding the Desktop file" sidebar, also earlier in this chapter, for instructions on slimming it down.

# Software Snafus

This part describes things that can go wrong while you're working: problems in programs, for example. See also "System Crashes and Freezes " and "Error Messages."

## Disappearing text

This one's covered under "The Top Ten Beginner Troubles (That Don't Actually Need Shooting)" at the beginning of this chapter.

## In FileMaker: Missing information

FileMaker, the world's most popular Mac database, sometimes misleads novices into thinking that their information has been lost. That impression is a result of FileMaker's clever ability to *hide* data. For example, you can ask your Rolodex file to show you only the names of people who weigh more than 250 pounds or something similar; the name and address information for everybody skinnier will be *hidden*.

To restore all names to the screen, choose Find All from the Select menu. They should reappear.

## In Excel: ##### in a cell

In Excel and other spreadsheets, it's a simple matter to make a cell wider or narrower. But if you make a cell so narrow that it chops off the number inside it, the program displays #####. (Other spreadsheet programs display something similar.)

You can see why it does this; otherwise, only *part* of the number would show up, possibly misleading you into thinking (for example) that your quarterly earnings are only $56, instead of $56,456,890.

## In HyperCard: No menu bar

Actually, in certain HyperCard documents, the menu bar has been deliberately hidden by the programmer. The combination of keys ⌘-Q still quits the program, though.

If you'd like the menu bar to reappear, press ⌘-spacebar.

## Miscellaneous crashes, freezes, beeps, and goofy or sluggish behavior

For details on freezes and crashes, see "System Crashes and Freezes" earlier in the chapter.

*First resort:* If this behavior seems to be happening regularly, try the Shift-key trick I'm such a fan of. That is, turn your Mac off. When you turn it on again, press the Shift key continuously until you see the words "Extensions Off" (or the Desktop, whichever you notice first).

If the problems have gone away, then, as noted earlier in the chapter, two of your extension programs (in the Extensions folder of the System folder) are fighting each other. Or maybe one of them is out of date or buggy. Anyway, the Shift-key trick turns *all* of those extensions off so that you can at least pinpoint the general source of your problems.

Of course, now you have to begin the tedious process of figuring out *which* extensions were giving you grief. You have to repeatedly restart the Mac with different combinations of extensions in the Extensions folder until you sleuth out the culprit(s).

*Second resort:* Something may have gotten messed up in the program itself. Find the original master disks and install the program onto your hard disk again. (Throw away the copy you've been using.)

*Third resort:* Call the company that makes the program. It's their job.

*Fourth resort:* If everything on your Mac has seemed to be getting slower and slower lately, see the sidebar "Defragmenting your disk," later in this chapter.

*Last resort:* It's extremely unlikely, but possible that your Mac has been invaded by a computer virus. Basically, though, the problem is almost never related to a virus. You can find out for sure by running a virus-checker program, like Disinfectant or Symantec Anti-Virus (both listed in Appendix B, the Resource Resource).

# Hard-Disk Horrors

If you're like many Mac users, you wind up storing your whole life on that disk: appointments, finances, explosive secret diary, the works. That's a lot of trust to place in an inanimate mechanical device that's all moving parts. Back up your work all the time — and rely on this section when things go wrong.

## The hard-drive icon doesn't show up

If it's an external drive, either it isn't on, it isn't plugged in right, or its SCSI setup isn't right (see "Scuzzy SCSI" in this chapter). If we're talking about the drive inside your Mac, it's probably a SCSI problem.

It's theoretically possible that your drive is broken, too. Bummer.

## Sluggish behavior

If copying, launching, and quitting programs (and opening and closing windows) seem to be taking longer than when you first bought your Mac, it's probably time to give your hard disk a physical. See the sidebar "Defragmenting your disk."

## You threw something away by mistake

*First resort:* If you haven't chosen Empty Trash from the Special menu, you're in good shape. Just double-click the Trash icon. Its window opens so that you can rescue any files therein by dragging them back to your hard-disk icon.

*Last resort:* If you've already emptied the Trash, you're not out of luck. Chances are very good that you can still recover the last several dozen files that you threw away, using a *data-recovery program* like Norton Utilities or Mac Tools Deluxe. The more you've used your Mac since you threw something away, the less chance you have of getting it back. See Appendix B, the Resource Resource, for information on getting these programs, and see their manuals for instructions.

## Defragmenting your disk

Over time, you create and throw away a lot of files.

Your hard drive, if you'll indulge me, is like a closet maintained by a guy who's always in a hurry. When guests are coming over, he cleans up the living room and throws everything into the closet, although not particularly neatly. Every now and then, when he gets time, he unpacks the closet and repacks it neatly, putting everything in a tidy, organized place.

The hard drive, too, is in a hurry. When you ask it to save a file, it doesn't wait around: It shoves that file wherever it can find space. Sometimes that even means sticking the file in *two* places, splitting it up as necessary. Over time, more and more files are stored on your hard disk in pieces. It's no

big deal: when you need that file again, the hard drive remembers where all the pieces are and is perfectly able to bring the file back to the screen.

But all this hunting for pieces slows the drive down. And like our busy closet keeper, it's very satisfying, every six months or so, to reorganize the files on your disk so that they're each in one piece, neatly placed end-to-end on the hard drive surface.

There are two ways to *defragment* your drive (which is the term for it). First, you can copy everything onto other disks, erase the hard drive, and copy the files back onto it. Second, you can buy a program just for defragmenting your drive. These programs are called things like Norton Utilities and DiskExpress.

# Hardware Headaches

These aren't the most common glitches you're likely to encounter, but they're just as frustrating.

## The mouse/trackball is sluggish, jerky, or sticky

This is a very common problem. Like children, mops, and mimes, a mouse does its work by rolling around on the ground. It's bound to get dirty.

To clean it, turn it upside down in your hand. Very firmly rotate the round collar counterclockwise so that you can remove it. (Same idea on a PowerBook. On a Duo, you might think the collar ring is impossible to turn, but it can be done. Push really hard against the soft curves of the ring around the trackball.)

Dump the rubber or plastic ball into your hand, wash it off under the faucet, and let it air-dry completely.

In the meantime, go to work inside the socket where the ball usually is. With tweezers or something, pull out any obvious dust bunnies and hairballs. The main thing, though, is those three little rollers inside the cavity: you'll probably see a stripe of accumulated gunk around their circumferences. With patience, a scissors blade, and a good light, scrape off that stuff, preferably making an effort not to let it fall inside the cavity. Keep turning the mouse right side up and tapping it on the table to dislodge stuff.

When you put it all back together, you and your mouse will both be much happier.

## Double-clicking doesn't work

You're probably double-clicking too slowly, or else you're moving the mouse a little bit during the double-click process.

## The cursor freezes on the screen and won't move

This is a system freeze, or system hang. Read all about it under "System Crashes and Freezes" in this chapter.

Then again, your mouse (or keyboard) cable may have come loose. Plug everything in firmly.

## Something really weird starts suddenly: Beeps and menus get stuck down

If it's not your Mac, or if it *is* your Mac and you just aren't very tuned in, the culprit may be a little add-on program that makes menus jump down when the cursor touches them, even when you're *not* pressing the mouse button. I've always thought this kind of program is somewhat cruel, but some people claim that it saves them some effort.

If you're using a trackball, you may be the victim of a similarly stupid feature: a button on the trackball that, when clicked, makes the Mac think you're pressing the mouse button *all the time*. For the rest of your computing day, the Mac will think that the button is down, even if you frantically click the *regular* mouse button or try to quit the program or anything. Only when you again touch the click lock button does the Mac free the pointer from its bondage.

## Nothing appears when you type

***First resort:*** Well, obviously, you can't just type at any time and expect to see text appear. You have to be either in a word processor or in a text-editing area (like a dialog box or in the little text-editing rectangle when you're renaming an icon).

*Second resort:* Check the cable between the keyboard and the Mac. Make sure it's *very* firmly plugged in at both ends.

Incidentally, the keyboard and mouse cables are especially sensitive to being plugged and unplugged while the computer is on. Be religious about shutting off the Mac before plugging and unplugging them. (That's especially true of SCSI cables. The same is *not* particularly true of modem and printer cables, though.)

## Keyboard shortcuts aren't working

Suppose that you try to press ⌘-P to print or ⌘-Q to quit, and nothing happens. Chances are pretty good that your Caps Lock key is engaged, and you're not sending the Mac the signal you think you're sending. (Of course, well-written programs should be aware of that and not care whether the Caps Lock is down or not.)

On the other hand, the Option, ⌘, and Control keys *are* awfully close together, and they *are* awfully similar. It happens all the time: somebody complains that a keyboard shortcut isn't working, and it turns out that he is pressing Control, not Option . . . or whatever. Look twice to make sure.

## Your monitor shimmers

Of course, I don't mean that your monitor *itself* jiggles; I mean the picture.

*First resort:* Your screen's being subjected to some kind of electrical interference, such as a lamp, a fan, or an air conditioner running on the same circuit. Try a different plug, a different monitor location, or a different career.

*Last resort:* You live in an earthquake zone. Move to the Midwest.

# Chapter 12
# Beyond Point-and-Click: Where to Go from Here

●●●●●●●●●●●●●●●●●●●●●●●●●●●●●●●●●●●●●●●●●●●●●●●●●●●●●●

●●●●●●●●●●●●●●●●●●●●●●●●●●●●●●●●●●●●●●●●●●●●●●●●●●●●●●

## *Credit Card Workout #5: Upgrades and Accelerators*

As I warned you in Chapter 1, your Mac's life span is limited — not in terms of usefulness but in terms of cutting-edgeness. As new models roll out of Silicon Valley, you'll find that your Mac model, though once top-of-the-line, becomes bottom-of-the-heap insultingly quickly.

The advice I'm about to give you may be difficult to follow, but it's something I firmly believe: If the Mac does what you need it to do, *you don't have to keep up with technology.* The impulse to keep your Mac current for its own sake will be strong, but I promise you that your personal worth does *not* ride on the processor speed of your Mac.

A woman in my building uses a 1984 Mac with one-eighth of a meg of memory. She owns one program — the very first version of MacWrite. She's in heaven.

Now then. If some *software* comes out that requires a more powerful Mac, and you require that program, that's a different story. At that point you have a couple of options:

▸ You can upgrade or accelerate your Mac by having a dealer install a more powerful circuit board inside. These upgrades are provided both by Apple and by other companies. Needless to say, Apple's upgrades are twice as expensive as non-Apple ones; what you're basically buying is the logo — and, if your Mac is still under warranty (or Apple's extended warranty

> program, called AppleCare), an Apple upgrade won't nuke your safety net. A non-Apple upgrade probably *will* cancel your warranty — but if your Mac's warranty has already expired, there's no reason not to consider it.
>
> ✔ You can sell your old Mac and buy a more recent model. Believe it or not, this is often the more economical route. It's more effort, of course. But there are plenty of places to sell your Mac: the classifieds, user groups, bulletin boards at the library or the gym, and any of a number of national computer brokerages. These last advertise in *Macworld* and *MacUser* magazines.

# Where to Turn in Times of Trouble

You *do* own the world's most forgiving, self-explanatory computer. But sometimes things will go wrong.

Up until a couple years ago, your official Answer Person was supposed to be — ready for this? — the dealer from whom you bought your computer.

Yeah, right. Like this guy ever wants to see you again once the check clears.

Fortunately, Apple has gone from providing an absolutely wretched service plan to an absolutely spectacular one. Any time during the first year you own your Mac, they'll send somebody *to you* to fix the thing if it breaks. In your house. For free.

And if it's a PowerBook, they'll send an overnight-package person to your door to pick up the laptop, pay for the overnight freight to Texas, fix it there, and overnight it right back to you. For free.

The magic phone number to get this kind of help, cleverly enough, is 800-SOS-APPL. Get it?

For software and System 7 questions, Apple provides a couple somewhat less free phone numbers. Their $2-per-minute help line is 900-535-2775. Or you can listen to some canned questions-and-answers at 408-257-7700, for which you're charged nothing but the long-distance call.

Otherwise, as I've no doubt etched permanently into your brain by now, your next resort should be a local user group, if you're lucky enough to live in a pseudo-metropolitan area. A user group, of course, doesn't exist to answer *your* personal questions; you still have to do some phoning and hobnobbing and research. But a user group *is* a source of sources. You can call up and find out who will know the answer to your question.

The other great source of help, as I've said, is an electronic meeting place like America Online, where you may get your question answered instantly — and if not, you can post your question on a bulletin board for somebody to answer overnight. As a matter of fact, *I'm* there, ready to receive your praise or, if it must be, your wrath, for stuff I've gotten you into. My e-mail address there is Pogue.

As for your continuing education — after you spend a month's salary on a computer, I'll bet you can afford $20 more for a subscription to *Macworld* or *MacUser* magazine. I'll warn you that huge chunks of these rags will go right over your head. Heck, chunks of them go over *my* head. But in every single issue, you'll find at least one really useful item. You can learn all kinds of things just by reading the ads. And if you're not in touch with the computer nerd world at least by that tenuous thread — via magazine — then you might miss stuff like free offers, recall notices, warnings, and other consumer-oriented jazz.

And there are books. The publisher of this book has decided that, by gum, there's a market for this stuff, so he persuaded me to write two more. Like *More Macs For Dummies,* which is just like this book except more.

And when you *really* become an expert, you'll be ready for *Macworld Macintosh Secrets,* which has 1,000 pages, three software disks, and requires a forklift to move.

# *Save Changes Before Closing?*

If you do decide to pursue this Macintosh thing, I've listed the phone numbers of major user groups, dial-up services, and magazines in Appendix B, the Resource Resource, along with contact information for the products I've mentioned.

But wait a minute — the point of this book wasn't to convert you into a full-time Mac rabbit. It was to get you off the ground. To give you just enough background so you'll know why the computer's beeping at you. To show you the basics and help you figure out what the beanie heads are talking about.

Don't let them intimidate you. So *what* if you don't know the lingo or have the circuitry memorized? If you can turn the thing on, get something written up and printed, and get out in time to enjoy the sunshine, you qualify as a real Mac user.

Any dummy knows that.

# Top Ten Topics Not Covered in This Book

Here's a who's who of topics I don't think any new Mac user needs to bother with. If you have the slightest interest in any of them, the shelves are full of geekier books than this one.

1. Networking.

2. Programming.

3. Any add-on that costs over $2,000.

4. Color separations.

5. Multimedia. Nobody even knows what it is.

6. Hard-disk partitioning. Too many syllables.

7. Publish and Subscribe. If you really want to get into it, it's in your Mac manuals.

8. How data is stored on a disk. If you never need to know something, why bring it up?

9. Security. There are all kinds of fancy ways to lock up your Mac. If you're really interested, call up Mac Connection and ask about what they can sell you.

10. The terms *ROM, interleave, AUTOEXEC.BAT, SIMM, initiate, user-definable, SIMM, DRAM, implement, CDEV, nanosecond, kerning, VRAM, magneto-optical, token-ring, Ethernet, directory,* or *DOS.*

# Appendix A
# How to Buy (and Set Up) a Macintosh

• • • • • • • • • • • • • • • • • • • • • • • • • • • • • • • • • • • • • • • • • • • • • • • • •

*G*etting started with a Mac really involves three steps (or four, if you count reading this book): deciding which model to get, figuring out where to buy it, and setting it up. This delightful appendix will guide you through all three with as few tension headaches as possible.

## The Only Three Specs That Matter (Besides the Price)

You'll hear all kinds of numbers and specifications tossed around when you go Mac shopping. But the only three that matter are (1) hard disk space, (2) memory, (3) the processor chip model.

> ✔ **Hard disk space.** The first number that matters is the *size of the hard disk inside the Mac.* The size is measured in *megabytes,* or, if you're at a cocktail party, you can say *megs* for short. Larger disks are more expensive.
>
> How much do you need? Well, the stuff you'll be creating (letters, manuscripts, whatever) is pretty small; a 500-page book might take up *one* megabyte of your hard disk. But today's *software programs,* like a word processing program, are huge; count on each one taking up a megabyte or

---

### What the hey?

I'm perfectly aware that these are strange, alien terms unless you've already looked over Chapter 1½, where hard disks and memory are discussed in nauseating detail. Essentially, the bigger the hard disk, the more stuff (text, pictures, music, numbers, whatever) you can store. And memory is related to the computer's capacity to run programs — the more memory, the more you can do with your software programs.

two by itself. Whether you understand any of this or not, believe it: a hard disk fills up quickly. Get at least an 80MB hard disk (or at least 40MB on a PowerBook).

The first question you might ask in the computer store, then, is — "Yo. Does this Mac have an 80-, 120-, or 230-megabyte hard disk?" No salesperson will take *you* for a ride.

✔ **Memory.** When you press Play on a VCR, it reads the videocassette's contents and throws the video information up onto the TV screen. When the TV is off, you can't watch your movie, but you sleep well knowing it's still safely stored on the tape.

Similarly, your Macintosh reads what's on the *hard disk,* and throws an electronic copy of it up on your computer screen, where you can look at it, make changes, whatever. While it's on the screen, it's *in memory.* (Details on this stuff in Chapter 1½.)

What's confusing about memory is that it's measured in the *same units* as hard-drive space — megabytes. But memory is much more expensive than disk space, so you get a lot less of it. Where hard drives are typically 80MB or 120MB, a Mac usually comes with 4MB or 8MB of memory. The more you have, the more you can do with your computer simultaneously (type into one window, draw in another, and so on). In general, you need at least 4MB of memory to do anything useful.

Intelligent Computer Comment Number Two, then, is: "How much RAM do I get in this Mac? Two megs? Forget it! I can't even *breathe* in two megs."

By the way, newspaper ads often give you both of these first critical numbers (memory and disk space) at once. You might read, for example, "Mac Classic 2/40." In your newfound savvy, you know that this computer has 2MB of *memory* and a 40MB *hard drive* for permanent storage. A Mac Classic 4/80 is better.

✔ **Processor model number**. The third important number is the name of the primary processor chip. (As endless *Newsweek* articles and specials on *Nova* have no doubt informed you, a *chip* is a rat's nest of tiny circuits, etched into a piece of silicon the size of a couple of postage stamps.) The heart of a Macintosh is a chip, about an inch square, that's actually manufactured in the millions by a completely different company. (It's Motorola; that's why *Apple* stock goes down when there are negative headlines about Motorola.)

The higher the model number of this chip, the faster the Mac. There are three models of processor chip used in recent Macs: 68000, 68030, and 68040. You don't have a choice for a specific model of Mac. The Classic, for example, has a 68000 chip, and that's all there is to it. All other current models use the 68030 or 68040 chip. (Except . . . well, read the section later in this chapter called " . . . And the PowerPC.")

Actually, there's a *fourth* variable that accounts for the performance differences among Mac models — the *clock speed* of that chip.

That's something like the blood pressure. It's how fast the data moves through the machine's circuits. The range of speeds, measured (get this) in *megahertz,* is from 16 to 40 (Mac Plus and Quadra, respectively).

That explains why the Classic II, the IIsi, and the IIci (for example) all have different prices and run at different speeds, even though they all use the same Motorola 68030 chip.

Just one more thing: in order to make newcomers feel as much like outsiders as possible, the computer stores and newspaper ads run this information together into a cryptic little line. This is pretty important information for comparison shoppers, so I thought a translation might be in order.

You might read, for example, about a Mac with a "33 MHz '040" chip. In other words, it's a 68040 processor, like the Quadras, running at 33 MHz. Since the megahertz (speed) scale runs from 16 to 40, you can tell that this is a pretty fast Mac.

# *Macintosh as a Second Language*

Let's see how much of that tech-talk you were able to absorb.

*In today's newspaper:* "SPECIAL SALE: 33 MHz '030 Performa 550 8/230."

Stay calm. Don't let your eyes glaze over. You *do* know what this means. Take it morsel by morsel.

Translation: The "33 MHz '030" part is the speed measurement. Remember that the clock speed is the MHz (megahertz) part, and the scale goes from 16 to 40. And the chip numbers are 68000, 68030, and 68040 — so *'030* indicates a chip with middle-of-the-line power.

Then there's the Mac model number (Performa 550). These numbers are purely marketing designations by Apple, and have nothing to do with the Macs' relative speeds or anything. Just ignore it.

Finally, you see how much memory and hard-drive space you get in this computer. Both are measured in megabytes (MB); the memory comes before the slash, the hard drive size after.

*In the grocery:* "Nice to see you! Say, you ought to come over to my house. My husband just got a Macintosh PowerBook 165c 4/40. It's neato."

*Translation:* Well, you'll find out from the discussion below that a PowerBook with a *c* in its name has a color screen. So her husband got a middle-of-the-laptop-line color laptop computer with 4MB of RAM (just enough) and a 40MB hard drive — the 4/40 configuration. (He'll probably fill up that baby's hard drive with stuff in about three months.)

*In* Entertainment Weekly: "The film's special effects were created using a Macintosh IIfx with an installed 040 accelerator card."

*Translation:* OK, well, you'll find out later in this chapter that the IIfx is a powerful machine, but it comes with a 68030 processor. The special-effects people needed more horsepower, so they expanded it — they opened the lid and slipped in a circuit board (which they purchased from a non-Apple company that makes such things). This circuit board has a 68040 chip on it — the same one that makes the Quadra such a racehorse — so these special-effects wizards essentially turned their not-quite-top-of-the-line IIfx into a real workstation.

*On a bulletin board:* "FOR SALE: Macintosh Plus. Color monitor, 2 expansion slots. $3,000. Call Sid."

*Translation:* This guy has no idea what he's talking about. The Plus is black-and-white, it has no expansion slots, and that's about six times too much to pay for a used machine!

If you understand that much, the worst is over. You're ready to begin your assault on the computer marketplace — informed, armed, and ready for anything.

# The Product Line

Look, it's hopeless to try to keep up with Apple in a Mac book. Since the Macintosh first appeared on the scene, there have been 50 different models.

There are something like 20 still being made by Apple — at *this* writing. Each one is available in several different configurations of features. For heaven's sake, they introduce a half dozen new models *twice a year!* Who can keep them straight, let alone get them printed into a book that stays current?

Still, I think you should have some idea of what's happening on the Mac shelf when you walk into the store. One reason it's especially futile to keep track of the Macs in this world is that Apple often gives several *different names* to the *same machine!* I mean, the Quadra 605, the Macintosh LC 475, and the Performa 476 are *identical Macs.*

Why on earth would Apple do something so silly? Because Apple thinks that there are three distinct ways people buy computers. Kids, of course, buy them through their schools; the Macs for sale there are all called LC-something. Business people buy computers at computer stores; their machines are all called Quadra-something (or PowerBook-something). And Mr. and Mrs. Family buy their computers at Sears and electronics stores; their Macs are all called Performa-something. So Apple figures: may as well sell the same models in as many different ways as possible!

Of course, this strategy is something new for Apple. Before they came up with this scheme, their were a zillion other, now defunct model lines. Remember the olden days of 1993? Remember those crazy Mac II-series machines? And how about those nutty Classics? And oh, yeah — that wacky Centris line!

Anyway, here are some representative model names, past and present, along with what you might use them for. Remember that, for a little diñero, you can upgrade almost any Mac at any time to make it faster. Also remember that within each family, higher numbers usually indicate faster, more recent models.

## *Black-and-white one-piece*

Macintosh Plus

Macintosh SE and SE/30

Macintosh Classic and Classic II

Performa 200

These one-piece models, called *compact Macs* by Apple, are about two feet tall. All you do is plug in the keyboard and the power cord, and you're off and running. All of these models, which now cost from $400 to about $900, have been discontinued by Apple. (Techie note: They all run at a speed of 16 MHz; all are based on the 68000 processor, except the '030-based Classic II/Performa 200.)

The screen is built in. Apple calls it a nine-inch screen, but they're measuring diagonally. It's actually about seven inches wide and five inches tall, so you can see a five-inch-tall slice of a page all the way across.

One-piece Macs are inexpensive and relatively transportable (there's a handle built into the top). They weigh about 15 pounds, you can get a carrying case for them, and they fit into the overhead rack of an airplane, just barely. Especially if you take out the little foam pillows first. (Of the rack, I mean. Not the computer.)

For word processing, the screen size is perfectly adequate. But art and graphic design people go nuts if they can't see an entire page on the screen at once.

### What they're good for

Word processing; mail-merge (form letters); typing-instruction programs; black-and-white painting programs; dialing over the phone lines using a modem; Rolodex and calendar programs; simple database files; designing flyers; HyperCard stacks, such as kids' programs; checkbook programs.

## Color one-piece

Color Classic

Color Classic II (overseas only)

LC 520 (Performa 550)

They're bigger, heavier, and more expensive (in the $1,200–1,500 range) than the black-and-white compact Macs. On the other hand, they're fast, easily expandable, and have a built-in, gorgeous, *color* screen. And they're relatively fast, since they're based on the 68030 chip at a speed of 16 or 25 MHz. The LC 520 also has built-in stereo speakers and a built-in CD-ROM player (see Chapter 7). Its screen measures 14 inches diagonally; the Color Classic's screen is 10 inches.

### What they're good for

Everything listed for the previous models, plus: Color games; kids' programs (especially CD-ROM discs, in the case of the LC 520); basic color painting and drawing; playback of QuickTime digital movies, complete with sound and video in a small window.

# The LC series

Macintosh LC

Macintosh LC II (Performa 405, 410, 430)

Macintosh LC III (Performa 450, 460, 466, 467)

Macintosh LC 475 (Performa 475, 476)

The LC (for *low-cost color*) Macs are two-piece Macs. In other words, you have to buy two pieces of equipment: the computer itself and a separate screen (the *monitor*). When computer nerds want to show off, they call the part that's *not* the monitor a *CPU*. Got that? You have two pieces to buy — a monitor and a CPU. (CPU stands for *Central Processing Unit*. Now *that* makes everything clear, doesn't it?)

Now, you're not going to be able to transport *this* baby without the original shipping cartons (and a luggage cart). But buying a separate monitor grants you the power of choice: large or small, black-and-white or color, tall or wide. (Also Apple and non-Apple, for that matter — the golden rule is that anything with the Apple logo on it costs 15 percent more than the same gadget from somebody else.)

The two-piece Macs (called *modular* by Apple) are also easily expandable. The lid pops right off, just like the lid of a shoebox. Of course, the inside of the computer looks nothing like the inside of a shoebox. There are a lot of wires and chips and stuff, but they're very neatly arranged, and whatever you want to install (more memory, an accelerator card, whatever) slips into a very obvious place. (Each LC has one *slot* — a rectangular socket into which you can plug a special-feature circuit board, like an accelerator or a video card.)

Today, Apple thinks of the LCs as its educational line. An LC is no longer considered a cheapo wimp machine, either; the LC 475, for example, is the exact same computer as the Quadra 605, a respectably horsepowered machine. (Techie note: The LC models' speeds vary widely within the family, ranging from the LC, with an '020 chip, to the LC 475, with its '040 chip; speeds run from 16 to 33 MHz.) Prices for new and used LC computers range from $800 to $1,400 or so.

The LC and LC II are, in fact, exactly the same (slowish) speed. The LC III, on the other hand, is over twice as fast. If, as an LC or LC II owner, the thought of getting a faster computer has entered your head at all, roll this little concept around on your mental tongue: for about $500, you can get an Apple upgrade that turns your Mac into a shiny new LC III, which will feel positively turbo-charged to the touch.

### What they're good for

Everything listed for the previous models, plus: page layout and graphic design (since you can attach a big screen); music recording from a synthesizer; basic spreadsheets. (The LC 475, of course, has the horsepower necessary for more challenging tasks; see "What they're good for" following the Mac II-series discussion, next, for example.)

## Mac II series

Macintosh II, IIx, IIfx, IIcx, IIsi, IIci, IIvx

Macintosh IIvi (overseas only)

Macintosh IIvx (Performa 600)

All of these models have been discontinued. These, too, are modular Macs (see the description of the LC series, above). Furthermore, most of these Macs have multiple expansion slots. The prices for used II-series Macs are between $1,000 and $2,000. (Techie details: All but the '020-based Mac II contain a 68030 chip running at speeds between 16 and 40 MHz. You can get a built-in CD-ROM player on the IIvx/Performa 600.)

### What they're good for

Everything listed for the previous models, plus: complex spreadsheets; pro-level page layout; medium and complex databases; music notation (sheet music); QuickTime digital movie recording (with the addition of a $400 expansion card) and editing; sending electronic mail to other Macs in the office.

# The Quadra series

Macintosh Quadra 605

Macintosh Quadra 610 (Centris 610)

Macintosh Quadra 650 (Centris 650)

Macintosh Quadra 700, 800, 900, 950

If the PowerBooks are laptops, then these are *floortops;* most of them are so massive and powerful-looking that you're supposed to put them under your desk.

The name *Quadra* comes from the chip these Macs are based on: the '040, which, when it first debuted, made everybody's hair stand on end with its blistering speed. Only a couple of years later, this speed has almost become status quo; except for the PowerBooks, the majority of current Mac models is now based on the '040 processor.

Anyway, the Quadras introduced one other notable feature: you can get other Mac devices, like CD-ROM players and removable SyQuest cartridge drives, built right in. A Quadra 600-series Mac can house one such device; Quadras 800 and higher are huge Macs, with enough room for two such built-in gadgets. Most Quadra models also come with a feature called *Ethernet;* much as it might sound like the webbing of choice for anesthesiologists, it is in fact a fast and fancy system of wiring Macs together in an office (for sending electronic messages back and forth, sharing files, and so on).

Prices for Quadras range from $1,000 for the recent, slimline 605 model to $5,000 for the top-of-the-line, feature-packed 950 ready for use as the backbone for a whole office.

## What they're good for

Everything listed for the previous models, plus: color photo retouching and Photoshop (a professional painting program) art; 3-D graphics "rendering" (on-screen model making); morphing (making QuickTime movies that melt one image magically into another, as in Michael Jackson's "Black and White" video);

high-level statistical analysis; programming; and serving as an office "server" (a central Mac whose files can be accessed by every desktop Mac in the office).

## The AV series

Macintosh Quadra 660AV (Centris 660AV)

Macintosh Quadra 840AV

AV stands for audio-visual, and that describes these Macs perfectly. They can actually *speak* anything you type out for them, using a voice that actually has some expression and lilt (although it does sound like it has a permanent stuffy nose). They can also take orders from you: the microphone picks up any commands you speak, and executes them. Of course, it ain't exactly taking dictation; its comprehension of things you say to it is, for the most part, limited to menu commands in your programs. And how does it know when you're addressing *it,* instead of just chattering away on the phone? Because you preface each command with your Mac's name. "Xerxes, empty the trash," you might say. (One guy I know thought it was hysterically funny to name his Mac "Simon Says." That way, his AV wouldn't respond if he said "Close window." It would only react if he said "*Simon says* Close window!")

These are very fast Macs — particularly the Quadra 840AV, which has a 68040 chip that runs at a wild 40 MHz. Yet the prices aren't particularly numbing: a Quadra 660AV is around $2,500, and a Quadra 840AV is about $3,500.

### What they're good for

Everything listed for the previous models, plus a few specialized tasks that only AV Macs can perform: hooking up a VCR to record what you see on the screen; hooking up a cable and watching TV on your monitor; connecting a telephone line and using the Mac as a glorified answering machine/speakerphone; making QuickTime movies from a videotape or the TV without buying any extra equipment; with the purchase of a $100 adapter, serving as a full-fledged fax/ modem (see Chapter 7).

## PowerBooks

PowerBook 100, 140, 170

PowerBook 145, 145b, 160, 165, 180

PowerBook 165c, 180c

PowerBook Duo 210, 230, 250, 270c

These Macs are called PowerBooks. They're dark gray, two inches thick, weigh under seven pounds, and are every bit as powerful as the models we've been discussing. They open like a book when you're using them; one side has the keyboard, and the other has the screen. You can plug a PowerBook in or use the battery, which lasts about two hours per charge. (Airport waiting lounges, public restrooms, bus terminals . . . you'd be amazed at how good you'll become at finding power outlets on the road once you own a PowerBook. See Chapter 10 for a detailed discussion of these amazing gadgets.)

Typing on a PowerBook is slightly less comfortable than on a desktop Mac; you pay more, and you can only expand one with considerable hassle and expense (unless you have a Duo Dock; see Chapter 10). But a PowerBook is indispensable for anyone who travels. And a PowerBook is definitely the Mac to have if you're trying to catch the eye of an attractive stranger across the aisle. (Especially if you've got one with a color screen.)

What on earth could account for all the different models and prices (from $1,200 to $3,800)? After all, they all use a 68030 processor. First, there's color; the model numbers followed by the letter *c* have color screens, which are more expensive (and guzzle battery power faster) than black-and-white screens. Second, there's something called *built-in video*. The more expensive PowerBooks have a jack on the back into which you can plug in a regular Mac monitor, so that you can plug in your huge, heavy, full-page color monitor whenever you're not on a plane somewhere. The less expensive PowerBooks (140, 145b) lack this back-panel jack, Jack.

Finally, there are the Duos. I'm a wild, hysterical fan of these amazing four-pound PowerBooks, actually. They're much smaller and lighter than regular PowerBooks because you can leave a lot of the electronics — the floppy-disk drive and the back-panel jacks — at home on your desk, and just take the computer itself with you to do your work. Consult Chapter 10 to find out all the witty and interesting things you can attach to the back of a Duo to turn it into a more full-fledged Mac, complete with big screen, mouse, and full-size keyboard.

### What they're good for

Everything listed for the Mac II-series Macs — but you can do any of it while sitting comfortably on a plane, train, or La-Z-boy recliner.

## ...And the PowerPC

Apple's 1994 Mac models won't be based on those 68000-series processor chips like all previous ones. Instead, these new Macs will contain an *extremely* fast, very high-tech new chip called the PowerPC chip.

These Macs, which will probably be called Quadras (and look like Quadras), will work fine with all normal Mac programs. But the speed won't exactly pin your ears back; when you run these programs, you'll think you're using an LC III or something.

But if you upgrade your programs to special PowerPC versions, they'll *really* scream; these specially written programs will run three times *faster* than on the fastest of today's Quadras. (Some of the programs that will be available on Day 1 in PowerPC-ready versions are Photoshop, Illustrator, Freehand, ClarisWorks, QuarkXpress, and others.) These new Mac models will cost between $2,000 and $4,000; as 1994 progresses, Apple hopes to introduce more and more models, built on faster and faster PowerPC chips.

If you've already bought a Quadra or Centris Mac, you'll be able to upgrade your computer to have a PowerPC chip when the time comes.

### What they're good for

Everything listed for the previous models — but *faster*.

## Buying a Monitor

If you've decided to become the proud owner of a two-piece Mac (a Mac II-something, a Quadra, Centris, LC or equivalent), you have to decide what kind of screen (monitor) to get.

You can classify monitors either by shape or by display color. For instance, you can get a *portrait* or *full-page* display, which is big enough to show you a full 8½-inch × 11-inch page at a time (below left).

There are also *two-page* displays, which (needless to say) show two side-by-side pages at a time (above middle). The most popular Apple color monitors, on the other hand, have a screen just shy of nine inches wide and seven inches tall. They're called *landscape* monitors because they're wider than they are tall, and they don't quite show you a full page at a time (above right). These Apple color monitors are referred to as the 12-inch, 13-inch, and 14-inch displays. The old 12-inch monitor is cheap, but avoid it; everyone I know who has one complains about it. The 13-inch is fantastic but pricier. For about half as much you can get a slightly lower quality 14-inch monitor which, despite its name, shows exactly the same amount of screen area as the 13-inch.

For writing, virtually any size screen will do. Even if you can only see half a page at a time, you can always *scroll* the display up or down, to see what you wrote on the previous (or next) page. If you plan to do any graphic design — that is, page layout of brochures or newsletters — you'll probably want at least a full-page display. And if you're going to do professional page design work, such as laying out a book, then get a two-page display.

## Black-and-white, grayscale, color

The least expensive screens show you black writing against a white background, just like a typewriter. For writing, finances, spreadsheets, music, databases, calendars, Rolodexes, and 90 percent of the other day-to-day Mac tasks, black-and-white is all you'll ever need. Black-and-white screens are also the fastest; you almost never have to wait for the computer to "paint" the screen from top to bottom, as you do when you're working in color.

---

## Nauseating detail about monochrome

The computer nerds refer to black-and-white screens as *monochrome* monitors. Joke's on them, though. *Monochrome* doesn't actually mean black-and-white. Technically speaking, it means a color monitor with only one color — black. In other words, a grayscale monitor, which is something totally different.

---

The next step up is a *grayscale* monitor. These monitors don't just have black and white; they can also display any shade of gray. Particularly in larger sizes, these Macs are less expensive than color monitors, yet they can still give your icons a nice 3-D look.

Color monitors are the most expensive, and they make everything appear on the screen slightly slower. There are some things that absolutely demand a color monitor: games, color graphics, presentations and some business charts, digital movies (called QuickTime movies), and so on. Otherwise, color is purely a luxury. Everything on the screen appears more 3-D. Certain programs make clever use of color — for example, a drafting program might display light blue graph paper lines behind the black lines you draw.

In the olden days (in other words, last year), that would have been the end of the color story. You got to see great, rich, stunning color on the screen, but everything you printed came out in black and white. Color printers cost way too much for any individual to buy.

Recently, though, the prices of color printers have plummeted. Now you can buy a high-quality color printer for $4,000, or one with a more limited palette of colors for $1,000. I wouldn't advise getting a color printer for everyday correspondence and such, but if you're ever hired to design rough sketches for a movie poster or something, keep those cheapie color printers in mind.

## A little bit about 8-bit color

If you decide to get a color monitor, your decision-making isn't over yet. The techno-bullies of the world have foisted several different *kinds* of color upon us: *8-bit, 16-bit,* or *24-bit* color. All you need to know is that 16-bit and 24-bit color is relatively more expensive, slower to appear on the screen, and much more realistic. *Realistic* is a term that only matters if you plan to work with photos or movies on the screen. If not, 24-bit is for the pros, and it's overkill for everyone else. (An additional note: Most current Macs give you 8-bit color; all you have to do is plug your monitor into a built-in jack. If you one day decide that you can't live without photo-realistic colors on your screen, you can buy and install a *video card* [a circuit board] to get 16-bit or 24-bit color — you don't need a whole new monitor.)

## One less thing to buy — maybe

In the olden days, color Macs didn't have built-in color-monitor circuitry. You'd have to pay $400 for a video card *and* buy a monitor.

Nowadays, Apple is more generous: they've built the required circuitry for basic (8-bit) color into all current Macs (and even some discontinued ones like the IIsi and the IIci). Today, the primary reason to buy a video card is to gain 16-bit or 24-bit (more realistic) color.

Be ye warned, though. By using the Mac's own brain to process the visual information (instead of shoving it over to a video card to do), you slow down your Mac. If you're shopping for a new Mac and plan to use its built-in video feature instead of buying a card, try one at a computer store to make certain you won't be impatient waiting for the screen picture to update itself.

When you're choosing a monitor, remember that a color monitor is *also* a grayscale monitor *and* a black-and-white monitor. (An on-screen control panel lets you switch from one mode to another.) As you read this book, look over the possibilities of color and see if any of them appeal to you. Otherwise, black and white is the faster, less expensive way to go.

## For pixel weenies only

You really, really want to know where terms like *8-bit* and *24-bit* come from? Don't say you weren't warned.

Remember color theory from high school physics? Mixing the three primary colors red, yellow, and blue is supposed to be able to produce any color in the rainbow.

Well, to display a color picture, the Mac has to remember the precise amount of those colors to mix for *each individual dot on the screen*. Think about it: dot number 15 is 21 percent red, 79 percent blue, and so on, for each dot. That's an awful lot of information to store for each of 307,200 dots.

To save expense, trouble, and memory, the most popular Mac monitors only reserve 8 bits of the Mac's brain to describe the color of each dot. (You can think of a *bit* as one word of computer description, a unit of electronic information.) So even though a particular dot can be any color under the rainbow, the *total number of colors* that can appear on an 8-bit color monitor is 256. That may sound like a lot of colors, but there are thousands more shades needed to produce a convincing rainbow.

The pros, then, get much more expensive monitors that use far more information to describe the color of each dot — 16 or 24 bits, in fact. With that much description power, the Mac can display *millions* of different colors at once. In fact, every dot on the screen could be a different color, and you'd still have millions of colors to choose from that couldn't fit on the screen.

All this thinking and describing the Mac has to do for 24-bit color (sometimes stupidly called 32-bit color, by the way — it's the same thing) means the screen gets painted pretty slowly. Of course, the Basic Rule of Computing states that whenever there's a computing inconvenience, some company will invent an expensive gizmo that solves it. The slow speed of 24-bit monitors is no exception: For a couple grand more, you can get an *accelerated* graphics card, which makes it possible to see 24-bit images almost as quickly as 8-bit ones on an *unac*celerated screen.

# Where to Buy Your Mac

I'm going to assume that you're not in Donald Trump's tax bracket and that you're looking for ways to get the most Mac for the least lira.

## The Apple university discount

First of all, you should know that Apple grants hefty Mac discounts to students and teachers. In Apple's younger, healthier days, it was 40 percent; it's not quite as much of a giveaway today, but there's still no possible way to find lower prices on Mac equipment. If you're affiliated with a college, find out if the school's bookstore is a member of this delightful program.

## Mail order

If you're not fortunate enough to be a student or faculty member, the next least-expensive way to get a new Mac is probably through a mail-order catalog. These outfits take out big ads in the Macintosh magazines like *Macworld* (which, I say with no small conflict of interest, is my favorite) and *MacUser*. Of course, you can't exactly browse the merchandise, and so it's assumed that you already know what you want when you call up one of these places.

If everything goes smoothly, mail order can be a nifty deal: You save hundreds by avoiding sales tax, you get a pretty good price, and you don't have to haul anything home in the car. The trouble with mail order, though, is that things can get pretty ugly if things *don't* go right. What if the thing is broken when it arrives? Suddenly, you've got the burden of packing it up, shipping it back to the company, and persuading them to replace the equipment (*if* they'll even consider it). Mail order is for gamblers: You can score big, but you can also get shafted, and you won't have anywhere to turn for help.

## Computer stores

A computer store, on the other hand, is likely to have higher prices. You'll have to pay sales tax. But you also get a human being to blame when things get fouled up.

Unfortunately, buying a computer at a store is still a crapshoot: good dealers are relatively rare, and lousy dealers are everywhere. There's a notorious New York City dealership, for example, that makes a regular practice of advertising rock-bottom prices. Then, when you show up, they mention that you'll "probably also want to buy" several items normally included in the package — the mouse, for example, or a cartridge if you're buying a printer.

So how are you supposed to know good dealers (and their repair guys) from bad? There's only one way: ask around. Of course, depending on where you live, getting the word-of-mouth report may be easier said than done. If you're at a loss as to whom you should ask, start by finding the nearest Macintosh user group (by calling Apple's user group listing hotline, 800-538-9696).

## *Consumer stores*

There they are, right next to the blenders and microwaves: the Macintosh Performa series. These Macs are *only* sold through non-computer stores like Sears, Silo, Price Club, and office-supply stores. Because the usual clerks can't be expected to know anything about computers, Apple covers you with toll-free phone numbers — one to call with questions and one to call if something breaks.

The Performas are essentially the same machines as Macs sold under other names in usual computer stores. And they're priced about the same, but they come with free software. Their special version of System 7 makes using them even easier — but at the expense of some minor features (see Chapter 9 for details). If you don't mind that, and aren't too grossed out by the word Performa, then the Performas are a good deal.

## *Used Macs*

Finally, you can buy a used Mac. Once again, the luck of the draw determines how satisfied you'll be. To a certain extent, you can tell how much abuse a Mac has had by looking at it. But a visual exam won't tell you about the funny noise the hard drive makes only after it's been on for 20 minutes, or the monitor that's been in for repair three times already, or the ball of cat hair wedged inside the disk drive.

In other words, there are three rules for buying used equipment. First, determine that you're willing to forgo the comfy Apple warranty for the sake of saving money. Second, be sure the asking price really is low enough that the savings is meaningful, particularly with discontinued Mac models like the SE/30 or the LC. (Some naïve sellers, who don't understand the Inviolable Rule of Instant Obsolescence, think they can recoup their full purchase price when they sell their used Mac. Don't fall for it — be sure you've compared the asking price with a computer store's new Mac price.)

And finally, test the Mac as much as possible before you buy it. Above all, test the disk drive (by inserting a floppy disk and copying a file onto it), the printer port (by printing something), and the mouse (by rolling it around on the desk).

## Credit cards

It doesn't thrill me to break the news to you, but you're going to be spending a lot of money even *after* buying your Mac. We haven't even discussed buying a keyboard yet. (Here's the discussion: Wherever you're buying your Mac, you can also buy a keyboard. But it'll cost about $50 more than a keyboard from a mail-order company.) And you're going to need software. As hobby costs go, computing isn't exactly crocheting.

As long as you're committed to this plunge, a word of solemn advice: Put everything on a credit card, especially when you're buying by mail order. Thousands of Mac users have avoided getting ripped off by the occasional fly-by-night operation because they charged it. (As you probably know, the credit card company doesn't pay your bill if you're disputing the charge — an incredible layer of protection between you and companies that send you the wrong item, a broken one, and so on.)

# I Took Off the Shrink-Wrap! Now What?

Setting up the Mac should take less than 20 minutes. All you have to do is plug in three cables. (If you have a two-piece Mac, you also have to set up the monitor. And if you have a printer, you have to hook that up, too — see Chapter 4.)

## Ergo . . . ergonomics

First, figure out where you're going to put the most expensive appliance you've ever bought. In my opinion, the principal principle is: When you're seated at your desk, and you're in typing position, *your elbows can't be lower than your wrists.* Otherwise, if you plan to do a lot of work at the computer, you may wind up with a nasty and painful ailment, called Carpal Tunnel Syndrome, which never goes away until you stop using the computer.

The next ergonomic lesson is one learned from painful experience by thousands of home-office users: Don't put the monitor in front of a sunny window. It turns out that your pupils shrink to accommodate the bright window light. But since you're trying to focus on the relatively dim Mac screen, your optic system gets confused and strained, and it's hello, headache.

Finally, I suppose I should mention ELF. No, this elf isn't the little man inside the Mac who runs around obeying your every command. It stands for Extremely Low-Frequency radiation. There are a few scientists who've been saying (without much hard proof one way or another) that electrical appliances emit a very subtle, low dose of radiation. If you sit very close to an appliance for a very long period of time, the theory says that your cancer risk increases. (Computers are supposedly the biggest risk — not many people sit all day hunched in front of their *blenders.*)

*Macworld* magazine tests discovered that you have to sit *really* close to your Mac to get any of this radiation. In fact, by the time you move 28 inches away, the level of ELF radiation is zero. That's arm's length. If ELF radiation concerns you, then just stay arm's length from the nearest monitor and you'll be OK. (Furthermore, all of this applies primarily to two-piece Macs; the compact Macs don't emit anything but good vibes.)

## Getting plugged

Of course, your manuals are the best instructions for setting up the Mac. But here are the basics.

Everything plugs into the back of the Mac. Take a look, there's a whole assortment of plugs back there. They're labeled with little symbolic pictures, called *icons.* (Get used to icons. They're the cornerstone of the Mac's graphic nature.) The next section shows the back of a typical Mac and what you can plug in.

If your new Mac is a laptop (the PowerBook), there's nothing to set up. Plug it in, open the back panel, hit the round On/Off button, and flip back to Chapter 1.

If your Mac *isn't* a PowerBook, study the diagram on the next page. Using it as your guide, plug the power cord into the power jack and the keyboard into the ADB port. Most people then plug the mouse into the other side of the keyboard. But some Macs have a second ADB port for the mouse; do whatever feels good.

If you have any form of Classic, Mac Plus, SE, LC 520, or Performa 200, your installation is complete. Flip back to Chapter 1.

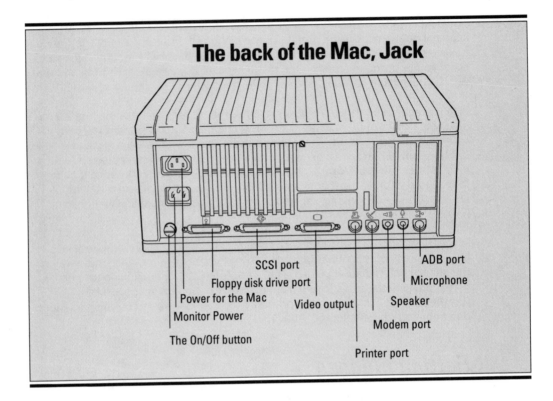

### The back of the Mac, Jack

SCSI port
Floppy disk drive port
Power for the Mac
Monitor Power
The On/Off button
Video output
Modem port
Printer port
Speaker
Microphone
ADB port

If you have a two-piece Mac, and your monitor *didn't* come with a separate circuit board (video card), plug the monitor's two cables into the monitor power and video out jacks, as shown in the following diagram. You're all set.

(If you bought an old, used Mac that requires a video card, you have to open the cover and install it. Follow the instructions that came with it. Call whoever sold it to you if you need help.)

You're ready for business. For instructions on hooking up your printer, see Chapter 4.

## *Switching the Mac on*

Quick! Flip to Chapter 1!

# *Top Ten Things You Get Free with Your Mac*

Enjoy this list. This is probably the last time you'll get anything free in your entire computing career.

1. A mouse.

2. A floppy-disk drive built into the front.

3. HyperCard Player. (See Chapter 5.)

4. A one-year warranty that covers parts and labor at *any* Apple dealership — or at your house or office.

5. A set of white System software disks (except Performa models).

6. A power cord.

7. A coupon for a free mouse pad or subscription to *Macworld* magazine.

8. Instruction manuals.

9. A guided tour disk ("Macintosh Basics" or "Mouse Practice").

10. A registration card. Fill it out, send it in.

# Appendix B
# The Resource Resource

## Magazines

*Macworld*
800-234-1038

*MacUser*
800-627-2247

*MacWeek*
609-461-2100

## User Groups

Apple User-Group
Info Line
800-538-9696

Arizona Macintosh
User's Group
602-553-8966

Boston Computer Society
BCS/Mac
617-625-7080

BMUG
415-849-9114

Apple Corps of Dallas
214-357-9185

Houston Area Apple
Users' Group
713-522-2179

Los Angeles Macintosh
Users' Group
213-278-5264

New Jersey Macintosh
Users' Group
201-893-5274

New York Macintosh
Users' Group
212-645-2265

## Products Mentioned in This Book

**1-2-3 for Macintosh**
Lotus Corp.
617-577-8500

**911 Utilities**
Datawatch Corporation
Triangle Software
Division
919-490-1277
919-490-6672 (FAX)

**Adobe Type Manager (ATM)**
Adobe Systems
415-961-4400
800-833-6687
800-521-1976 ext. 4400
(to order ATM for $7.50)

**After Dark**
Berkeley Systems, Inc.
510-540-5535
510-540-5115 (FAX)

**Amazing Paint**
PrairieSoft
515-225-3720.
515-225-2422 (FAX)

**America Online**
America Online Inc.
800-827-6364

**Animation Works**
Gold Disk
416-602-4000
800-465-3375
416-602-4001 (FAX)

**Baseline Publishing**
901-682-9676
800-926-9677
901-682-9691 (FAX)

**Bernoulli**
Iomega Corporation
801-778-1000
800-456-5522

**Capture**
Mainstay
818-991-6540
818-991-4587 (FAX)

**ClarisWorks**
Claris Corp.
408-727-8227
408-987-3932 (FAX)

**CompuServe**
617-661-9440
800-873-1032

**Connectix Corp.**
800-950-5880
415-571-5100
415-571-5195 (FAX)

**DeskPaint**
Zedcor, Inc.
602-881-8101
800-482-4567

**DeskWriter**
Hewlett-Packard
415-857-1501
800-752-0900
415-857-5518 (FAX)

**Disinfectant**
Freeware: John Norstad,
author. Available from
any on-line modem
service, or send a self-
addressed stamped
sturdy envelope and an
800K disk to the following
address. People outside
the U.S. may send an
international postal reply
coupon instead of U.S.
stamps (available from
any post office).
John Norstad
Academic Computing and
Network Services
Northwestern University
2129 Sheridan Road
Evanston, IL 60208

**DiskDoubler**
Symantec Corp.
408-253-3570
800-441-7234

**Encore**
Passport Designs
415-726-0280
415-726-2254 (FAX)

**Excel**
Microsoft Corp.
206-882-8080
800-426-9400
206-936-7329 (FAX)

**EZ Vision**
Opcode Systems, Inc.
415-856-3333
415-856-3332 (FAX)

**Finale**
Coda Music Technology
612-854-1288
800-843-2066
612-854-4631 (FAX)

**Flight Simulator**
Microsoft Corp.
206-882-8080
800-426-9400
206-936-7329 (FAX)

**FreeHand**
Aldus Corp.
206-622-5500

**Gatekeeper**
Available from on-line
services

**GreatWorks**
Symantec Corp.
408-253-3570
800-441-7234

**Hard Disk ToolKit**
FWB Incorporated
415-474-8055
415-775-2125 (FAX)

**HyperCard**
Apple Computer
408-996-1010
800-776-2333
408-974-6726 (FAX)

**Illustrator**
Adobe Systems
415-961-4400
800-833-6687

**KidPix**
Broderbund Software,
Inc.
415-382-4400
800-521-6263
415-382-4419 (FAX)

**Last Resort**
Working Software
408-423-5696
800-229-9675
408-423-5699 (FAX)

**MacConnection**
800-800-4444

**MacLink Plus**
DataViz
203-268-0030
800-733-0030
203-268-4345 (FAX)

**MacRecorder**
Macromedia
415-442-0200
800-288-4797
415-442-0190 (FAX)

**MacTools Deluxe**
Central Point Software
503-690-8090
800-964-6896

**MacWarehouse**
800-255-6227

**Mac Zone**
800-248-0800

**MacPaint**
Claris Corp.
408-727-8227
408-987-3932 (FAX)

**MasterJuggler**
ALSoft
713-353-4090
800-257-6381
713-353-9868 (FAX)

**MenuFonts**
Dubl-Click Software, Inc.
818-888-2068

**MicroPhone**
Software Ventures
415-644-3232
800-336-3478
510-848-0885 (FAX)

**ModuNet**
Data Spec
818-772-9977
800-431-8124
818-718-8626 (FAX)

**MusicProse**
Coda Music Software
612-854-1288
800-843-2066
612-854-4631 (FAX)

**Movie Movie**
Sigma Designs
510-770-0100
800-845-8086

**MyAdvancedLabelMaker**
MySoftware Company
415-325-9372

**Nisus**
Nisus Software
619-481-1477
800-922-2993
619-481-6154 (FAX)

**Norton Utilities for the Macintosh (NUM)**
Symantec Corp.
408-253-3570
800-441-7234

**Now Up-to-Date**
Now Software
503-274-2800

**Now Utilities, Now Compress**
Now Software
503-274-2800

**PageMaker**
Aldus Corp.
206-622-5500

**Persuasion**
Aldus Corp.
206-622-5500

**PhoneNet**
Farallon
510-596-9100
800-344-7489
510-596-9020 (FAX)

**Photoshop**
Adobe Systems
415-961-4400
800-833-6687

**PowerBook Battery Recharger**
Lind Electronics Design
612-927-6303
800-659-5956
612-927-7740 (FAX)

**PowerBook Car/Boat Adapter**
Empire Engineering
805-543-2816
805-543-2820 (FAX)

**Power Partner (battery pack)**
Interex
316-524-4747

**QuarkXPress**
Quark Inc.
303-934-2211
800-356-9363

**Quicken**
Intuit
415-322-0573
800-624-8742

**QuicKeys**
CE Software
515-224-1995
515-224-4534 (FAX)

**Resolve**
Claris Corp.
408-727-8227
408-987-3932 (FAX)

**Screenshot**
Baseline Publishing
901-682-9676
800-926-9677
901-682-9691 (FAX)

**SilverLining**
La Cie
503-520-9000
800-999-0143
503-520-9100 (FAX)

**Studio/1**
Electronic Arts
415-571-7171
800-245-4525
415-571-8004 (FAX)

**StuffIt**
Aladdin Systems, Inc.
408-761-6200
408-761-6206 (FAX)

**Suitcase**
Symantec Corp.
408-253-3570
800-441-7234

**Super QuickDex**
Casady & Greene, Inc.
408-484-9228
800-359-4920

**SuperPaint**
Aldus Corp.
206-622-5500

**Symantec Utilities for the Macintosh (SAM)**
Symantec Corp.
408-253-3570
800-441-7234

**SyQuest**
SyQuest Technologies
510-226-4000
800-245-2278
510-226-4100 (FAX)

**Talking Moose**
Baseline Publishing
901-682-9676
800-926-9677
901-682-9691 (FAX)

**Thunder 7**
Baseline Publishing
901-682-9676
800-926-9677
901-682-9691 (FAX)

**Trax**
Passport Designs
415-726-0280
415-726-2254 (FAX)

**UltraPaint/ArtWorks**
Deneba Software
305-596-5644
800-622-6827

**VideoSpigot**
SuperMac Technology
800-345-9777
408-245-2202

**Virex**
Datawatch Corporation
Triangle Software
Division
919-490-1277
919-490-6672 (FAX)

**Voice Impact**
Articulate Systems
617-935-5656
800-443-7077

**White Knight**
The FreeSoft Company
412-846-2700
412-847-4436 (FAX)

**Wingz**
Informix
913-599-7100
800-438-7627

**Word**
Microsoft Corp.
206-882-8080
800-426-9400
206-936-7329 (FAX)

**WordPerfect for the Macintosh**
WordPerfect Corp.
801-225-5000
800-321-4566

**WriteNow**
WordStar International, Inc.
800-523-3520

# Appendix C
# The Techno-Babble
# Translation Guide

## accelerator

The pedal you press while driving to pick up your very first Mac. Also, an expensive circuit board you can install to make your Mac faster and slightly less obsolete.

## active window

The window in front. Usually, only one window can be active; you can recognize it by the stripes across the title bar, like this:

## ADB

An acronym for Apple Desktop Bus, which describes the cables and jacks used by the keyboard and mouse: *Could you believe that dimwit!? He plugged his printer into the ADB port!*

## alert box

A message that appears on the screen; the Mac's attempt to maintain an open and communicative relationship with you. Unfortunately, as happens so often in relationships, the Mac tends to communicate only when something is wrong. An alert box is marked either with the International Exclamation Point or a warning hand, like this:

## Apple menu

The menu at the far left of your menu bar, marked by a piece of black or multi-colored fruit. In the Apple menu, you'll find a listing of your desk accessories (miniprograms like the Calculator), as well as any files, folders, documents, control panels, and even disks (or their aliases) you care to see there. (To add something to the Apple menu, drop its icon into the Apple Menu Items folder within your System Folder.)

## AppleShare

Some kind of trademarked name for the way interconnected Macs communicate with each other. You'll never need to know this.

## AppleTalk

Another trademarked name, also having to do with Macs talking to each other. You *may* need to know this term if you have a laser printer because AppleTalk is the language it speaks to your Mac. AppleTalk must be "active" to print; choose the Chooser from the  menu, and you'll see where you turn AppleTalk on or off. (PowerBook user alert: Turn AppleTalk off for the plane rides — you'll gain a whole half-hour of battery life.)

## application

Nerd word for *program*.

## Application menu

The rightmost menu on the menu bar (if you have System 7), marked by an icon. This menu lists whichever programs you have open and shows a check mark next to the frontmost program. You can switch from one program to another by choosing their names from the Application menu.

## ASCII

The most interesting thing about this term (which means "text file") is its weird pronunciation: *ASKie*. Good name for a Labrador, don't you think?

## ATM

Short for Adobe Type Manager, a piece of software that makes certain fonts look really great on the screen (and in nonlaser printouts). It's free, for only $7.50.

## background printing

A feature that returns control of the Mac to you immediately after you use the Print command; the Mac will print your document taking its own sweet time, always giving priority to what you're doing on the screen. The alternative, known as *background printing is off*, takes less time to print — but takes over the Mac, preventing you from working, displaying a "now printing" message until the printing is over.

## baud rate

The speed of a modem (see *modem*). Directly related to the price.

## BBS

An electronic bulletin board system. That's where a Mac in somebody's house is connected to a phone line or two, so that you can dial in with your modem (see *modem*) and post messages for other people to see. You can also read their messages. Good place to advertise that you're selling your used Mac stuff and to get dates.

## beta test

Means "test," but adding a Greek word makes it more important-sounding. Used exclusively when applied to software: When a program is still so buggy and new that a company doesn't dare sell it, they give it away (to people who are then called "beta testers") in hopes of being told what the bugs are.

## binary

Capable of counting only up to 2: how a computer thinks. Or anything that can only be in one of two conditions, like a Morse code signal, a light switch, or a public restroom.

## bit

You'd think it was the past tense of *byte* (see next page). Actually, it's a tiny piece of computer information not even big enough to bother with.

## bitmap

A particular arrangement of black dots on your white screen. To your eye, a particular bitmap might look like the letter A (bit-mapped text) or a coffee mug (a bitmapped graphic); to the computer, it's just a bunch of dots whose exact positions it has to memorize.

## boot

(1) Western footwear. (2) To start up the computer. (3) To fire somebody for having accidentally erased the hard drive: *He was booted out of here so fast, you could have heard a résumé drop.*

## bps

Bits per second. The technically proper way to measure the speed of a *modem* (instead of *baud*, which everybody still says from force of habit).

# bug

A programming error in a piece of software, caused by a programmer too wired on Jolt and pizza, that makes the program do odd or tragic things when you're working to beat a deadline.

# bus

A form of public transportation. Any other questions?

# button

There are two you'll have to deal with: the big square one on the mouse, or the many oval or round ones you'll see on the screen that offer you options.

# byte

A piece of computer information made up of bits. Now *that* made everything clear, didn't it?

# CAD

Computer-aided design (i.e., architectural programs).

# Caps Lock

A key on your keyboard responsible for messing up pages and pages of manuscript if you're one of those people who doesn't look up much from the keyboard. It makes every letter you type come out as a capital. Doesn't affect numbers. Press it once to get the capitals; press it again to return to normal.

# CD-ROM

A computer compact disc, requiring a special $400 player. CD-ROMs can show pictures, play music or voices, display short animations or movies, or display reams and reams of text. (A typical CD holds 600 megs of information; compare with the measly 230-meg hard disks that come in the more expensive Macs.)

# cdev

Short for control panel.

# Chooser

A desk accessory, therefore listed in the  menu, that lets you specify what kind of printer you have. Failure to use this thing when you first set up your Mac is the Number One reason beginners can't print.

# click

(v.) The cornerstone of the Macintosh religion: to point the cursor at an on-screen object and then press and release the mouse button.

# clip art

Instead of possessing actual artistic ability, graphic designers can buy (or otherwise acquire) collections of ready-made graphics — little cutesy snowmen, city skylines, Santa Clauses, whatever — that they can use to dress up their newsletters, party invitations, or threatening legal notices.

# Clipboard

The invisible holding area where the Mac stashes any text or graphics that you copy using the Copy command. The contents of the Clipboard get vaporized when you turn off the Mac (or copy something new).

# close box

The little square in the upper-left corner of a window (as opposed to the little square who sold you the Macintosh) which, when clicked, closes the window.

# color separation

The technique used in offset printing, where four separate metal plates (each one sopped in ink of a different color) are used to print a full-color image.

## command

Something you'd like the Mac to do, like Print or Save or Make Me Rich.

## Command key

The one on your keyboard that has a ⌘ symbol on it. When it's pressed, the letter keys on your keyboard perform commands instead of typing letters: ⌘-P = Print, ⌘-S = Save, ⌘-Q = Quit, and ⌘-Z = undo (well, they can't *all* be mnemonic).

## Control key

A keyboard key that does absolutely nothing.

## control panel

A little window full of settings that pertain to some aspect of the Mac's operation. There's a control panel for the mouse, another for the keyboard, another for the monitor, and so on. To view the selection of control panels, choose (what else?) Control Panels from the ⌘ menu.

## Copy

Do you really need a definition of *copy?*

## CPU

What it *stands for* is central processing unit. What it *means* is the actual computer — in the case of two-piece Macs, the box that contains the real brains, as distinguished from things like the monitor, the printer, and the keyboard.

## CRT

Man, those geeks really get into cryptic acronyms for simple things, don't they? CRT is the screen. If you must know, it stands for cathode ray tube.

## cursor

The pointer on the screen, whose position you control by moving the mouse across the desk.

## DA

Short for desk accessory.

## daisy chaining

The act of stringing together a bunch of different add-on appliances, like a CD player, a hard disk, or a scanner, by plugging one into the back of the next, very much like an elephant conga line.

## data

Isn't he that white-makeup guy on *Star Trek: The Next Generation?*

## database

An electronic list of information — like a mailing list — that can be sorted very quickly or searched for a specific name.

## defragment

To restore something that's all broken up and scrambled into one continuous chunk. Usually refers to the information in memory or on a hard disk, but can also be applied to hamburger meat.

## Delete key

In the typewriter days, this key was named Backspace. In my opinion, it still *should* be called that. I make it a habit to magic-marker the word *Backspace* on every keyboard I encounter.

## desktop

(1) The top of your desk, where the Mac sits, as in *I don't want a laptop; I want a desktop computer.* (2) (Capitalized) The home-base environment, where you see the Trash can and icons and all that stuff. Also known as the Finder. (3) The actual, usually gray, background of that home-base view. You can drag

an icon out of its window and onto this gray tablecloth and announce to your coworker that you've just placed an icon on the desktop.

## desktop file

A file the Mac maintains for its own use, in which it stores information like what your icons should look like and which kinds of documents can be opened by which programs. This file is invisible — but when it becomes damaged or bloated and starts causing problems, it's not quite invisible enough for most people.

## desktop publishing

The act of cranking out nice-looking printouts from your Mac, instead of paying to have it typeset. Despite the fact that the PowerBook is equally adept at creating beautiful printouts, the term *laptop publishing* still hasn't quite caught on.

## dialog box

The message box the Mac puts on the screen when it needs more information from you (like the one that appears when you print, asking how many copies you want). Because the Mac doesn't, thank God, actually talk back to you, and instead just listens to what *you* say, a better name might be *therapist box*.

## digitize

Computerese for *digest*. It's what happens to sound, pictures, video, or any other kind of real-world sensory experience after the Mac converts it into its own internal numerical digestive tract.

## digitizing board

A circuit board that converts video or TV pictures into files on your Mac.

## disk

Oh, come on, you know *this* word.

## disk cache

A secret feature for making your Mac faster at the expense of memory; the Mac memorizes a few things you do a lot and keeps them in a wad of memory called the disk cache, where they'll be immediately accessible. You set the size of the disk cache (the amount of memory reserved) using the Memory control panel.

## disk drive

The machinery that actually reads what's on a disk. If we're talking hard disk, the disk and the drive are built into a single unit. If we're talking floppy, the disk drive is the slot in the face of the Mac into which you insert a floppy disk.

## document

A file that you create with a program, like a memo (using a word processor), a logo (using a graphics program), or a spreadsheet (using a spreadsheet program).

## dot-matrix

A kind of low-quality printer and the printouts it makes. The ImageWriter printer is a dot-matrix printer.

## dots per inch

A gauge of visual clarity, both on printouts and on the screen. The Mac's crystal-clear screen became famous for having a very high resolution — 72 dots per inch, or 72 *dpi*. A laser printer is much sharper, though, capable of printing at 300 dpi.

## double-click

One of the most basic Mac skills without which you can't do anything but stare at the blank screen. Involves placing the on-screen pointer on an icon and, without moving it, pressing the mouse button twice quickly. If you double-click an icon, it always opens into a window; double-click a word to select it.

## download

To transfer a file from one computer to another over the phone wires. If you're on the receiving end, you *download* the file. If you're on the sending end, you *upload* the file. If you're the phone company, you *love* the file.

## downloadable font

Every laser printer comes with a basic set of typefaces built into it. You're welcome to use fonts that aren't in that built-in set, but the Mac has to send them to the printer (it has to *download* them) before the printer can start spitting out pages.

## drag

(1) To position the cursor on something, press the mouse button and move the mouse while the button is still down. (2) What it is when your disk drive breaks the day after the warranty expires.

## drawing program

A graphics program that creates circles, squares, and lines. The Mac stores each object you draw as an object unto itself, rather than storing the status of each screen dot; see *painting program* and *bitmap.*

## driver

A smallish file on your disk that tells the Mac how it's supposed to relate to a specific piece of equipment, like a printer or a scanner, that it's never heard of before. A translator.

## E-mail

Electronic mail. Messages that you read and write on the Mac screen, without ever printing them. May also be short for Earth-mail since no paper (and no rain forest acreage) is involved.

## Enter key

A key, obviously, with the word "Enter" on it. It almost always does the same thing as the Return key.

## expansion slot

The new notch you have to use on your belt when you've been putting on weight. Also, the socket for an add-on circuit board inside most Mac models.

## extended keyboard

A slightly more expensive keyboard than the "standard" one; the extended one has a row of function keys (F1, F2) across the top, which don't do anything, and a little bank of keys that say PgUp, PgDown, and stuff.

## extension

Miniprogram that you install by dropping it into your System Folder (whereupon the Mac puts it into the Extensions folder). From that moment on, the extension will run itself when you turn on the Mac and be on all the time. Examples: virus protectors and screen savers.

## fax/modem

Like a modem (see *modem*) but costs more and also lets you send or receive faxes from your Mac screen.

## field

Computerese for *blank,* like a blank on a form.

## file

The generic word for one of the little icons in your Macintosh. There are two kinds of files: *programs,* that you purchase to get work done, and *documents,* which are created by programs. See also *program* and *document.*

# file compression

Making a file take up less disk space by encoding it into a more compact format, using (what else?) a *file-compression program* like StuffIt or DiskDoubler. The trade-off: stuffing something down (and later expanding it when you need it again) takes a few seconds.

# File Sharing

A built-in feature of System 7, wherein you can make any file, folder, or disk available for other people to go rooting through (as long as they're connected to your Mac by network wiring).

# Finder

The "home-base" view when you're working on your Mac. It's the environment where you see the Trash, your icons, and how little space you've got left on your disk. Also known as the Desktop or "that place with all the little pictures."

# FKEY

One of those cool techno-sounding words that nobody's ever pinned down to one meaning. Can refer to (1) the row of keys across the top of some keyboards, the *function* keys, labeled F1, F2, and so on. Or (2) a special built-in keyboard shortcut involving the ⌘ and Shift keys plus a number; the ⌘-Shift-3 function key, for example, takes a snapshot of the screen, and ⌘-Shift-1 ejects a floppy disk.

# flat-file database

A shopping list, Rolodex, or phone book; a simple collection of information. On a Mac, you can do things to your database like search or sort; *flat-file* means it doesn't have fancy interconnections to other lists, like a "relational" database does.

# floppy disk

The hard 3½-inch square thing you put into your disk drive slot. Comes in three capacities: 400K (single-sided), 800K (double-sided), and 1,400K (quadruple-sided, or high-density). When magnetized by being placed too near an appliance, often used as a windshield scraper.

# folder

In the Mac world, a little filing-folder icon into which you can drop other icons, like your work, for organizational purposes. When you double-click a folder, it opens into a window. Also, the name of the high-speed machine that creases and envelope-stuffs the junk mail you're going to start getting from computer companies.

# font

(1) Apple's usage: a single typeface. (2) Everyone else's usage: a typeface family or package.

# Font/DA Mover

An obsolete, obtuse, and obstinate utility program that came with every Mac for years. Used for adding or removing fonts to/from your Mac (and adding or removing desk accessories). With System 7, thank God, the Font/DA Mover is history.

# fragmentation

When something gets broken up into little pieces. Usually refers to the files on your hard disk (which, over time, get stored in little pieces all over the disk, making it slower) or the memory in your computer (see *defragment*). Also can apply to your window after you throw the computer through it in frustration.

# freeze

When your cursor becomes immovable on your screen, and you can't type anything, and your Mac locks up, and you get furious because you lose everything you've typed in the last ten minutes.

## Function key

See *FKEY*.

## gray scale

A form of color image or color monitor, where all the colors are different shades of gray, like all the images in this book.

## grow box

Slang for Resize Box. (See *resize box.*)

## hang

(1) Freeze (see *freeze*). (2) Knack: *Hey, I'm actually getting the hang of this. I'm no dummy!*

## hard copy

A synonym for *printout,* used primarily by the kind of people who have carphones and say "let's interface on this."

## hard disk

A hard drive.

## hard drive

A hard disk. That is, the spinning platters, usually inside your Mac but also purchasable in an external form, that serve as a giant-sized floppy disk where your computer files get stored.

## hardware

The parts of your computer experience you can feel, and touch, and pay for. Contrast with *software.*

## header

Something that appears at the top of every page of a document, like "Chapter 4: The Milkman's Plight" or "Final Disconnection Notice."

## highlight

To select, usually by clicking or dragging with the mouse. In the Mac world, text and icons usually indicate that they're selected, or highlighted, by turning black. In the barbecue world, things indicate that they're, um, *ready* by turning black.

## HyperCard

A program that once came with every Mac. Sort of a Rolodex gone mad. Can be an appointment book, a diary, a kid's game . . . whatever you make of it.

## icon

A teensy picture, an inch tall, used as a symbol for a file, a folder, or a disk.

## ImageWriter

A low-cost, high-noise, low-speed, low-quality Apple dot-matrix printer.

## INIT

The dweeb's word for *extension* (see that).

## insertion point

In word processing, the blinking, short vertical line that's always somewhere in your text. It indicates where your next typing (or backspacing) will begin.

## K

Short for *kilobyte,* a unit of size measurement for computer information. A floppy disk usually holds 800K or 1,400K of data. All the typing in this book fills about 1,500K. A full-screen color picture is around 1,000K of information. When your hard disk gets accidentally erased, it's got 0K (but that's not OK).

## kerning

In type-intensive Mac work like creating a newspaper headline, the act of squishing two letters slightly closer together to make better use of space so that you can fit the phrase AN ALIEN FATHERED MY 2-HEADED BABY on one line.

# landscape

The natural environment you gradually forget about as you become addicted to the Mac. Also used to describe the sideways orientation of a piece of paper.

# laptop

Where a PowerBook computer is when you're working on the plane.

# laser printer

An expensive printer that creates awesome-looking printouts.

# launch

To open a program: *He just sits at that computer all day long, moving icons around, because he hasn't figured out how to launch a program yet.*

# LCD

The technology that creates the flat screen on the PowerBook laptop computer, marked by the tendency for the pointer to fade out if moved too quickly. Stands for either "Liquid Crystal Display" or "Lost the Cursor, Dammit."

# leading

(*LEDding*): The vertical distance between lines of text in a document. Single-spaced and double-spaced are measurements of leading. *His term paper was 33 pages short, so he increased the leading and hoped the professor wouldn't notice.*

# LocalTalk

The hardware portion of a Macintosh network: the connectors and cables that plug one Mac into another.

# macro

A predefined series of actions the Mac does automatically when you press a single key — like launching the word processor, typing "Help! I've been inhabited by a Mac polter-geist," and printing it — all by itself. Requires a special macro program.

# MacroMaker

A macro program that used to come free with your Mac. Doesn't work with System 7.

# math coprocessor

The kid whose algebra homework you used to copy. Oh, all right: it's actually a specialized little chip inside certain high-level Macs that kicks in to handle certain very specific number-crunching tasks (like data analysis and stuff). Does nothing for word processing and other normal tasks.

# MB

Short for *megabyte*.

# megabyte

Another unit of disk-storage space or memory measurement (see *K*). Used to measure hard disks and other large storage devices. There are about 1,000K in a megabyte.

# memory

The electronic holding area, which only exists when the Mac is turned on, where your document lives while you're working on it. Expensive and limited in each Mac.

# menu

A list of commands, neatly organized by topic, that drops down from the top of the Mac screen (when you click its title).

# menu bar

The white strip that's always at the top of the Mac screen, containing menu titles. Not to be confused with *bar menu,* or wine list.

# modem

A phone attachment for your Mac, so you can send files and messages to other computer users all over the world, and prevent anyone else in the house from using the phone.

## modifier keys

Keys that mess up what the letter keys do. Famous example: the Shift key. Other examples: ⌘ (Command), Option, Control, and Caps Lock.

## monitor

What you should do to your blood pressure when you find out how much computer screens (monitors) cost and weigh.

## mouse

The little handheld gray thing that rolls around on your desk and controls the movement of the cursor and is such an obvious target for a rodent joke that I won't even attempt it.

## mouse button

The square or rounded plastic button at the far end of the top of the mouse.

## mouse pad

A piece of plastic-topped foam rubber that protects the mouse and desk from each other and gives the mouse good traction. Often bears a logo or slogan like "Sony Disks: We're always floppy."

## MultiFinder

Before Apple invented System 7, you could only run one program at a time. To paste a graphic into a letter, you'd have to quit your graphics program, launch the word processor, and paste the picture. Using MultiFinder, a special optional software add-on, you could have the graphics and word processing programs both open at once. (In System 7, you can *always* have more than one program open provided you have enough memory.)

## multimedia

Something involving more than one medium, I guess. Mainly an advertising gimmick.

## network

What you create when you connect Macs to each other so that you can send messages or transfer files from one to another without having to get up and run down the hall with a floppy disk in your hand (a networking system fondly called *SneakerNet*).

## NuBus

The special kind of expansion slot (see *expansion slot*) found in any Mac II-style computer. Contrast with *PDS*, the slot found in a Macintosh LC. And no, there was never an OldBus.

## OCR

Short for optical character recognition, where you run an article you tore out of *Entertainment Weekly* through a scanner, and the Mac translates it into a word processing document on your screen, so you can edit it and remove all references to Cher.

## on-line

Hooked up: *Let's get this relationship on-line.*

## painting program

(1) A program with the word Paint in the title (like MacPaint or UltraPaint) that creates artwork by turning individual white dots black on the screen (by creating a *bitmap*; see that). (2) An adult education course for would-be watercolorers.

## partition

To use special formatting software that tricks the Mac into thinking that your hard disk is actually *two* (or more) disks, each with its own icon on the screen. Like subdividing a movie theatre into a duplex, but less expensive.

## PDS

Stands for processor direct slot, and is the kind of *expansion slot* (see that) in a Mac LC. Incompatible with *NuBus* (see that, too).

## peripheral

(1) Add-on: a printer, scanner, CD drive, dust cover. (2) The kind of vision by which you'll see your spouse leave you forever because you're too consumed by the Mac.

## PICT

A confusing-sounding acronym for the most common kind of picture file: *Just paste that image of Sculley's head into your word processor, Frank; it's only a PICT file, for heaven's sake.*

## pixel

One single dot out of the thousands that make up the screen image. Supposedly derived from *pi*cture *el*ement, which doesn't explain how the X got there.

## pop-up menu

Any menu that doesn't appear at the top of the screen. Usually marked by a down-pointing black triangle. Doesn't actually pop *up;* usually drops down.

## port

(1) A jack or connection socket in the back of your Mac. (2) Where boaters dock so they can recharge their PowerBook batteries.

## portrait

A right side-up piece of paper; the opposite of *landscape* (see that). Also a right side-up monitor that can show a full page at once (as in "a portrait display monitor").

## PostScript

A technology, a printer, a trademark, a kind of font, a computer code language for displaying or printing text or graphics, a way of life. All of it means high-quality type and graphics, and all of it means heaping revenues for Adobe, the company that invented it.

## PRAM

Parameter RAM . . . the little piece of memory maintained by your Mac's battery that helps explain why the Mac always knows the date and time even when it's been turned off.

## Print Monitor

A program that launches itself, unbidden, whenever you try to print something when Background Printing is turned on (see *background printing*). Print Monitor is also the program that tries to notify you when something goes wrong with the printer, like when a piece of paper gets horribly mangled inside.

## printer font

The printer half of a PostScript font (the other half is the *screen font*). Must be in your System Folder, and you must have one printer font for each style (bold, italic, and so on). An eternal nuisance.

## program

A piece of software, created by a programmer, that you buy in order to make your Mac do something specific: graphics, music, word processing, number crunching, or whatever.

## Publish and Subscribe

A fancy new version of copy-and-paste that's part of System 7. Lets you paste information (like a graphic) from one document into another (like a memo), such that when you make a change to the original (the graphic), the copy (the memo) is changed automatically.

## radio button

What you see in groups of two or more when the Mac is forcing you to make a choice between mutually exclusive options:

> A System error has occurred. What result
> would you like?
>
> ○ Loud, static buzzing
> ◉ Quietly blink to black
> ○ A two-minute fireworks display

# RAM

Term for memory (see *memory*) designed to intimidate non-computer users.

# RAM disk

A way to trick the Mac into thinking that it has an extra floppy disk inserted, but the disk is actually a chunk of memory set aside to *resemble* a disk (complete with an icon on the screen). A built-in option on the PowerBooks, Centrises, Quadras, and some other models.

# reboot

Restart.

# rebuilding the Desktop

One of several desperate methods that can be used in the event of something screwy going wrong with the Mac. Involves holding down the ⌘ and Option keys while the Mac is starting up.

# record

(n.) Other than its obvious definitions, the computer word *record* refers to one "card" in a database, such as one person's address information. Contrast with *field*, which is one *blank* (like a ZIP code) within a record.

# relational database

A complex information list that you hire somebody to come in and set up for you, where each list of information (like a mailing list) is interconnected to another list (like People Who Never Pay on Time).

# removable cartridge

Like a hard drive with free refills: a storage device (usually made by SyQuest or Bernoulli) that accepts huge-capacity disks, so you never run out of disk space (until you run out of the ability to buy more cartridges).

# ResEdit

A free program that lets anybody do some hacking to any program — changing what the menus say, altering the keyboard shortcuts, or really screwing up the works.

# resize box

The small square at the lower-right corner of a window that, when dragged, changes the size and shape of your window.

# resolution

(1) A number, measured in dots per inch, that indicates how crisply a printer or a monitor can display an image. (2) A New Year's vow, like "I will spend five minutes away from the computer each day for family, exercise, and social activity."

# restart switch

A little plastic switch, marked by a left-pointing triangle, on the case molding of most Macs that, when pressed, safely turns the Mac off and on again.

# ROM

A mediation mantra you can use when contemplating the ROM chips, where the Mac's instructions to itself are permanently etched.

# sans serif

A font, like Helvetica or Geneva, with no little "hats" and "feet" at the tip of each letter.

## scanner

A machine that takes a picture of a piece of paper (like a Xerox machine), and then displays the image on your Mac screen for editing.

## Scrapbook

A desk accessory, found in your  menu, used for permanent storage of graphics, text, and sounds. (Not the same as the Clipboard, which isn't permanent, and only holds one thing at a time.) To get something into the Scrapbook, copy it from a document, open the Scrapbook, and paste it. To get something out of the Scrapbook, use the scroll bar until you see what you want, and copy it (or cut it).

## screen saver

A program that darkens your screen after you haven't worked for several minutes. Designed to protect an unchanging image from burning into the screen, but used more often as a status symbol.

## scroll

To bring a different part of a document into view, necessitated by the fact that most computer monitors aren't large enough to display all 60 pages of your annual report at once.

## SCSI

Stands for Small Computer something Interface. The second S may stand for *standard* or *system* or *serial* or something else, depending on whom you ask. Only used in the following five terms.

## SCSI address

Refers to a number you have to give each SCSI device (see *SCSI device*) plugged into your Mac, using a little switch or thumb-wheel on the back. Can be between 0 and 7, except that the Mac is always 7 and the internal hard disk is always 0. If two SCSI devices have the same SCSI address, you're in big trouble.

## SCSI cable

A fat cable with a 25- or 50-pin connector at the end. Used to join SCSI devices to each other. Total length of all your SCSI cables can't be more than about 20 feet, or you're in big trouble.

## SCSI device

A scanner, CD player, external hard drive, printer (sometimes), removable-cartridge drive, external floppy-disk drive (sometimes), or other piece of equipment that you attach to the wide SCSI port in the back of your Mac. When you attach more than one of them (by plugging each into the back of the previous one), you have to obey certain rules (outlined in Chapter 11), or you're in big trouble.

## SCSI port

The wide connector in the back of your Mac.

## SCSI terminator

A plug that is supposed to go on the last SCSI device attached to your Mac. If you don't use one, you're in big trouble; although sometimes you're in big trouble if you *do* use one. See Chapter 11.

## serif

(n., adj): A term used to describe a font that has little ledges, like little "hats" and "feet," at the tip of each letter, like Times or this font.

## shareware

Programs that are distributed for free, via electronic bulletin board or on a floppy disk from user groups. The programmer requests that you send $10 or $20 to him or her, but only if you really like the program.

## Shut Down

The command in the Special menu that turns off your Mac.

## SIMM

It stands for Single In-line Memory Module, which I suggest you immediately forget, and it refers to memory chips.

## sleep

A command, and a condition, that applies only to PowerBooks or the Mac Portable. Sort of like Off, except that the Mac remembers everything you had running on the screen. So when you want to use the computer again, you just touch a key, and the whole computer wakes up, the screen lights up, and you're in business again. Used to conserve battery power.

## slot

An *expansion slot*. See that.

## software

The real reason you got a computer. Software is computer code, the stuff on disks: programs (that let you create documents) and documents themselves. Software tells the hardware what to do.

## spooler

A program that allows *background printing* (see that).

## spreadsheet

A program like an electronic ledger book, so you can type in columns of numbers and have them added up automatically.

## stack

A document created by the HyperCard program.

## startup disk

*A* startup disk is a floppy or hard disk that contains a System Folder (including a particular set of fonts, desk accessories, and settings for running your Mac). *The* startup disk is the one you've designated to be in control (in the event that there's more than one to choose from). The Startup Disk *control panel* is what you use to specify *the* startup disk.

## stationery pad

A System 7 feature. Click a document icon, choose Get Info from the File menu, select Stationery Pad. From now on, when you double-click that icon, it won't open; instead, an exact *copy* of it opens. Saves you the hassle of pasting the same logo into every memo you write because you can paste it into your Stationery Pad document just once.

## StyleWriter

A low-cost, quiet, high-quality, slow-speed Apple inkjet printer.

## submenu

In some menus, you're forced to choose from an additional set of options, which are marked in the menu by a right-pointing triangle. When your pointer is on the main menu command, the submenu pops out:

## SuperDrive

The kind of floppy-disk drive found on every Macintosh except the Plus and early Mac II's and SE's. Called Super because it can read high-density (1.4MB) floppy disks instead of the un-super 800K disks and because it can theoretically read IBM-format disks.

## System 6

One version of the Mac's controlling software. Faster, but harder to use, than System 7. Requires 1MB of memory, or less.

## System 7

The more recent version of the Mac's controlling software. More attractive, easier to use, more powerful, and slower than System 6. Requires at least 2MB of memory and, because it's a lot of software, requires a hard disk (it doesn't fit on a floppy).

## System 7.1

The first version of the Mac system software that's not free; you have to pay $35 for it. Adds two features to System 7: a Fonts folder that contains all manner of font files (TrueType, screen fonts, printer fonts); and WorldScript, the ability to convert all Mac screen elements into a different language, like Japanese (requires special drop-in language modules). System 7.1 is also modular; you can add new features to it just by dropping in plug-in software tidbits as they become available.

## system crash

Where something goes so wrong inside your Mac that a bomb appears on the screen with a message "Sorry, a System error has occurred" — or not. Sometimes the whole screen just freaks and makes buzzing noises and gets filled with static, like a TV station going off the air.

## System disk

A *startup disk* (see that entry).

## System file

The most important individual file inside a System Folder. Contains the Mac's instructions to itself, and stores your fonts, sounds, and other important customization information. A Mac without a System file is like a broke politician: It can't run.

## System Folder

The all-important folder that the Mac requires in order to run. Contains all kinds of other stuff also defined in this glossary: the System file, the Finder, fonts, desk accessories, printer fonts, and so on. Always identified by a special folder icon:

System Folder

## telecommunication

Communicating with other computers over the phone lines. Requires a modem.

## telecommute

To work in T-shirt and slippers in a messy apartment, spending not one penny on transportation, and sending work in to the office over the phone wires. Requires a modem and an ability to be alone for days on end without going insane.

### terminator

See *SCSI terminator.* Or see an Arnold Schwarzenegger movie.

### third party

(1) A company other than Apple: *You didn't get a mouse pad with your Mac? Well, of course not; you buy that from a third party.* You, by the way, are the second party. (2) The New Year's Eve get-together at which you get the drunkest.

### TIFF

Stands for tagged image file format, and is the kind of graphics-file format created by a scanner.

### title bar

The strip at the top of a window, where the window's name appears. Shows thin horizontal stripes if the window is *active* (in front of all the others).

### toner

The powder that serves as the "ink" for a laser printer. Runs out at critical moments.

### trackball

An alternative to the mouse. Looks like an 8-ball set into a pedestal, which you roll to move the pointer.

### TrueType

A special font format from Apple that ensures high-quality type at any size, both on the screen and on any printer. Rival to PostScript but costs much less (nothing, in fact: comes with System 7).

### user group

A local computer club that usually meets once a month and acts as a local source of information, and a place to unload your obsolete equipment to unsuspecting newcomers.

### video card

A circuit board required by most Mac II-series Macs in order to see anything at all on the monitor; something else you have to buy.

### virtual memory

A chunk of hard-disk space the Mac sets aside, if you wish, to act as emergency memory.

### virus

Irritating, self-duplicating computer program designed (by the maladjusted jerk who programmed it) to gum up the works of your Mac. Easily prevented by using Disinfectant or another virus barrier.

### window

A square view of Mac information; in the Finder, a window is a table of contents for a folder or a disk. In a program, a window displays your document.

### word wrap

A word processor's ability to place a word on the next line as soon as the first line becomes full.

### WYSIWYG

Short for What You See Is What You Get, one supposed reason for the Mac's superiority over other computers. Means that your printout will precisely match what you see on the screen. Isn't always true.

### zoom box

The tiny square in the upper-right corner of a window (in the title bar) that, when clicked, makes the window jump to full size.

# Index

# Order Form

**Order Center: (800) 762-2974** (8 a.m.-5 p.m., PST, weekdays) or (415) 312-0650

**For Fastest Service:** Photocopy This Order Form and FAX it to : (415) 358-1260

| Quantity | ISBN | Title | Price | Total |
|----------|------|-------|-------|-------|
|          |      |       |       |       |
|          |      |       |       |       |
|          |      |       |       |       |
|          |      |       |       |       |
|          |      |       |       |       |
|          |      |       |       |       |
|          |      |       |       |       |
|          |      |       |       |       |
|          |      |       |       |       |
|          |      |       |       |       |
|          |      |       |       |       |
|          |      |       |       |       |
|          |      |       |       |       |
|          |      |       |       |       |

## Shipping & Handling Charges

| Subtotal | U.S. | Canada & International | International Air Mail |
|----------|------|------------------------|------------------------|
| Up to $20.00 | Add $3.00 | Add $4.00 | Add $10.00 |
| $20.01-40.00 | $4.00 | $5.00 | $20.00 |
| $40.01-60.00 | $5.00 | $6.00 | $25.00 |
| $60.01-80.00 | $6.00 | $8.00 | $35.00 |
| Over $80.00 | $7.00 | $10.00 | $50.00 |

In U.S. and Canada, shipping is UPS ground or equivalent.
For Rush shipping call (800) 762-2974.

Subtotal _____

CA residents add applicable sales tax _____

IN residents add 5% sales tax _____

Canadian residents add 7% GST tax _____

Shipping _____

TOTAL _____

---

**Ship to:**

Name _____

Company_____

Address_____

City/State/Zip _____

Daytime Phone _____

---

Payment: ❑ Check to IDG Books (US Funds Only)   ❑ Visa   ❑ MasterCard   ❑ American Express

Card # _____ Exp. _____ Signature _____

Please send this order form to: IDG Books, 155 Bovet Road, Suite 310, San Mateo, CA 94402.
Allow up to 3 weeks for delivery. Thank you!

**BOBFD**